A Gift To

_____

_____

From

_____

_____

Date

_____

THE
BIBLE
IN 366 DAYS

YOUTH EDITION

CHRISTIAN ART
PUBLISHERS

Originally published by Christelike Uitgewersmaatskappy
under the title *Die Bybel in 366 dae vir jongmense*

© 2009

English edition
© 2010 Christian Art Publishers
PO Box 1599, Vereeniging, 1930, RSA

First edition 2010

Cover designed by Christian Art Publishers

Images used under license from Shutterstock.com

Scripture quotations are taken from the *Holy Bible*,
New Living Translation®, second edition, copyright © 1996, 2004.
Used by permission of Tyndale House Publishers, Inc.,
Carol Stream, Illinois 60188. All rights reserved.

Set in 9 on 12 pt Arial
by Christian Art Publishers

Printed in China

ISBN 978-1-77036-440-0

14   15   16   17   18   19   20   21   22   23   –   15   14   13   12   11   10   9   8   7   6

Your word is a lamp to guide my feet
and a light for my path.

– Psalm 119:105

January

Start at the beginning

God created the heavens and the earth. Early in the Bible we learn that it is not about us, but about God and how and why He created the earth and us.

1 ¹In the beginning God created the heavens and the earth.

²⁶Then God said, "Let us make human beings in our image, to be like us. They will reign over the fish in the sea, the birds in the sky, the livestock, all the wild animals on the earth, and the small animals that scurry along the ground."

²⁷God created human beings in his own image. In the image of God he created them; male and female he created them.

²⁸Then God blessed them and said, "Be fruitful and multiply. Fill the earth and govern it. Reign over the fish in the sea, the birds in the sky, and all the animals that scurry along the ground." ²⁹Then God said, "Look! I have given you every seed-bearing plant throughout the earth and all the fruit trees for your food. ³⁰And I have given every green plant as food for all the wild animals, the birds in the sky, and the small animals that scurry along the ground—everything that has life." And that is what happened.

³¹Then God looked over all he had made, and he saw that it was very good! And evening passed and morning came, marking the sixth day.

2 ¹So the creation of the heavens and the earth and everything in them was completed. ²On the seventh day God had finished his work of creation, so he rested from all his work. ³And God blessed the seventh day and declared it holy, because it was the day when he rested from all his work of creation.

Genesis 1:1, 26-2:3

A perfect match

God knows that people need more than just animals for company – they need a soulmate. That's why God made a mate for Adam who took his breath away! Since then every man and woman looks for their perfect match.

¹⁵The LORD God placed the man in the Garden of Eden to tend and watch over it. ¹⁶But the LORD God warned him, "You may freely eat the fruit of every tree in the garden—¹⁷except the tree of the knowledge of good and evil. If you eat its fruit, you are sure to die."

¹⁸Then the LORD God said, "It is not good for the man to be alone. I will make a helper who is just right for him." ¹⁹So the LORD God formed from the ground all the wild animals and all the birds of the sky. He brought them to the man to see what he would call them, and the man chose a name for each one. ²⁰He gave names to all the livestock, all the birds of the sky, and all the wild animals. But still there was no helper just right for him.

²¹So the LORD God caused the man to fall into a deep sleep. While the man slept, the LORD God took out one of the man's ribs and closed up the opening. ²²Then the LORD God made a woman from the rib, and he brought her to the man.

²³"At last!" the man exclaimed. "This one is bone from my bone, and flesh from my flesh! She will be called 'woman,' because she was taken from 'man.'"

²⁴This explains why a man leaves his father and mother and is joined to his wife, and the two are united into one.

Genesis 2:15-24

Here comes big trouble

Adam and Eve ate their way out of Paradise ... and into unhappiness. Since then, things have never been the same. Today people try to play God too, with the same disastrous consequences!

¹The serpent was the shrewdest of all the wild animals the LORD God had made. One day he asked the woman, "Did God really say you must not eat the fruit from any of the trees in the garden?"

²"Of course we may eat fruit from the trees in the garden," the woman replied. ³"It's only the fruit from the tree in the middle of the garden that we are not allowed to eat. God said, 'You must not eat it or even touch it; if you do, you will die.'"

⁴"You won't die!" the serpent replied to the woman. ⁵"God knows that your eyes will be opened as soon as you eat it, and you will be like God, knowing both good and evil."

⁶The woman was convinced. She saw that the tree was beautiful and its fruit looked delicious, and she wanted the wisdom it would give her. So she took some of the fruit and ate it. Then she gave some to her husband, who was with her, and he ate it, too. ⁷At that moment their eyes were opened, and they suddenly felt shame at their nakedness. So they sewed fig leaves together to cover themselves.

⁹Then the LORD God called to the man, "Where are you?"

¹⁰He replied, "I heard you walking in the garden, so I hid. I was afraid because I was naked."

¹¹"Who told you that you were naked?" the LORD God asked. "Have you eaten from the tree whose fruit I commanded you not to eat?"

Genesis 3:1-7, 9-11

A family is a wonderful thing when you all work together, and every family's uniqueness must be celebrated – but jealousy makes you nasty. That's why it is better to be a grace giver (like God was to Cain) and not a grace killer (like Cain was to Abel).

⁶"Why are you so angry?" the LORD asked Cain. "Why do you look so dejected? ⁷You will be accepted if you do what is right. But if you refuse to do what is right, then watch out! Sin is crouching at the door, eager to control you. But you must subdue it and be its master."

⁸One day Cain suggested to his brother, "Let's go out into the fields." And while they were in the field, Cain attacked his brother, Abel, and killed him.

⁹Afterward the LORD asked Cain, "Where is your brother? Where is Abel?"

"I don't know," Cain responded. "Am I my brother's guardian?"

¹⁰But the LORD said, "What have you done? Listen! Your brother's blood cries out to me from the ground!"

¹³Cain replied to the LORD, "My punishment is too great for me to bear! ¹⁴You have banished me from the land and from your presence; you have made me a homeless wanderer. Anyone who finds me will kill me!"

¹⁵The LORD replied, "No, for I will give a sevenfold punishment to anyone who kills you." Then the LORD put a mark on Cain to warn anyone who might try to kill him.

Genesis 4:6-10, 13-15

A rainbow full of promise

People are often promise breakers. Rainbows remind us that God is a promise keeper. That's why we should be like Noah and obey God when He asks us to do something – even if other people think we have lost our minds. (A boat? Where's the water?) God knows best. The best is to do what God says!

6 [11]Now God saw that the earth had become corrupt and was filled with violence. [12]God observed all this corruption in the world, for everyone on earth was corrupt. [13]So God said to Noah, "I have decided to destroy all living creatures, for they have filled the earth with violence. Yes, I will wipe them all out along with the earth!

[14]"Build a large boat from cypress wood and waterproof it with tar, inside and out. Then construct decks and stalls throughout its interior.

9 [11]"Yes, I am confirming my covenant with you. Never again will floodwaters kill all living creatures; never again will a flood destroy the earth.

[16]"When I see the rainbow in the clouds, I will remember the eternal covenant between God and every living creature on earth."

Genesis 6:11-14; 9:11, 16

Put your hand in God's and see the world

When you walk with God you step out of your comfort zone and begin to see unfamiliar, new things. They are only unknown to you though, because everything on earth was created by God. Trust Him and see His wonderful world.

[1]The LORD had said to Abram, "Leave your native country, your relatives, and your father's family, and go to the land that I will show you. [2]I will make you into a great nation. I will bless you and make you famous, and you will be a blessing to others. [3]I will bless those who bless you and curse those who treat you with contempt. All the families on earth will be blessed through you."

[4]So Abram departed as the LORD had instructed, and Lot went with him. Abram was seventy-five years old when he left Haran. [5]He took his wife, Sarai, his nephew Lot, and all his wealth—his livestock and all the people he had taken into his household at Haran—and headed for the land of Canaan. When they arrived in Canaan, [6]Abram traveled through the land as far as Shechem. There he set up camp beside the oak of Moreh. At that time, the area was inhabited by Canaanites.

[7]Then the LORD appeared to Abram and said, "I will give this land to your descendants." And Abram built an altar there and dedicated it to the LORD, who had appeared to him.

Genesis 12:1-7

Mission impossible?
Never!

The bottom line of this story and the rest of the Bible is: Nothing is impossible for God. An old woman (and later a virgin, Mary) became pregnant. Our intellect battles to understand that, but if you don't believe it yet you won't believe it easily. *Mission impossible* is always *mission possible* for God.

¹The LORD kept his word and did for Sarah exactly what he had promised. ²She became pregnant, and she gave birth to a son for Abraham in his old age. This happened at just the time God had said it would. ³And Abraham named their son Isaac. ⁴Eight days after Isaac was born, Abraham circumcised him as God had commanded. ⁵Abraham was 100 years old when Isaac was born.

⁶And Sarah declared, "God has brought me laughter. All who hear about this will laugh with me. ⁷Who would have said to Abraham that Sarah would nurse a baby? Yet I have given Abraham a son in his old age!"

Genesis 21:1-7

H.A.L.T.,
think and do

Shout H.A.L.T. next time you (like Esau) begin to do something stupid – like trading a precious long-term treasure for a short-term pleasure like lentil soup. H.A.L.T. stands for **H**ungry. **A**ngry. **L**onely. **T**ired. Whenever you feel like this, say H.A.L.T. before you do something you'll regret later.

29One day when Jacob was cooking some stew, Esau arrived home from the wilderness exhausted and hungry. 30Esau said to Jacob, "I'm starved! Give me some of that red stew!" (This is how Esau got his other name, Edom, which means "red.")

31"All right," Jacob replied, "but trade me your rights as the firstborn son."

32"Look, I'm dying of starvation!" said Esau. "What good is my birthright to me now?"

33But Jacob said, "First you must swear that your birthright is mine." So Esau swore an oath, thereby selling all his rights as the firstborn to his brother, Jacob.

34Then Jacob gave Esau some bread and lentil stew. Esau ate the meal, then got up and left. He showed contempt for his rights as the firstborn.

Genesis 25:29-34

Heaven is sometimes closer than you think

In a dark moment in his life Jacob made this huge faith discovery. It's amazing that we find God when we least expect to find Him, but when we need Him the most. Look for the "ladder" that links heaven and earth.

¹¹At sundown he arrived at a good place to set up camp and stopped there for the night. Jacob found a stone to rest his head against and lay down to sleep. ¹²As he slept, he dreamed of a stairway that reached from the earth up to heaven. And he saw the angels of God going up and down the stairway.

¹³At the top of the stairway stood the LORD, and he said, "I am the LORD, the God of your grandfather Abraham, and the God of your father, Isaac. The ground you are lying on belongs to you. I am giving it to you and your descendants. ¹⁴Your descendants will be as numerous as the dust of the earth! They will spread out in all directions—to the west and the east, to the north and the south. And all the families of the earth will be blessed through you and your descendants. ¹⁵What's more, I am with you, and I will protect you wherever you go. One day I will bring you back to this land. I will not leave you until I have finished giving you everything I have promised you."

¹⁶Then Jacob awoke from his sleep and said, "Surely the LORD is in this place, and I wasn't even aware of it!" ¹⁷But he was also afraid and said, "What an awesome place this is! It is none other than the house of God, the very gateway to heaven!"

²⁰Then Jacob made this vow: "If God will indeed be with me and protect me on this journey, and if he will provide me with food and clothing, ²¹and if I return safely to my father's home, then the LORD will certainly be my God."

Genesis 28:11-17, 20-21

What a terrible discovery. You think you are marrying the love of your life, Rachel, but when you lift the veil you see her older sister whom no one wants! But for true love you will put up with dishonesty and trickery. Love has its own reasons that your mind cannot understand.

¹⁴Laban exclaimed, "You really are my own flesh and blood!"

After Jacob had stayed with Laban for about a month, ¹⁵Laban said to him, "You shouldn't work for me without pay just because we are relatives. Tell me how much your wages should be."

¹⁶Now Laban had two daughters. The older daughter was named Leah, and the younger one was Rachel. ¹⁷There was no sparkle in Leah's eyes, but Rachel had a beautiful figure and a lovely face. ¹⁸Since Jacob was in love with Rachel, he told her father, "I'll work for you for seven years if you'll give me Rachel, your younger daughter, as my wife."

²⁵But when Jacob woke up in the morning—it was Leah! "What have you done to me?" Jacob raged at Laban. "I worked seven years for Rachel! Why have you tricked me?"

²⁶"It's not our custom here to marry off a younger daughter ahead of the firstborn," Laban replied. ²⁷"But wait until the bridal week is over, then we'll give you Rachel, too—provided you promise to work another seven years for me."

²⁸So Jacob agreed to work seven more years. A week after Jacob had married Leah, Laban gave him Rachel, too. ²⁹(Laban gave Rachel a servant, Bilhah, to be her maid.) ³⁰So Jacob slept with Rachel, too, and he loved her much more than Leah. He then stayed and worked for Laban the additional seven years.

Genesis 29:14-18, 25-30

This is one wrestling match you can't win

Jacob is a schemer and a wrestler, but God, his Superior, catches hold of him. After his big wrestling match, Jacob walked with a limp to remind him – and others – that if you wrestle with God, you will not be left untouched. Limping, yet blessed with a new name and a life-changing walk with God.

[24]This left Jacob all alone in the camp, and a man came and wrestled with him until the dawn began to break. [25]When the man saw that he would not win the match, he touched Jacob's hip and wrenched it out of its socket. [26]Then the man said, "Let me go, for the dawn is breaking!"

But Jacob said, "I will not let you go unless you bless me."

[27]"What is your name?" the man asked.

He replied, "Jacob."

[28]"Your name will no longer be Jacob," the man told him. "From now on you will be called Israel, because you have fought with God and with men and have won."

[29]"Please tell me your name," Jacob said.

"Why do you want to know my name?" the man replied. Then he blessed Jacob there.

[30]Jacob named the place Peniel (which means "face of God"), for he said, "I have seen God face to face, yet my life has been spared." [31]The sun was rising as Jacob left Peniel, and he was limping because of the injury to his hip. [32](Even today the people of Israel don't eat the tendon near the hip socket because of what happened that night when the man strained the tendon of Jacob's hip.)

Genesis 32:24-32

Being the pet favorite is bad for you

The problem with favorites is that if you are someone's 'favorite' then you think everything revolves around you. Then it's easy for you to get into trouble with other people. The problem begins with those who show preferential treatment. The solution is to treat everyone like they are special – then everyone is a favorite!

³Jacob loved Joseph more than any of his other children because Joseph had been born to him in his old age. So one day Jacob had a special gift made for Joseph—a beautiful robe. ⁴But his brothers hated Joseph because their father loved him more than the rest of them. They couldn't say a kind word to him.

⁵One night Joseph had a dream, and when he told his brothers about it, they hated him more than ever. ⁶"Listen to this dream," he said. ⁷"We were out in the field, tying up bundles of grain. Suddenly my bundle stood up, and your bundles all gathered around and bowed low before mine!"

⁸His brothers responded, "So you think you will be our king, do you? Do you actually think you will reign over us?" And they hated him all the more because of his dreams and the way he talked about them.

Genesis 37:3-8

Bloom where you're planted

It doesn't matter what life throws at you, make the best of every opportunity. If you are in a bad situation where someone is harassing you (like Potiphar's wife), or even if you're in jail, bloom where God plants you so that everyone will know that you belong to His family.

[2] The LORD was with Joseph, so he succeeded in everything he did as he served in the home of his Egyptian master.

[4] Potiphar put him in charge of his entire household and everything he owned. [5] From the day Joseph was put in charge of his master's household and property, the LORD began to bless Potiphar's household for Joseph's sake. [6] Joseph was a very handsome and well-built young man, [7] and Potiphar's wife soon began to look at him lustfully. "Come and sleep with me," she demanded.

[8] But Joseph refused. "Look," he told her, "my master trusts me with everything in his entire household. [9] No one here has more authority than I do. He has held back nothing from me except you, because you are his wife. How could I do such a wicked thing? It would be a great sin against God." [10] She kept putting pressure on Joseph, but he refused to sleep with her.

[17] Then she told Potiphar her story. "That Hebrew slave you've brought into our house tried to come in and fool around with me," she said. [18] "But when I screamed, he ran outside, leaving his cloak with me!"

[19] Potiphar was furious when he heard his wife's story about how Joseph had treated her. [20] So he took Joseph and threw him into the prison where the king's prisoners were held, and there he remained.

Genesis 39:2, 4-10, 17-20

The perfect revenge: forgiveness

The sweetest revenge that you can take is to forgive the person unconditionally. Life is way too short to be bitter and mad the whole time. Forgive like Joseph and live like God intended: without the baggage of hate weighing you down!

¹Joseph could stand it no longer. There were many people in the room, and he said to his attendants, "Out, all of you!" So he was alone with his brothers when he told them who he was. ²Then he broke down and wept. He wept so loudly the Egyptians could hear him, and word of it quickly carried to Pharaoh's palace.

³"I am Joseph!" he said to his brothers. "Is my father still alive?" But his brothers were speechless! They were stunned to realize that Joseph was standing there in front of them. ⁴"Please, come closer," he said to them. So they came closer. And he said again, "I am Joseph, your brother, whom you sold into slavery in Egypt. ⁵But don't be upset, and don't be angry with yourselves for selling me to this place. It was God who sent me here ahead of you to preserve your lives. ⁶This famine that has ravaged the land for two years will last five more years, and there will be neither plowing nor harvesting. ⁷God has sent me ahead of you to keep you and your families alive and to preserve many survivors. ⁸So it was God who sent me here, not you! And he is the one who made me an adviser to Pharaoh—the manager of his entire palace and the governor of all Egypt.

⁹"Now hurry back to my father and tell him, 'This is what your son Joseph says: God has made me master over all the land of Egypt. So come down to me immediately!'"

Genesis 45:1-9

Not 20/20 vision,
but 50/20 vision

20/20 vision describes someone who has perfect eyesight. 50/20 vision describes someone who is sensitive to God's hand in his life. Why? Genesis 50:20 says, "You intended to harm me, but God intended it all for good." REMEMBER, God can bring good out of a seemingly hopeless situation.

[14]After burying Jacob, Joseph returned to Egypt with his brothers and all who had accompanied him to his father's burial. [15]But now that their father was dead, Joseph's brothers became fearful. "Now Joseph will show his anger and pay us back for all the wrong we did to him," they said.

[16]So they sent this message to Joseph: "Before your father died, he instructed us [17]to say to you: 'Please forgive your brothers for the great wrong they did to you—for their sin in treating you so cruelly.' So we, the servants of the God of your father, beg you to forgive our sin." When Joseph received the message, he broke down and wept. [18]Then his brothers came and threw themselves down before Joseph. "Look, we are your slaves!" they said.

[19]But Joseph replied, "Don't be afraid of me. Am I God, that I can punish you? [20]You intended to harm me, but God intended it all for good. He brought me to this position so I could save the lives of many people. [21]No, don't be afraid. I will continue to take care of you and your children." So he reassured them by speaking kindly to them.

Genesis 50:14-21

Smarter than God?

The most clever person with the smartest plan can never outwit God. How amazing is it that Moses was saved by Pharaoh's daughter and then brought up by his own mother? God always sees the bigger picture. What a great God we worship!

[1]About this time, a man and woman from the tribe of Levi got married. [2]The woman became pregnant and gave birth to a son. She saw that he was a special baby and kept him hidden for three months. [3]But when she could no longer hide him, she got a basket made of papyrus reeds and waterproofed it with tar and pitch. She put the baby in the basket and laid it among the reeds along the bank of the Nile River. [4]The baby's sister then stood at a distance, watching to see what would happen to him.

[5]Soon Pharaoh's daughter came down to bathe in the river. When the princess saw the basket among the reeds, she sent her maid to get it for her. [6]When the princess opened it, she saw the baby. The little boy was crying, and she felt sorry for him. "This must be one of the Hebrew children," she said.

[7]Then the baby's sister approached. "Should I go and find one of the Hebrew women to nurse the baby for you?" she asked.

[8]"Yes, do!" the princess replied. So the girl went and called the baby's mother.

[9]"Take this baby and nurse him for me," the princess told the baby's mother. So the woman took her baby home and nursed him.

[10]Later, when the boy was older, his mother brought him back to Pharaoh's daughter, who adopted him as her own son. The princess named him Moses, for she explained, "I lifted him out of the water."

Exodus 2:1-10

Take off your shoes – you're standing on holy ground

God has to help us to see the burning bush before it burns up completely. Then we are able to shout out in surprise, "This place is filled with holiness and I didn't even know it!" Remember, the earth is filled with heaven. Bramble bushes are on fire all around us. But only those who see them take off their shoes.

¹One day Moses was tending the flock of his father-in-law, Jethro, the priest of Midian. He led the flock far into the wilderness and came to Sinai, the mountain of God. ²The angel of the LORD appeared to him in a blazing fire from the middle of a bush. Moses stared in amazement. Though the bush was engulfed in flames, it didn't burn up. ³"This is amazing," Moses said to himself. "Why isn't that bush burning up? I must go see it."

⁴When the LORD saw Moses coming to take a closer look, God called to him from the middle of the bush, "Moses! Moses!"

"Here I am!" Moses replied.

⁵"Do not come any closer," the LORD warned. "Take off your sandals, for you are standing on holy ground. ⁶I am the God of your father—the God of Abraham, the God of Isaac, and the God of Jacob." When Moses heard this, he covered his face because he was afraid to look at God.

Exodus 3:1-6

When God calls you to do something, you often think of excuses to get out of doing it. But your best excuses fall flat against God's answers. Eventually you realize that you must simply do what God asks – because your excuses are just challenges for God to overcome. He wants to use you – and He will use you.

¹But Moses protested again, "What if they won't believe me or listen to me? What if they say, 'The Lᴏʀᴅ never appeared to you'?"

²Then the Lᴏʀᴅ asked him, "What is that in your hand?"

"A shepherd's staff," Moses replied.

³"Throw it down on the ground," the Lᴏʀᴅ told him. So Moses threw down the staff, and it turned into a snake! Moses jumped back.

⁴Then the Lᴏʀᴅ told him, "Reach out and grab its tail." So Moses reached out and grabbed it, and it turned back into a shepherd's staff in his hand.

¹⁰But Moses pleaded with the Lᴏʀᴅ, "O Lord, I'm not very good with words. I never have been, and I'm not now, even though you have spoken to me. I get tongue-tied, and my words get tangled."

¹¹Then the Lᴏʀᴅ asked Moses, "Who makes a person's mouth? Who decides whether people speak or do not speak, hear or do not hear, see or do not see? Is it not I, the Lᴏʀᴅ? ¹²Now go! I will be with you as you speak, and I will instruct you in what to say."

¹³But Moses again pleaded, "Lord, please! Send anyone else."

Exodus 4:1-4, 10-13

Is your God great enough?

God gives you enough for each day. We can trust Him because He carries our interests close to His heart. But don't try to cheat, because you will get caught out. Then everyone will know that your image of God is not big enough.

[14]When the dew evaporated, a flaky substance as fine as frost blanketed the ground. [15]The Israelites were puzzled when they saw it. "What is it?" they asked each other. They had no idea what it was. And Moses told them, "It is the food the LORD has given you to eat. [16]These are the LORD instructions: Each household should gather as much as it needs. Pick up two quarts for each person in your tent."

[17]So the people of Israel did as they were told. Some gathered a lot, some only a little. [18]But when they measured it out, everyone had just enough. Those who gathered a lot had nothing left over, and those who gathered only a little had enough. Each family had just what it needed.

[19]Then Moses told them, "Do not keep any of it until morning." [20]But some of them didn't listen and kept some of it until morning. But by then it was full of maggots and had a terrible smell. Moses was very angry with them.

[21]After this the people gathered the food morning by morning, each family according to its need. And as the sun became hot, the flakes they had not picked up melted and disappeared.

Exodus 16:14-21

10 ways to an abundant life

God gave His people the Ten Commandments so that they would know how to live in the Promised Land. Today they are ten of the best guidelines on how to stand out as a follower of Christ and not blend in with the rest of the world!

²"I am the LORD your God, who rescued you from the land of Egypt, the place of your slavery. ³You must not have any other god but me. ⁴You must not make for yourself an idol of any kind or an image of anything in the heavens or on the earth or in the sea. ⁵You must not bow down to them or worship them, for I, the LORD your God, am a jealous God who will not tolerate your affection for any other gods. I lay the sins of the parents upon their children; the entire family is affected—even children in the third and fourth generations of those who reject me.

⁷"You must not misuse the name of the LORD your God. The LORD will not let you go unpunished if you misuse his name.

⁸"Remember to observe the Sabbath day by keeping it holy. ⁹You have six days each week for your ordinary work, ¹⁰but the seventh day is a Sabbath day of rest dedicated to the LORD your God. On that day no one in your household may do any work.

¹²"Honor your father and mother. Then you will live a long, full life in the land the LORD your God is giving you.

¹³"You must not murder. ¹⁴You must not commit adultery. ¹⁵You must not steal. ¹⁶You must not testify falsely against your neighbor.

¹⁷"You must not covet your neighbor's house. You must not covet your neighbor's wife, male or female servant, ox or donkey, or anything else that belongs to your neighbor."

Exodus 20:2-5, 7-10, 12-17

Looking for a scapegoat!

Everyone loves looking for a scapegoat they can blame for their sins and mistakes. Christians, however, know that there is only one Scapegoat who can take away all our sins: the crucified Jesus Christ. On Golgotha, in AD 33, your sins were taken away forever. Don't drag them around with you or place the blame on anyone else.

³"When Aaron enters the sanctuary area, he must follow these instructions fully. He must bring a young bull for a sin offering and a ram for a burnt offering. ⁴He must put on his linen tunic and the linen undergarments worn next to his body. He must tie the linen sash around his waist and put the linen turban on his head. These are sacred garments, so he must bathe himself in water before he puts them on. ⁵Aaron must take from the community of Israel two male goats for a sin offering and a ram for a burnt offering.

⁶"Aaron will present his own bull as a sin offering to purify himself and his family, making them right with the LORD. ⁷Then he must take the two male goats and present them to the LORD at the entrance of the Tabernacle. ⁸He is to cast sacred lots to determine which goat will be reserved as an offering to the LORD and which will carry the sins of the people to the wilderness of Azazel. ⁹Aaron will then present as a sin offering the goat chosen by lot for the LORD. ¹⁰The other goat, the scapegoat chosen by lot to be sent away, will be kept alive, standing before the LORD. When it is sent away to Azazel in the wilderness, the people will be purified and made right with the LORD."

Leviticus 16:3-10

Handle with care: image of God

Treat everyone who crosses your path as if he is a "God-carrier." Every person is made in the image of God and must therefore be treated with the utmost respect and love. This passage from Leviticus has a list to help you see the good (image of God) in every person.

¹³"Do not defraud or rob your neighbor. Do not make your hired workers wait until the next day to receive their pay.

¹⁴"Do not insult the deaf or cause the blind to stumble. You must fear your God; I am the LORD.

¹⁵"Do not twist justice in legal matters by favoring the poor or being partial to the rich and powerful. Always judge people fairly.

¹⁶"Do not spread slanderous gossip among your people. Do not stand idly by when your neighbor's life is threatened. I am the LORD.

¹⁷"Do not nurse hatred in your heart for any of your relatives. Confront people directly so you will not be held guilty for their sin.

¹⁸"Do not seek revenge or bear a grudge against a fellow Israelite, but love your neighbor as yourself. I am the LORD."

Leviticus 19:13-18

Amazing blessings from an amazing God

Someone once reassuringly said that it is good to know that 90% of the things we worry about don't ever happen. Numbers 6 would have added: not because that's part of life, but because God is loving and kind.

²²Then the LORD said to Moses, ²³"Tell Aaron and his sons to bless the people of Israel with this special blessing:
    ²⁴'May the LORD bless you and protect you.
    ²⁵'May the LORD smile on you and be gracious to you.
    ²⁶'May the LORD show you his favor and give you his peace.'
    ²⁷Whenever Aaron and his sons bless the people of Israel in my name, I myself will bless them."

Numbers 6:22-27

Complaining makes you tired

Moses was wearied by the Israelites' continuous whining about how good it had been in Egypt. They forgot: "Yesterday is history. Tomorrow is a mystery. Today is a gift. That's why it's called the 'present.'" That's why we must learn from yesterday. Don't longingly look back at the past, but live full out for today and face tomorrow with hope!

⁴Then the foreign rabble who were traveling with the Israelites began to crave the good things of Egypt. And the people of Israel also began to complain. "Oh, for some meat!" they exclaimed. ⁵"We remember the fish we used to eat for free in Egypt. And we had all the cucumbers, melons, leeks, onions, and garlic we wanted. ⁶But now our appetites are gone. All we ever see is this manna!"

⁷The manna looked like small coriander seeds, and it was pale yellow like gum resin. ⁸The people would go out and gather it from the ground. They made flour by grinding it with hand mills or pounding it in mortars. Then they boiled it in a pot and made it into flat cakes. These cakes tasted like pastries baked with olive oil. ⁹The manna came down on the camp with the dew during the night.

¹⁰Moses heard all the families standing in the doorways of their tents whining, and the LORD became extremely angry. Moses was also very aggravated. ¹¹And Moses said to the LORD, "Why are you treating me, your servant, so harshly? Have mercy on me! What did I do to deserve the burden of all these people?"

Numbers 11:4-11

Look with eyes of faith

The majority is not always right, especially if their fear makes challenges look gigantic! The minority use eyes of faith and know that with God's help they can do anything. If you walk with God then you are always in the majority, even though you may look like the minority!

²⁵After exploring the land for forty days, the men returned ²⁶to Moses, Aaron, and the whole community of Israel at Kadesh in the wilderness of Paran. They reported to the whole community what they had seen and showed them the fruit they had taken from the land. ²⁷This was their report to Moses: "We entered the land you sent us to explore, and it is indeed a bountiful country—a land flowing with milk and honey. Here is the kind of fruit it produces. ²⁸But the people living there are powerful, and their towns are large and fortified. We even saw giants there, the descendants of Anak! ²⁹The Amalekites live in the Negev, and the Hittites, Jebusites, and Amorites live in the hill country. The Canaanites live along the coast of the Mediterranean Sea and along the Jordan Valley."

³⁰But Caleb tried to quiet the people as they stood before Moses. "Let's go at once to take the land," he said. "We can certainly conquer it!"

³¹But the other men who had explored the land with him disagreed. "We can't go up against them! They are stronger than we are!" ³²So they spread this bad report about the land among the Israelites: "The land we traveled through and explored will devour anyone who goes to live there. All the people we saw were huge. ³³Next to them we felt like grasshoppers, and that's what they thought, too!"

Ten of the best with one difference

The difference is the Sabbath! Exodus says that the reason for a day of rest is Creation – think of everything God created. For Deuteronomy, however, it is the re-creation – being saved from slavery in Egypt – which symbolizes our salvation from sin and into a land of new life.

¹Moses called all the people of Israel together and said, "Hear the decrees and regulations I am giving you today, so you may learn them and obey them!

⁶"I am the LORD your God, who rescued you from the land of Egypt. ⁷You must not have any other god but me. ⁸You must not make for yourself an idol of any kind. ⁹You must not bow down to them or worship them, for I, the LORD your God, am a jealous God who will not tolerate your affection for any other gods.

¹¹"You must not misuse the name of the LORD your God. The LORD will not let you go unpunished if you misuse his name.

¹²"Observe the Sabbath day by keeping it holy. ¹⁵Remember that you were once slaves in Egypt, but the LORD your God brought you out with his strong hand and powerful arm. That is why the LORD your God has commanded you to rest on the Sabbath day.

¹⁶"Honor your father and mother, as the LORD your God commanded you. Then you will live a long, full life in the land the LORD your God is giving you.

¹⁷"You must not murder. ¹⁸You must not commit adultery. ¹⁹You must not steal. ²⁰You must not testify falsely against your neighbor. ²¹You must not covet your neighbor's wife. You must not covet your neighbor's house or land or anything else that belongs to your neighbor."

Deuteronomy 5:1, 6-9, 11-12, 15-21

Be sure to share and live it

A meaningful life begins here: realize that there is only one God and love Him with your whole being. Also, remember that you are here to spread the gospel to the next generation.

⁴"Listen, O Israel! The LORD is our God, the LORD alone. ⁵And you must love the LORD your God with all your heart, all your soul, and all your strength. ⁶And you must commit yourselves wholeheartedly to these commands that I am giving you today.

⁷"Repeat them again and again to your children. Talk about them when you are at home and when you are on the road, when you are going to bed and when you are getting up. ⁸Tie them to your hands and wear them on your forehead as reminders. ⁹Write them on the doorposts of your house and on your gates.

¹⁰"The LORD your God will soon bring you into the land he swore to give you when he made a vow to your ancestors Abraham, Isaac, and Jacob. It is a land with large, prosperous cities that you did not build. ¹¹The houses will be richly stocked with goods you did not produce. You will draw water from cisterns you did not dig, and you will eat from vineyards and olive trees you did not plant. When you have eaten your fill in this land, ¹²be careful not to forget the LORD, who rescued you from slavery in the land of Egypt."

Deuteronomy 6:4-12

Remember
to remember!

People sometimes have such short memories – they forget things so easily. Especially bad things, and God's hand in their lives. In good times it is easy to think that you are great and to say, "Look at all I've done!" But Moses reminds us to remember Who helped us get there.

⁴"For all these forty years your clothes didn't wear out, and your feet didn't blister or swell. ⁵Think about it: Just as a parent disciplines a child, the LORD your God disciplines you for your own good.

⁶"So obey the commands of the LORD your God by walking in his ways and fearing him.

¹⁷"He did all this so you would never say to yourself, 'I have achieved this wealth with my own strength and energy.' ¹⁸Remember the LORD your God. He is the one who gives you power to be successful, in order to fulfill the covenant he confirmed to your ancestors with an oath."

Deuteronomy 8:4-6, 17-18

Choose a
L.O.C.-life!

Who won't choose life instead of death? Yet there are some people who are dead long before they are dead and buried. Life begins with a L.O.C.-choice for God and a L.O.C.-lifestyle: Loving God, Committed to God, Obedient to God.

[15]"Now listen! Today I am giving you a choice between life and death, between prosperity and disaster. [16]For I command you this day to love the LORD your God and to keep his commands, decrees, and regulations by walking in his ways. If you do this, you will live and multiply, and the LORD your God will bless you and the land you are about to enter and occupy.

[19]"Today I have given you the choice between life and death, between blessings and curses. Now I call on heaven and earth to witness the choice you make. Oh, that you would choose life, so that you and your descendants might live!

[20]"You can make this choice by loving the LORD your God, obeying him, and committing yourself firmly to him. This is the key to your life. And if you love and obey the LORD, you will live long in the land the LORD swore to give your ancestors Abraham, Isaac, and Jacob."

Deuteronomy 30:15-16, 19-20

There is no one like God

We are the apple of God's eye. Therefore we can be certain that if we need help, there is no one like God. He rides on the clouds to come to our rescue. This is the kind of help that really works because God Himself helps us.

32 ¹⁰He found them in a desert land, in an empty, howling wasteland. He surrounded them and watched over them; he guarded them as he would guard his own eyes.

¹¹Like an eagle that rouses her chicks and hovers over her young, so he spread his wings to take them up and carried them safely on his pinions.

¹²The LORD alone guided them; they followed no foreign gods.

33 ²⁶"There is no one like the God of Israel. He rides across the heavens to help you, across the skies in majestic splendor.

²⁷"The eternal God is your refuge, and his everlasting arms are under you. He drives out the enemy before you; he cries out, 'Destroy them!'"

Deuteronomy 32:10-12, 33:26-27

Food for the journey

> Pack the following "food" in the backpack of your life: Look for God's fresh signs every day (Josh. 1:3). Remember to stand out (v. 7). Success depends on how much you read God's Word (v. 8). Never give up (v. 9).

³"I promise you what I promised Moses: 'Wherever you set foot, you will be on land I have given you.'

⁵"No one will be able to stand against you as long as you live. For I will be with you as I was with Moses. I will not fail you or abandon you.

⁶"Be strong and courageous, for you are the one who will lead these people to possess all the land I swore to their ancestors I would give them. ⁷Be strong and very courageous. Be careful to obey all the instructions Moses gave you. Do not deviate from them, turning either to the right or to the left. Then you will be successful in everything you do.

⁸"Study this Book of Instruction continually. Meditate on it day and night so you will be sure to obey everything written in it. Only then will you prosper and succeed in all you do. ⁹This is my command—be strong and courageous! Do not be afraid or discouraged. For the LORD your God is with you wherever you go."

Joshua 1:3, 5-9

February

The mighty wall comes tumbling down

The wall of Jericho was the strongest city wall in the ancient world. No unwelcome element could get in – that's why it was one of the safest cities to live in. But for God it was child's play to make the great wall come tumbling down like building blocks. Even today, God's methods can leave your mind boggling in amazement.

¹Now the gates of Jericho were tightly shut because the people were afraid of the Israelites. No one was allowed to go out or in.

²But the LORD said to Joshua, "I have given you Jericho, its king, and all its strong warriors. ³You and your fighting men should march around the town once a day for six days. ⁴Seven priests will walk ahead of the Ark, each carrying a ram's horn. On the seventh day you are to march around the town seven times, with the priests blowing the horns. ⁵When you hear the priests give one long blast on the rams' horns, have all the people shout as loud as they can. Then the walls of the town will collapse, and the people can charge straight into the town."

²⁰When the people heard the sound of the rams' horns, they shouted as loud as they could. Suddenly, the walls of Jericho collapsed, and the Israelites charged straight into the town and captured it.

²⁷So the LORD was with Joshua, and his reputation spread throughout the land.

Joshua 6:1-5, 20, 27

You can't hide your sin for long

Sin doesn't just affect the person who sinned but also the people that person knows. Here, Achan did a silly thing – as if he thought God couldn't see his sin! Because of this the whole of Israel was affected until he confessed his sin. Always think before you do anything wrong – because your actions affect others too.

¹But Israel violated the instructions about the things set apart for the LORD. A man named Achan had stolen some of these dedicated things, so the LORD was very angry with the Israelites. Achan was the son of Carmi, a descendant of Zimri son of Zerah, of the tribe of Judah.

²Joshua sent some of his men from Jericho to spy out the town of Ai, east of Bethel, near Beth-aven. ³When they returned, they told Joshua, "There's no need for all of us to go up there; it won't take more than two or three thousand men to attack Ai. Since there are so few of them, don't make all our people struggle to go up there."

⁴So approximately 3,000 warriors were sent, but they were soundly defeated. The men of Ai ⁵chased the Israelites from the town gate as far as the quarries, and they killed about thirty-six who were retreating down the slope. The Israelites were paralyzed with fear at this turn of events, and their courage melted away.

Joshua 7:1-5

Choose today whom you will serve

Joshua wants to know: What are your priorities? Is your faith just an afterthought or is it the ruling principle in your life; a way to live and the basis on which your whole life is fixed? You cannot choose when and how you will die, but you can decide how you will live!

[14]"So fear the LORD and serve him wholeheartedly. Put away forever the idols your ancestors worshiped when they lived beyond the Euphrates River and in Egypt. Serve the LORD alone. [15]But if you refuse to serve the LORD, then choose today whom you will serve. Would you prefer the gods your ancestors served beyond the Euphrates? Or will it be the gods of the Amorites in whose land you now live? But as for me and my family, we will serve the LORD."

[16]The people replied, "We would never abandon the LORD and serve other gods. [17]For the LORD our God is the one who rescued us and our ancestors from slavery in the land of Egypt. He performed mighty miracles before our very eyes. As we traveled through the wilderness among our enemies, he preserved us."

[21]But the people answered Joshua, "No, we will serve the LORD!"

[22]"You are a witness to your own decision," Joshua said. "You have chosen to serve the LORD."

"Yes," they replied, "we are witnesses to what we have said."

Joshua 24:14-17, 21-22

As soon as Gideon realized that he was not alone and that the Almighty God was with him, his fear and uncertainty turned into courage and certainty. Whenever you are scared or in doubt and want to run away, remember the Lord's words to Gideon – they are still true today, "I will be with you" (v. 16).

[12]The angel of the LORD appeared to him and said, "Mighty hero, the LORD is with you!"

[13]"Sir," Gideon replied, "if the LORD is with us, why has all this happened to us? And where are all the miracles our ancestors told us about? Didn't they say, 'The LORD brought us up out of Egypt'? But now the LORD has abandoned us and handed us over to the Midianites."

[14]Then the LORD turned to him and said, "Go with the strength you have, and rescue Israel from the Midianites. I am sending you!"

[15]"But Lord," Gideon replied, "how can I rescue Israel? My clan is the weakest in the whole tribe of Manasseh, and I am the least in my entire family!"

[16]The LORD said to him, "I will be with you. And you will destroy the Midianites as if you were fighting against one man."

Judges 6:12-16

The story of our lives:
if it wasn't for God

Sometimes we think we are so strong and clever. Our memory spans can become really short when things are going well. God let only 300 men remain of an army of 22,000 so that no one would be able to doubt: It is not us, but God who let us win. So always remember, if it wasn't for God ...

[2] The LORD said to Gideon, "You have too many warriors with you. If I let all of you fight the Midianites, the Israelites will boast to me that they saved themselves by their own strength. [3] Therefore, tell the people, 'Whoever is timid or afraid may leave this mountain and go home.'" So 22,000 of them went home, leaving only 10,000 who were willing to fight.

[4] But the LORD told Gideon, "There are still too many! Bring them down to the spring, and I will test them to determine who will go with you and who will not." [5] When Gideon took his warriors down to the water, the LORD told him, "Divide the men into two groups. In one group put all those who cup water in their hands and lap it up with their tongues like dogs. In the other group put all those who kneel down and drink with their mouths in the stream." [6] Only 300 of the men drank from their hands. All the others got down on their knees and drank with their mouths in the stream.

[7] The LORD told Gideon, "With these 300 men I will rescue you and give you victory over the Midianites. Send all the others home." [8] So Gideon collected the provisions and rams' horns of the other warriors and sent them home. But he kept the 300 men with him.

Judges 7:2-8

A weak side makes your strong side weak too

Strong Samson was known for killing 1,000 men with a donkey's jawbone. But his weakness was a pretty woman. He never built up his character — and it cost him. Your reputation can be destroyed in the blink of an eye if you do not allow God to build up and strengthen your character.

¹⁶Delilah tormented him with her nagging day after day until he was sick to death of it.

¹⁷Finally, Samson shared his secret with her. "My hair has never been cut," he confessed, "for I was dedicated to God as a Nazirite from birth. If my head were shaved, my strength would leave me, and I would become as weak as anyone else."

¹⁸Delilah realized he had finally told her the truth, so she sent for the Philistine rulers. "Come back one more time," she said, "for he has finally told me his secret." So the Philistine rulers returned with the money in their hands. ¹⁹Delilah lulled Samson to sleep with his head in her lap, and then she called in a man to shave off the seven locks of his hair. In this way she began to bring him down, and his strength left him.

²⁰Then she cried out, "Samson! The Philistines have come to capture you!"

When he woke up, he thought, "I will do as before and shake myself free." But he didn't realize the LORD had left him.

²¹So the Philistines captured him and gouged out his eyes. They took him to Gaza, where he was bound with bronze chains and forced to grind grain in the prison.

²²But before long, his hair began to grow back.

Judges 16:16-22

God's solution is sometimes closer than you think

Naomi lost her family (her husband and both her sons died) in a foreign land. She felt like God had abandoned her, but she didn't realize God's solution was in her daughter-in-law, Ruth, who stuck by her side. God uses other people to show you His love and mercy. So keep your eyes open.

¹⁴And again they wept together, and Orpah kissed her mother-in-law good-bye. But Ruth clung tightly to Naomi. ¹⁵"Look," Naomi said to her, "your sister-in-law has gone back to her people and to her gods. You should do the same."

¹⁶But Ruth replied, "Don't ask me to leave you and turn back. Wherever you go, I will go; wherever you live, I will live. Your people will be my people, and your God will be my God. ¹⁷Wherever you die, I will die, and there I will be buried. May the LORD punish me severely if I allow anything but death to separate us!" ¹⁸When Naomi saw that Ruth was determined to go with her, she said nothing more.

¹⁹So the two of them continued on their journey. When they came to Bethlehem, the entire town was excited by their arrival. "Is it really Naomi?" the women asked.

²⁰"Don't call me Naomi," she responded. "Instead, call me Mara, for the Almighty has made life very bitter for me. ²¹I went away full, but the LORD has brought me home empty. Why call me Naomi when the LORD has caused me to suffer and the Almighty has sent such tragedy upon me?"

Ruth 1:14-21

God always sees the bigger picture

There is one thing we can cling to in this life: God always sees the bigger picture. Our vision, just like Naomi's as she returned to Bethlehem is limited and small. We easily get caught in the here and now, but God saw that out of this family line would come not only King David, but also King Jesus!

¹³So Boaz took Ruth into his home, and she became his wife. When he slept with her, the LORD enabled her to become pregnant, and she gave birth to a son. ¹⁴Then the women of the town said to Naomi, "Praise the LORD, who has now provided a redeemer for your family! May this child be famous in Israel. ¹⁵May he restore your youth and care for you in your old age. For he is the son of your daughter-in-law who loves you and has been better to you than seven sons!"

¹⁶Naomi took the baby and cuddled him to her breast. And she cared for him as if he were her own. ¹⁷The neighbor women said, "Now at last Naomi has a son again!" And they named him Obed. He became the father of Jesse and the grandfather of David.

¹⁸This is the genealogical record of their ancestor Perez:

Perez was the father of Hezron. ¹⁹Hezron was the father of Ram. Ram was the father of Amminadab.

²⁰Amminadab was the father of Nahshon. Nahshon was the father of Salmon.

²¹Salmon was the father of Boaz. Boaz was the father of Obed.

²²Obed was the father of Jesse. Jesse was the father of David.

Ruth 4:13-22

Listen before you act

Always listen to another person's story first before you jump to conclusions. Eli saw Hannah and thought that she was drunk. But when he listened to her story he found out she was just heartbroken. People don't always want advice; sometimes they just want to know that someone is listening to them. If someone listens to you, you experience that God is listening too.

⁹Once after a sacrificial meal at Shiloh, Hannah got up and went to pray. Eli the priest was sitting at his customary place beside the entrance of the Tabernacle. ¹⁰Hannah was in deep anguish, crying bitterly as she prayed to the LORD. ¹¹And she made this vow: "O LORD of Heaven's Armies, if you will look upon my sorrow and answer my prayer and give me a son, then I will give him back to you. He will be yours for his entire lifetime, and as a sign that he has been dedicated to the LORD, his hair will never be cut."

¹²As she was praying to the LORD, Eli watched her. ¹³Seeing her lips moving but hearing no sound, he thought she had been drinking. ¹⁴"Must you come here drunk?" he demanded. "Throw away your wine!"

¹⁵"Oh no, sir!" she replied. "I haven't been drinking wine or anything stronger. But I am very discouraged, and I was pouring out my heart to the LORD. ¹⁶Don't think I am a wicked woman! For I have been praying out of great anguish and sorrow."

¹⁷"In that case," Eli said, "go in peace! May the God of Israel grant the request you have asked of him."

1 Samuel 1:9-17

Prayer puts God in the spotlight

Prayer helps you realize: God is God and I am dependent on Him. Hannah came to thank God for her son, Samuel (Samuel means *asked of God*), and there in the temple she prayed, "All that I have is thanks to God and His grace and goodness."

1²⁵After sacrificing the bull, they brought the boy to Eli. ²⁶"Sir, do you remember me?" Hannah asked. "I am the woman who stood here several years ago praying to the Lord. ²⁷I asked the Lord to give me this boy, and he has granted my request. ²⁸Now I am giving him to the Lord, and he will belong to the Lord his whole life." And they worshiped the Lord there.

2¹Then Hannah prayed: "My heart rejoices in the Lord! The Lord has made me strong. Now I have an answer for my enemies; I rejoice because you rescued me.

²"No one is holy like the Lord! There is no one besides you; there is no Rock like our God.

³"Stop acting so proud and haughty! Don't speak with such arrogance! For the Lord is a God who knows what you have done; he will judge your actions."

1 Samuel 1:25-2:3

Listen for God's voice

Sometimes we struggle to hear God's voice, especially to hear Him clearly! Eli gave some advice that we can still follow today:

1. Lie down (just like Samuel, we are too busy running around, we need to be still)
2. Listen (put your ear near God's heart, hear His heartbeat in the Bible)
3. Answer Him (God is calling us, for sure!)

[8]So the LORD called a third time, and once more Samuel got up and went to Eli. "Here I am. Did you call me?"

Then Eli realized it was the LORD who was calling the boy. [9]So he said to Samuel, "Go and lie down again, and if someone calls again, say, 'Speak, LORD, your servant is listening.'" So Samuel went back to bed.

[10]And the LORD came and called as before, "Samuel! Samuel!" And Samuel replied, "Speak, your servant is listening."

[19]As Samuel grew up, the LORD was with him, and everything Samuel said proved to be reliable. [20]And all Israel, from Dan in the north to Beersheba in the south, knew that Samuel was confirmed as a prophet of the LORD. [21]The LORD continued to appear at Shiloh and gave messages to Samuel there at the Tabernacle.

1 Samuel 3:8-10, 19-21

God doesn't look
at people like we do

The Hebrew word used to describe David is *haqqaton*. It implies something that is unimportant or meaningless. But God looks at people differently to how we look at each other. We should learn to look at people the way God looks at them. Everyone is important in God's eyes.

[7]But the LORD said to Samuel, "Don't judge by his appearance or height, for I have rejected him. The LORD doesn't see things the way you see them. People judge by outward appearance, but the LORD looks at the heart."

[10]In the same way all seven of Jesse's sons were presented to Samuel. But Samuel said to Jesse, "The LORD has not chosen any of these." [11]Then Samuel asked, "Are these all the sons you have?"

"There is still the youngest," Jesse replied. "But he's out in the fields watching the sheep and goats."

"Send for him at once," Samuel said. "We will not sit down to eat until he arrives."

[12]So Jesse sent for him. He was dark and handsome, with beautiful eyes. And the LORD said, "This is the one; anoint him."

[13]So as David stood there among his brothers, Samuel took the flask of olive oil he had brought and anointed David with the oil. And the Spirit of the LORD came powerfully upon David from that day on.

1 Samuel 16:7, 10-13

The bigger your God, the smaller the giant

The people were terrified of the giant Goliath. But David challenged him because he believed: The bigger the giant, the harder he hits the ground. David looked beyond the giant and saw God. Who you are in a certain situation is determined by what you see, and what you see determines your actions.

⁴⁰He picked up five smooth stones from a stream and put them into his shepherd's bag. Armed only with his shepherd's staff and sling, he started across the valley to fight the Philistine.

⁴¹Goliath walked out toward David, ⁴²sneering in contempt at this ruddy-faced boy. ⁴³"Am I a dog," he roared at David, "that you come at me with a stick?"

⁴⁵David replied to the Philistine, "You come to me with sword, spear, and javelin, but I come to you in the name of the LORD of Heaven's Armies—the God of the armies of Israel, whom you have defied. ⁴⁶Today the LORD will conquer you, and I will kill you and cut off your head. ⁴⁷And everyone assembled here will know that the LORD rescues his people, but not with sword and spear. This is the LORD's battle, and he will give you to us!"

⁴⁸As Goliath moved closer to attack, David quickly ran out to meet him. ⁴⁹Reaching into his shepherd's bag and taking out a stone, he hurled it with his sling and hit the Philistine in the forehead. The stone sank in, and Goliath stumbled and fell face down on the ground.

⁵⁰So David triumphed over the Philistine with only a sling and a stone, for he had no sword. ⁵¹Then David ran over and pulled Goliath's sword from its sheath. David used it to kill him and cut off his head.

1 Samuel 17:40-43, 45-51

Like David and Jonathan

The question is not, "Who is my best friend?" but rather, "Who am I a best friend to?" To be a friend you must do the following: Honor your friend in every situation. Praise your friend in his absence. Help your friend when he needs it. Laughter, tears and a listening ear are the things that bind friends together.

18 ¹After David had finished talking with Saul, he met Jonathan, the king's son. There was an immediate bond between them, for Jonathan loved David. ²From that day on Saul kept David with him and wouldn't let him return home.

³And Jonathan made a solemn pact with David, because he loved him as he loved himself. ⁴Jonathan sealed the pact by taking off his robe and giving it to David, together with his tunic, sword, bow, and belt.

20 ⁴¹As soon as the boy was gone, David came out from where he had been hiding near the stone pile. Then David bowed three times to Jonathan with his face to the ground. Both of them were in tears as they embraced each other and said good-bye, especially David.

⁴²At last Jonathan said to David, "Go in peace, for we have sworn loyalty to each other in the LORD's name. The LORD is the witness of a bond between us and our children forever." Then David left, and Jonathan returned to the town.

1 Samuel 18:1-4; 20:41-42

Guard your eyes and hands

Power is a tricky thing. It can mess with a person's head so that he thinks he can do whatever he wants. When David decided to sleep with Uriah's wife, Bathsheba, he began to concoct a plan on how to get himself out of trouble. But repentance always comes too late. Think carefully, focus on God before you act.

²Late one afternoon, after his midday rest, David got out of bed and was walking on the roof of the palace. As he looked out over the city, he noticed a woman of unusual beauty taking a bath. ³He sent someone to find out who she was, and he was told, "She is Bathsheba, the daughter of Eliam and the wife of Uriah the Hittite."

⁴Then David sent messengers to get her; and when she came to the palace, he slept with her. Then she returned home. ⁵Later, when Bathsheba discovered that she was pregnant, she sent David a message, saying, "I'm pregnant."

¹⁴So the next morning David wrote a letter to Joab and gave it to Uriah to deliver. ¹⁵The letter instructed Joab, "Station Uriah on the front lines where the battle is fiercest. Then pull back so that he will be killed." ¹⁶So Joab assigned Uriah to a spot close to the city wall where he knew the enemy's strongest men were fighting. ¹⁷And when the enemy soldiers came out of the city to fight, Uriah the Hittite was killed along with several other Israelite soldiers.

2 Samuel 11:2-5, 14-17

A story catches you off-guard

You can't hide sin from God. Nathan used a story to reveal David's misguided thinking of, "I am the king and I can do what I want." Stories have a way of breaking through people's best defence mechanisms. Through Nathan's story David realized his sin and confessed it to God.

¹So the LORD sent Nathan the prophet to tell David this story: "There were two men in a certain town. One was rich, and one was poor. ²The rich man owned a great many sheep and cattle. ³The poor man owned nothing but one little lamb he had bought. He raised that little lamb, and it grew up with his children. It ate from the man's own plate and drank from his cup. He cuddled it in his arms like a baby daughter. ⁴One day a guest arrived at the home of the rich man. But instead of killing an animal from his own flock or herd, he took the poor man's lamb and killed it and prepared it for his guest."

⁵David was furious. "As surely as the LORD lives," he vowed, "any man who would do such a thing deserves to die! ⁶He must repay four lambs to the poor man for the one he stole and for having no pity."

⁷Then Nathan said to David, "You are that man! The LORD, the God of Israel, says: I anointed you king of Israel and saved you from the power of Saul."

¹³Then David confessed to Nathan, "I have sinned against the LORD."

Nathan replied, "Yes, but the LORD has forgiven you, and you won't die for this sin."

2 Samuel 12:1-7, 13

Like father like son

God offered Solomon a wish, "What do you want Me to give you?" Solomon probably thought about all the possibilities, but eventually he wished to be like his father, David (v. 6). David was honest, upright and faithful to God and Solomon wanted to be like that too. Don't you?

⁵That night the LORD appeared to Solomon in a dream, and God said, "What do you want? Ask, and I will give it to you!"

⁶Solomon replied, "You showed faithful love to your servant my father, David, because he was honest and true and faithful to you. And you have continued your faithful love to him today by giving him a son to sit on his throne.

⁷"Now, O LORD my God, you have made me king instead of my father, David, but I am like a little child who doesn't know his way around. ⁹Give me an understanding heart so that I can govern your people well and know the difference between right and wrong. For who by himself is able to govern this great people of yours?"

¹⁰The Lord was pleased that Solomon had asked for wisdom. ¹¹So God replied, "Because you have asked for wisdom in governing my people with justice and have not asked for a long life or wealth or the death of your enemies—¹²I will give you what you asked for! I will give you a wise and understanding heart such as no one else has had or ever will have! ¹³And I will also give you what you did not ask for—riches and fame! No other king in all the world will be compared to you for the rest of your life! ¹⁴And if you follow me and obey my decrees and my commands as your father, David, did, I will give you a long life."

1 Kings 3:5-7, 9-14

True love wants only the best for the one you love

Problem: two women, one living baby and one dead baby. Both women claim that the living baby is their own, which is clearly impossible, so Solomon picks up a sword. One woman begs for the baby's life to be spared and the other woman says to cut the baby in half. It is clear who the mother is. Wisdom knows that love = sacrifice.

[16]Two women came to the king to have an argument settled. [17]One of them began, "this woman and I live in the same house. I gave birth to a baby while she was with me in the house. [19]But her baby died during the night when she rolled over on it. [20]Then she got up in the night and took my son from beside me while I was asleep. She laid her dead child in my arms and took mine. [21]And in the morning when I tried to nurse my son, he was dead! But when I looked more closely, I saw that it wasn't my son at all."

[22]Then the other woman interrupted, "It certainly was your son, and the living child is mine."

"No," the first woman said, "the living child is mine, and the dead one is yours." And so they argued back and forth before the king.

[25]Then the king said, "Cut the living child in two, and give half to one woman and half to the other!"

[26]Then the woman who was the real mother of the living child, and who loved him very much, cried out, "Oh no, my lord! Give her the child—please do not kill him!"

But the other woman said, "All right, he will be neither yours nor mine; divide him between us!"

[27]Then the king said, "Do not kill the child, but give him to the woman who wants him to live, for she is his mother!"

1 Kings 3:16-17, 19-22, 25-27

You have to make a choice

If there is just one believer against an army, then that one person with God is still in the majority. It starts with this: Listen to God, trust Him and do what He says. Only those who are obedient really believe, and only those who believe are truly obedient.

[20] Ahab summoned all the people of Israel and the prophets to Mount Carmel. [21] Elijah stood in front of them and said, "How much longer will you waver, hobbling between two opinions? If the LORD is God, follow him! But if Baal is God, then follow him!"

[22] Then Elijah said to them, "I am the only prophet of the LORD who is left, but Baal has 450 prophets. [23] Now bring two bulls. The prophets of Baal may choose whichever one they wish and cut it into pieces and lay it on the wood of their altar, but without setting fire to it. I will prepare the other bull and lay it on the wood on the altar, but not set fire to it. [24] Then call on the name of your god, and I will call on the name of the LORD. The god who answers by setting fire to the wood is the true God!" And all the people agreed.

[36] At the usual time for offering the evening sacrifice, Elijah the prophet walked up to the altar and prayed, "O LORD, prove today that you are God in Israel and that I am your servant. Prove that I have done all this at your command. [37] Answer me so these people will know that you, O LORD, are God and that you have brought them back to yourself."

[38] Immediately the fire of the LORD flashed down from heaven and burned up the young bull, the wood, the stones, and the dust. [39] And when all the people saw it, they fell face down on the ground and cried out, "The LORD—he is God!"

1 Kings 18:20-24, 36-39

When you are tired, you lose perspective

Sometimes after an emotional or physical high it is easy for a person to feel depressed or burnt out. Then you see the world through dark glasses. In times like these seek God's company, because He will pick you up and help you to see the sunny side of life again.

¹When Ahab got home, he told Jezebel everything Elijah had done, including the way he had killed all the prophets of Baal. ²So Jezebel sent this message to Elijah: "May the gods strike me and even kill me if by this time tomorrow I have not killed you just as you killed them."

³Elijah was afraid and fled for his life. He went to Beersheba, a town in Judah, and he left his servant there. ⁴Then he went on alone into the wilderness, traveling all day. He sat down under a solitary broom tree and prayed that he might die. "I have had enough, LORD," he said. "Take my life, for I am no better than my ancestors who have already died."

⁵Then he lay down and slept under the broom tree. But as he was sleeping, an angel touched him and told him, "Get up and eat!" ⁶He looked around and there beside his head was some bread baked on hot stones and a jar of water! So he ate and drank and lay down again.

⁷Then the angel of the LORD came again and touched him and said, "Get up and eat some more, or the journey ahead will be too much for you."

⁸So he got up and ate and drank, and the food gave him enough strength to travel forty days and forty nights to Mount Sinai, the mountain of God. ⁹There he came to a cave, where he spent the night.

1 Kings 19:1-9

There is only one living God

The purpose of a miracle (like with Naaman) is to glorify God; how great and merciful He is. That is why Elisha at first did not come out of his house to greet his visitor, who was a very important man. A believer's life should always carry this message: "There is a Savior, He alone does good works – not me!"

[7]When the king of Israel read the letter, he tore his clothes in dismay and said, "This man sends me a leper to heal! Am I God, that I can give life and take it away? I can see that he's just trying to pick a fight with me."

[8]But when Elisha, the man of God, heard that the king of Israel had torn his clothes in dismay, he sent this message to him: "Why are you so upset? Send Naaman to me, and he will learn that there is a true prophet here in Israel."

[9]So Naaman went with his horses and chariots and waited at the door of Elisha's house. [10]But Elisha sent a messenger out to him with this message: "Go and wash yourself seven times in the Jordan River. Then your skin will be restored, and you will be healed of your leprosy."

[11]But Naaman became angry and stalked away. "I thought he would certainly come out to meet me!" he said. "I expected him to wave his hand over the leprosy and call on the name of the LORD his God and heal me!"

[14]So Naaman went down to the Jordan River and dipped himself seven times, as the man of God had instructed him. And his skin became as healthy as the skin of a young child's, and he was healed!

2 Kings 5:7-11, 14

To have sight and yet not see is the worst

Dangers and crises can distract our attention so much that we no longer see God in our lives. In bad times, when everything is going wrong, we must pray these words of Elisha, "Lord, open my eyes so I may see."

[15]When the servant of the man of God got up early the next morning and went outside, there were troops, horses, and chariots everywhere. "Oh, sir, what will we do now?" the young man cried to Elisha.

[16]"Don't be afraid!" Elisha told him. "For there are more on our side than on theirs!" [17]Then Elisha prayed, "O LORD, open his eyes and let him see!" The LORD opened the young man's eyes, and when he looked up, he saw that the hillside around Elisha was filled with horses and chariots of fire.

[18]As the Aramean army advanced toward him, Elisha prayed, "O LORD, please make them blind." So the LORD struck them with blindness as Elisha had asked. [19]Then Elisha went out and told them, "You have come the wrong way! This isn't the right city! Follow me, and I will take you to the man you are looking for." And he led them to the city of Samaria.

[20]As soon as they had entered Samaria, Elisha prayed, "O LORD, now open their eyes and let them see." So the LORD opened their eyes, and they discovered that they were in the middle of Samaria.

[21]When the king of Israel saw them, he shouted to Elisha, "My father, should I kill them? Should I kill them?"

[22]"Of course not!" Elisha replied. "Do we kill prisoners of war? Give them food and drink and send them home again to their master."

2 Kings 6:15-22

Life is sometimes difficult, but God is with us 24/7

Jabez means "with pain." I don't think I would like to have that name: "Pain, come here." To live with a name like that can certainly weigh a person down; therefore Jabez just went on his knees and prayed. God heard him and did something about his prayers. Prayer always changes the pray-er!

[9]There was a man named Jabez who was more honorable than any of his brothers. His mother named him Jabez because his birth had been so painful.

[10]He was the one who prayed to the God of Israel, "Oh, that you would bless me and expand my territory! Please be with me in all that I do, and keep me from all trouble and pain!" And God granted him his request.

1 Chronicles 4:9-10

Listen to the right people's advice

Peer pressure has always been around. Rehoboam had to make a big decision. He asked the advice of the older people: they said, "Be kind to Jeroboam." But Rehoboam rejected the advice and asked his friends. They said, "Show him who's boss." He listened to them and his kingdom became divided.

[3]Jeroboam and all Israel went to speak with Rehoboam. [4]"Lighten the harsh labor demands and heavy taxes that your father imposed on us. Then we will be your loyal subjects."

[5]Rehoboam replied, "Come back in three days for my answer." [6]Then King Rehoboam discussed the matter with the older men who had counseled his father, Solomon. "What is your advice?" he asked. [7]The older counselors replied, "If you are good to these people and do your best to please them and give them a favorable answer, they will always be your loyal subjects."

[8]But Rehoboam rejected the advice of the older men and instead asked the opinion of the young men who had grown up with him and were now his advisers.

[10]The young men replied, "This is what you should tell those complainers who want a lighter burden: 'My little finger is thicker than my father's waist! [11]Yes, my father laid heavy burdens on you, but I'm going to make them even heavier! My father beat you with whips, but I will beat you with scorpions!'"

[12]Three days later Jeroboam and all the people returned to hear Rehoboam's decision, just as the king had ordered. [13]But Rehoboam spoke harshly to them, for he rejected the advice of the older counselors [14]and followed the counsel of his younger advisers.

2 Chronicles 10:3-8, 10-14

Too big for your boots

King Asa (like many of us) made the wrong as-
sumption. He thought that as a believer he was
free to do what he thought was good. But a believer
only has freedom as long as his actions reflect
God's love. Your actions must fit in with God's will.

¹In the thirty-sixth year of Asa's reign, King Baasha of Israel
invaded Judah and fortified Ramah in order to prevent anyone
from entering or leaving King Asa's territory in Judah.

²Asa responded by removing the silver and gold from the
treasuries of the Temple of the LORD and the royal palace. He
sent it to King Ben-hadad of Aram, along with this message:
³"Let there be a treaty between you and me. See, I am sending
you silver and gold. Break your treaty with King Baasha of Israel
so that he will leave me alone."

⁴Ben-hadad agreed to King Asa's request and sent the com-
manders of his army to attack the towns of Israel. They conquered the towns of Ijon, Dan, Abel-beth-maacah, and all the
store cities in Naphtali. ⁵As soon as Baasha of Israel heard what
was happening, he abandoned his project of fortifying Ramah
and stopped all work on it.

⁷Hanani the seer came to King Asa and told him, "Because
you have put your trust in the king of Aram instead of in the
LORD your God, you missed your chance to destroy the army of
the king of Aram. ⁸Don't you remember what happened to the
Ethiopians and Libyans and their vast army? At that time you
relied on the LORD, and he handed them over to you. ⁹The eyes
of the LORD search the whole earth in order to strengthen those
whose hearts are fully committed to him. What a fool you have
been! From now on you will be at war."

2 Chronicles 16:1-5, 7-9

Remember: it's God's power that gives you victory

How do we praise God? By trusting Him in everything, by calling on Him when we need help, by seeking Him when we need saving, by declaring with our hearts and mouths that He is the Giver of all that is good. To make God the theme of our song testifies that He is in control.

¹⁵He said, "Listen, all you people of Judah and Jerusalem! This is what the LORD says: Do not be afraid! Don't be discouraged by this mighty army, for the battle is not yours, but God's."

¹⁸Then King Jehoshaphat bowed low with his face to the ground. And all the people of Judah and Jerusalem did the same, worshiping the LORD. ¹⁹Then the Levites stood to praise the LORD, the God of Israel, with a very loud shout.

²⁰The next morning the army of Judah went out into the wilderness. On the way Jehoshaphat stopped and said, "Listen to me, all you people! Believe in the LORD your God, and you will be able to stand firm. Believe in his prophets, and you will succeed."

²¹After consulting the people, the king appointed singers to walk ahead of the army, singing to the LORD and praising him for his holy splendor. This is what they sang: "Give thanks to the LORD; his faithful love endures forever!"

²²At the very moment they began to sing and give praise, the LORD caused the armies of Ammon, Moab, and Mount Seir to start fighting among themselves. ²³The armies of Moab and Ammon turned against their allies from Mount Seir and killed every one of them. After they had destroyed the army of Seir, they began attacking each other.

2 Chronicles 20:15, 18-23

if only ...
but with God I can

Some people live their lives thinking, "If only I ... ". "If only ..." thoughts paralyze you. Josiah decided not to hold on to his past (his grandfather was a murderer and his father wasn't much better) but to walk with God into a new future.

¹Josiah was eight years old when he became king. ²He did what was pleasing in the LORD's sight and followed the example of his ancestor David. He did not turn away from doing what was right.

¹⁴While they were bringing out the money collected at the LORD's Temple, Hilkiah the priest found the Book of the Law of the LORD that was written by Moses.

¹⁹When the king heard what was written in the Law, he tore his clothes in despair. ²⁰Then he gave these orders to Hilkiah, Ahikam, Acbor, Shaphan, and Asaiah: ²¹"Go to the Temple and speak to the LORD for me and for all the remnant of Israel and Judah. Inquire about the words written in the scroll that has been found. For the LORD's great anger has been poured out on us because our ancestors have not obeyed the word of the LORD. We have not been doing everything this scroll says we must do."

³⁰And the king went up to the Temple of the LORD with all the people of Judah and Jerusalem. There the king read to them the entire Book of the Covenant that had been found in the LORD's Temple. ³¹The king took his place of authority beside the pillar and renewed the covenant in the LORD's presence. He pledged to obey the LORD by keeping all his commands, laws, and decrees with all his heart and soul. He promised to obey all the terms of the covenant that were written in the scroll.

2 Chronicles 34:1-2, 14, 19-21, 30-31

Honesty counts in your relationship with God

The Jews viewed Ezra as a second Moses. We read how he was honest before God and apologized to Him. Confession washes the windows of your soul clean and opens your eyes to God's grace. It also opens your soul's windows to do God's will.

[6]I prayed, "O my God, I am utterly ashamed; I blush to lift up my face to you. For our sins are piled higher than our heads, and our guilt has reached to the heavens. [7]From the days of our ancestors until now, we have been steeped in sin. That is why we and our kings and our priests have been at the mercy of the pagan kings of the land. We have been killed, captured, robbed, and disgraced, just as we are today.

[8]"But now we have been given a brief moment of grace, for the LORD our God has allowed a few of us to survive as a remnant. He has given us security in this holy place. Our God has brightened our eyes and granted us some relief from our slavery. [9]For we were slaves, but in his unfailing love our God did not abandon us in our slavery. Instead, he caused the kings of Persia to treat us favorably. He revived us so we could rebuild the Temple of our God and repair its ruins. He has given us a protective wall in Judah and Jerusalem.

[10]"And now, O our God, what can we say after all of this? For once again we have abandoned your commands!

[15]"O LORD, God of Israel, you are just. We come before you in our guilt as nothing but an escaped remnant, though in such a condition none of us can stand in your presence."

Ezra 9:6-10, 15

Planning without prayer is like building castles in the air

When you have a plan, pray over it like Nehemiah did. Then you can be confident that God's hand will be over your plans. When Nehemiah didn't know how to answer the king he quickly prayed to God. You can talk to God 24/7!

1 ⁴When I heard this, I sat down and wept. In fact, for days I mourned, fasted, and prayed to the God of heaven. ¹⁰"The people you rescued by your great power and strong hand are your servants."

2 ¹Early the following spring, during the twentieth year of King Artaxerxes' reign, I was serving the king his wine. I had never before appeared sad in his presence. ²So the king asked me, "Why are you looking so sad? You don't look sick to me. You must be deeply troubled."

Then I was terrified, ³but I replied, "Long live the king! How can I not be sad? For the city where my ancestors are buried is in ruins, and the gates have been destroyed by fire."

⁴The king asked, "Well, how can I help you?" With a prayer to the God of heaven, ⁵I replied, "If it please the king, and if you are pleased with me, your servant, send me to Judah to rebuild the city where my ancestors are buried."

⁶The king, with the queen sitting beside him, asked, "How long will you be gone? When will you return?" After I told him how long I would be gone, the king agreed to my request.

⁸"And please give me a letter addressed to Asaph, the manager of the king's forest, instructing him to give me timber. I will need it to make beams for the gates of the Temple fortress, for the city walls, and for a house for myself." And the king granted these requests, because the gracious hand of God was on me.

Nehemiah 1:4, 10; 2:1-6, 8

March

Put your heart into your work

If you do the right thing, God's thing, then your heart will be in your work – but you should also expect opposition. But if believers roll up their sleeves they can, in spite of the resistance, finish the work – because they know God will make sure they are successful!

¹Sanballat was very angry when he learned that we were rebuilding the wall. He flew into a rage and mocked the Jews, ²saying in front of his friends and the Samarian army officers, "What does this bunch of poor, feeble Jews think they're doing? Do they think they can build the wall in a single day by just offering a few sacrifices? Do they actually think they can make something of stones from a rubbish heap—and charred ones at that?"

³Tobiah the Ammonite, who was standing beside him, remarked, "That stone wall would collapse if even a fox walked along the top of it!"

⁴Then I prayed, "Hear us, our God, for we are being mocked. May their scoffing fall back on their own heads, and may they themselves become captives in a foreign land! ⁵Do not ignore their guilt. Do not blot out their sins, for they have provoked you to anger here in front of the builders."

⁶At last the wall was completed to half its height around the entire city, for the people had worked with enthusiasm.

Nehemiah 4:1-6

When God touches you

From early in the morning until the middle of the day the Israelites busied themselves with the best thing: God's Word. They were affected deeply by it and were moved to live like people of God. The people did what the Word said and their lives moved in the right direction – God's direction.

²So on October 8 Ezra the priest brought the Book of the Law before the assembly, which included the men and women and all the children old enough to understand. ³He faced the square just inside the Water Gate from early morning until noon and read aloud to everyone who could understand. All the people listened closely to the Book of the Law.

⁵Ezra stood on the platform in full view of all the people. When they saw him open the book, they all rose to their feet.

⁶Then Ezra praised the LORD, the great God, and all the people chanted, "Amen! Amen!" as they lifted their hands. Then they bowed down and worshiped the LORD with their faces to the ground.

⁹Then Nehemiah the governor, Ezra the priest and scribe, and the Levites who were interpreting for the people said to them, "Don't mourn or weep on such a day as this! For today is a sacred day before the LORD your God." For the people had all been weeping as they listened to the words of the Law.

¹⁰And Nehemiah continued, "Go and celebrate with a feast of rich foods and sweet drinks, and share gifts of food with people who have nothing prepared. This is a sacred day before our Lord. Don't be dejected and sad, for the joy of the LORD is your strength!"

Nehemiah 8:2-3, 5-6, 9-10

God is devoted to you, so be devoted to Him

You only begin to live when you realize who God is and live like He says you must live. You are only truly faithful if you obey His instructions. The credibility of God's family suffers when believers know God's commands but don't follow them.

9⁵Then the leaders of the Levites—Jeshua, Kadmiel, Bani, Hashabneiah, Sherebiah, Hodiah, Shebaniah, and Pethahiah—called out to the people: "Stand up and praise the LORD your God, for he lives from everlasting to everlasting!" Then they prayed: "May your glorious name be praised! May it be exalted above all blessing and praise!

⁶"You alone are the LORD. You made the skies and the heavens and all the stars. You made the earth and the seas and everything in them. You preserve them all, and the angels of heaven worship you."

10²⁸Then the rest of the people—the priests, Levites, gatekeepers, singers, Temple servants, and all who had separated themselves from the pagan people of the land in order to obey the Law of God, together with their wives, sons, daughters, and all who were old enough to understand—²⁹joined their leaders and bound themselves with an oath. They swore a curse on themselves if they failed to obey the Law of God as issued by his servant Moses. They solemnly promised to carefully follow all the commands, regulations, and decrees of the LORD our Lord.

Nehemiah 9:5-6; 10:28-29

Something is better than nothing

Nothing that happens in your life is ever a co-incidence. Mordecai reminded Esther of this. God works behind the scenes of our lives. He uses normal people like Esther, and you, to bring about His purpose. Then you can take risks – like appearing before the king – because God is in control. Do your bit and God will do the rest.

¹⁰Then Esther told Hathach to go back and relay this message to Mordecai: ¹¹"All the king's officials and even the people in the provinces know that anyone who appears before the king in his inner court without being invited is doomed to die unless the king holds out his gold scepter. And the king has not called for me to come to him for thirty days." ¹²So Hathach gave Esther's message to Mordecai.

¹³Mordecai sent this reply to Esther: "Don't think for a moment that because you're in the palace you will escape when all other Jews are killed. ¹⁴If you keep quiet at a time like this, deliverance and relief for the Jews will arise from some other place, but you and your relatives will die. Who knows if perhaps you were made queen for just such a time as this?"

¹⁵Then Esther sent this reply to Mordecai: ¹⁶"Go and gather together all the Jews of Susa and fast for me. Do not eat or drink for three days, night or day. My maids and I will do the same. And then, though it is against the law, I will go in to see the king. If I must die, I must die." ¹⁷So Mordecai went away and did everything as Esther had ordered him.

Esther 4:10-17

Hold on to God always

Satan, the Accuser, roamed around the earth and then returned to God, full of his old tricks. He said that he was not sure if God's children would still follow Him if they had to go through hard times. God said they would, and so Job was put to the test. Satan was about to be proved wrong!

⁶One day the members of the heavenly court came to present themselves before the LORD, and the Accuser, Satan, came with them. ⁷"Where have you come from?" the LORD asked Satan.

Satan answered the LORD, "I have been patrolling the earth, watching everything that's going on."

⁸Then the LORD asked Satan, "Have you noticed my servant Job? He is the finest man in all the earth. He is blameless—a man of complete integrity. He fears God and stays away from evil."

⁹Satan replied to the LORD, "Yes, but Job has good reason to fear God. ¹⁰You have always put a wall of protection around him and his home and his property. You have made him prosper in everything he does. Look how rich he is! ¹¹But reach out and take away everything he has, and he will surely curse you to your face!"

¹²"All right, you may test him," the LORD said to Satan. "Do whatever you want with everything he possesses, but don't harm him physically." So Satan left the LORD's presence.

²²In all of this, Job did not sin by blaming God.

Job 1:6-12, 22

Give me a break

Sometimes life pushes you into a corner and you can't see any way out. This is when you cry to God, "Lord, if I can just catch my breath, then I will be able to face life and carry on." Find your rest in God.

[15]"I would rather be strangled—rather die than suffer like this.

[16]"I hate my life and don't want to go on living. Oh, leave me alone for my few remaining days.

[17]"What are people, that you should make so much of us, that you should think of us so often?

[18]"For you examine us every morning and test us every moment.

[19]"Why won't you leave me alone, at least long enough for me to swallow!

[20]"If I have sinned, what have I done to you, O watcher of all humanity? Why make me your target? Am I a burden to you?

[21]"Why not just forgive my sin and take away my guilt? For soon I will lie down in the dust and die. When you look for me, I will be gone."

Job 7:15-21

When life knocks you down

A kinsman-redeemer in biblical times was a family member or someone who freed a slave or looked after a widow and her family. Job saw God as His Redeemer and knew that even if everybody else let him down, God would never let one of His children down. All believers can hold tightly to this promise.

¹⁹"My close friends detest me. Those I loved have turned against me. ²⁰I have been reduced to skin and bones and have escaped death by the skin of my teeth.

²¹"Have mercy on me, my friends, have mercy, for the hand of God has struck me.

²²"Must you also persecute me, like God does? Haven't you chewed me up enough?

²³"Oh, that my words could be recorded. Oh, that they could be inscribed on a monument, ²⁴carved with an iron chisel and filled with lead, engraved forever in the rock.

²⁵"But as for me, I know that my Redeemer lives, and he will stand upon the earth at last.

²⁶"And after my body has decayed, yet in my body I will see God!

²⁷"I will see him for myself. Yes, I will see him with my own eyes. I am overwhelmed at the thought!"

Job 19:19-27

Don't try to understand God - worship Him

Job asked God some questions and God's answer was something like this: "Spend a day or two in My shoes." God listed the things that Job would have to do. As the list grew, Job became aware of how great God really is. When he understood this he became very quiet and realized: He is a child of God, not God Himself!

38 ¹Then the LORD answered Job from the whirlwind: ²"Who is this that questions my wisdom with such ignorant words? ³Brace yourself like a man, because I have some questions for you, and you must answer them.

⁴"Where were you when I laid the foundations of the earth? Tell me, if you know so much.

⁵"Who determined its dimensions and stretched out the surveying line? ⁶What supports its foundations, and who laid its cornerstone ⁷as the morning stars sang together and all the angels shouted for joy?

⁸"Who kept the sea inside its boundaries as it burst from the womb, ⁹and as I clothed it with clouds and wrapped it in thick darkness? ¹⁰For I locked it behind barred gates, limiting its shores.

¹¹"I said, 'This far and no farther will you come. Here your proud waves must stop!'

¹²"Have you ever commanded the morning to appear and caused the dawn to rise in the east?"

40 ³Then Job replied to the LORD, ⁴"I am nothing—how could I ever find the answers? I will cover my mouth with my hand. ⁵I have said too much already. I have nothing more to say."

Job 38:1-12; 40:3-5

Everything is OK

Job's prayer is a turning point. Job didn't understand why so many bad things had happened to him, but he realized that God is always near and He protects His children because He loves them. Before this Job had only heard about these things second hand, but now he had personally experienced it and knew it was true!

¹Then Job replied to the LORD: ²"I know that you can do anything, and no one can stop you.

³"You asked, 'Who is this that questions my wisdom with such ignorance?' It is I—and I was talking about things I knew nothing about, things far too wonderful for me.

⁴"You said, 'Listen and I will speak! I have some questions for you, and you must answer them.'

⁵"I had only heard about you before, but now I have seen you with my own eyes.

⁶"I take back everything I said, and I sit in dust and ashes to show my repentance."

Job 42:1-6

The Word's road
or the lost road

The Hebrew word *Hagah* refers to what a lion does at his prey. It is the same word used in the Bible to describe what it means to meditate on the Word of God. Truly joyful people can ponder day and night on the Word with joy and excitement. They stand by the Word, almost like a lion that stands and purrs by his prey before he begins to eat it.

¹Oh, the joys of those who do not follow the advice of the wicked, or stand around with sinners, or join in with mockers. ²But they delight in the law of the LORD, meditating on it day and night.

³They are like trees planted along the riverbank, bearing fruit each season. Their leaves never wither, and they prosper in all they do.

⁴But not the wicked! They are like worthless chaff, scattered by the wind. ⁵They will be condemned at the time of judgment. Sinners will have no place among the godly.

⁶For the LORD watches over the path of the godly, but the path of the wicked leads to destruction.

Psalm 1:1-6

We might be small, but we are special

Here is the perfect example of what a song of praise should sound like. It celebrates the greatness and grace of God by focusing on who He is and all that He does, and shows how small we are compared to God. He is big, but even though His children are small, we are the crown of His creation.

[1]O LORD, our Lord, your majestic name fills the earth! Your glory is higher than the heavens. [2]You have taught children and infants to tell of your strength, silencing your enemies and all who oppose you.

[3]When I look at the night sky and see the work of your fingers—the moon and the stars you set in place—[4]what are mere mortals that you should think about them, human beings that you should care for them?

[5]Yet you made them only a little lower than God and crowned them with glory and honor. [6]You gave them charge of everything you made, putting all things under their authority—[7]the flocks and the herds and all the wild animals, [8]the birds in the sky, the fish in the sea, and everything that swims the ocean currents.

[9]O LORD, our Lord, your majestic name fills the earth!

Psalm 8:1-9

I believe in God, even when He's quiet

Sometimes we feel like God is missing in action. In times like these it is good to read Psalm 13, because this psalm shows you that it is good to ask questions. But you must ask God your questions. Behind all these questions lies a promise in verse 6: God listens to you and will help you.

[2]How long must I struggle with anguish in my soul, with sorrow in my heart? How long will my enemy have the upper hand?

[3]Turn and answer me, O LORD my God! Restore the sparkle to my eyes, or I will die. [4]Don't let my enemies gloat, saying, "We have defeated him!" Don't let them rejoice at my downfall.

[5]But I trust in your unfailing love. I will rejoice because you have rescued me. [6]I will sing to the LORD because he is good to me.

Psalm 13:2-6

Focus on God –
it makes life beautiful

Psalm 16:11 has two lovely images. "You will show me the way of life" means that God's presence is always there helping us. And the "pleasures" refer to His gifts and blessings. The high point in life is that we got the best deal: God's wonderful presence. He is everywhere we go.

[1]Keep me safe, O God, for I have come to you for refuge.

[2]I said to the LORD, "You are my Master! Every good thing I have comes from you." [3]The godly people in the land are my true heroes! I take pleasure in them! [4]Troubles multiply for those who chase after other gods. I will not take part in their sacrifices of blood or even speak the names of their gods.

[5]LORD, you alone are my inheritance, my cup of blessing. You guard all that is mine. [6]The land you have given me is a pleasant land. What a wonderful inheritance!

[7]I will bless the LORD who guides me; even at night my heart instructs me. [8]I know the LORD is always with me. I will not be shaken, for he is right beside me.

[9]No wonder my heart is glad, and I rejoice. My body rests in safety. [10]For you will not leave my soul among the dead or allow your holy one to rot in the grave. [11]You will show me the way of life, granting me the joy of your presence and the pleasures of living with you forever.

Psalm 16:1-11

God will never leave us

Jesus cried out the first verse of Psalm 22 when He was on the cross. Maybe you also sometimes feel cut off from God, but there's a big difference between what you feel and what is real. It doesn't matter how dark it is around you, God is with you 24/7. Jesus made sure of that on the cross!

¹My God, my God, why have you abandoned me? Why are you so far away when I groan for help? ²Every day I call to you, my God, but you do not answer. Every night you hear my voice, but I find no relief.

³Yet you are holy, enthroned on the praises of Israel. ⁴Our ancestors trusted in you, and you rescued them. ⁵They cried out to you and were saved. They trusted in you and were never disgraced.

⁶But I am a worm and not a man. I am scorned and despised by all! ⁷Everyone who sees me mocks me. They sneer and shake their heads, saying, ⁸"Is this the one who relies on the LORD? Then let the LORD save him! If the LORD loves him so much, let the LORD rescue him!"

⁹Yet you brought me safely from my mother's womb and led me to trust you at my mother's breast. ¹⁰I was thrust into your arms at my birth. You have been my God from the moment I was born.

¹¹Do not stay so far from me, for trouble is near, and no one else can help me.

Psalm 22:1-11

Psalm 23

Psalm 23 is probably the most well-known and beloved psalm. It is a psalm for all seasons of life. Remember that when the storm clouds of life begin to gather (v. 4), David no longer talks about God as "He," but "You" – as Someone David knows personally.

¹The LORD is my shepherd; I have all that I need. ²He lets me rest in green meadows; he leads me beside peaceful streams. ³He renews my strength. He guides me along right paths, bringing honor to his name.

⁴Even when I walk through the darkest valley, I will not be afraid, for you are close beside me. Your rod and your staff protect and comfort me.

⁵You prepare a feast for me in the presence of my enemies. You honor me by anointing my head with oil. My cup overflows with blessings.

⁶Surely your goodness and unfailing love will pursue me all the days of my life, and I will live in the house of the LORD forever.

Psalm 23:1-6

The whole universe belongs to God

Verse 1 of Psalm 24 is very important for how a believer views life. It reminds us that everything belongs to God. Verses 3-6 say that for the people who know this, their lives look different. The last verse is used in Jewish ceremonies to remind believers that they are gathered in the presence of God, and they should never forget that.

¹The earth is the LORD's, and everything in it. The world and all its people belong to him. ²For he laid the earth's foundation on the seas and built it on the ocean depths.

³Who may climb the mountain of the LORD? Who may stand in his holy place? ⁴Only those whose hands and hearts are pure, who do not worship idols and never tell lies. ⁵They will receive the LORD's blessing and have a right relationship with God their savior. ⁶Such people may seek you and worship in your presence, O God of Jacob.

⁷Open up, ancient gates! Open up, ancient doors, and let the King of glory enter. ⁸Who is the King of glory? The LORD, strong and mighty; the LORD, invincible in battle. ⁹Open up, ancient gates! Open up, ancient doors, and let the King of glory enter. ¹⁰Who is the King of glory? The LORD of Heaven's Armies—he is the King of glory.

Psalm 24:1-10

Good ...
better ... God

God hates sin. But where people reject and punish, God guides and teaches us in His love and mercy. He is a Fountain that pours out His goodness over sinners. It has nothing to do with our character, but everything to do with God's character.

¹O LORD, I give my life to you. ²I trust in you, my God! Do not let me be disgraced, or let my enemies rejoice in my defeat. ³No one who trusts in you will ever be disgraced, but disgrace comes to those who try to deceive others.

⁴Show me the right path, O LORD; point out the road for me to follow. ⁵Lead me by your truth and teach me, for you are the God who saves me. All day long I put my hope in you.

⁶Remember, O LORD, your compassion and unfailing love, which you have shown from long ages past. ⁷Do not remember the rebellious sins of my youth. Remember me in the light of your unfailing love, for you are merciful, O LORD.

⁸The LORD is good and does what is right; he shows the proper path to those who go astray. ⁹He leads the humble in doing right, teaching them his way. ¹⁰The LORD leads with unfailing love and faithfulness all who keep his covenant and obey his demands.

Psalm 25:1-10

Not scared of anything or anyone

Some psalms end with a reassuring answer or with praise for the answer. In this psalm, however, the psalmist holds tight to God. He pleads for everyone else to do the same, even if there is no answer in sight – because **light** (what God is) is always the symbol of all that is positive and good.

¹The LORD is my light and my salvation—so why should I be afraid? The LORD is my fortress, protecting me from danger, so why should I tremble?

¹⁰Even if my father and mother abandon me, the LORD will hold me close.

¹¹Teach me how to live, O LORD. Lead me along the right path, for my enemies are waiting for me. ¹²Do not let me fall into their hands. For they accuse me of things I've never done; with every breath they threaten me with violence.

¹³Yet I am confident I will see the LORD's goodness while I am here in the land of the living. ¹⁴Wait patiently for the LORD. Be brave and courageous. Yes, wait patiently for the LORD.

Psalm 27:1, 10-14

Grace lets
you celebrate

God is Someone who can turn complaining prayers into joy-filled prayers of thanksgiving. Therefore, our brokenness lets us realize that all we have is God. Hope is to realize that He is all that we need to get out of the situation. Tears take you to Last Chance Station, but God puts you on the train to Celebration.

¹I will exalt you, LORD, for you rescued me. You refused to let my enemies triumph over me. ²O LORD my God, I cried to you for help, and you restored my health. ³You brought me up from the grave, O LORD. You kept me from falling into the pit of death.

⁴Sing to the LORD, all you godly ones! Praise his holy name. ⁵For his anger lasts only a moment, but his favor lasts a lifetime! Weeping may last through the night, but joy comes with the morning.

⁶When I was prosperous, I said, "Nothing can stop me now!" ⁷Your favor, O LORD, made me as secure as a mountain. Then you turned away from me, and I was shattered.

⁸I cried out to you, O LORD. I begged the Lord for mercy, saying, ⁹"What will you gain if I die, if I sink into the grave? Can my dust praise you? Can it tell of your faithfulness? ¹⁰Hear me, LORD, and have mercy on me. Help me, O LORD."

¹¹You have turned my mourning into joyful dancing. You have taken away my clothes of mourning and clothed me with joy, ¹²that I might sing praises to you and not be silent. O LORD my God, I will give you thanks forever!

Psalm 30:1-12

There is no other hand as safe as God's

Jesus spoke some of these words on the cross. In Jewish tradition, little children learn Psalm 31:5 as a prayer before they go to bed: "Into Your hands I commit my spirit." When they wake up in the morning, they are taught to say, "Thank You, Lord, that You gave my life back to me."

²Turn your ear to listen to me; rescue me quickly. Be my rock of protection, a fortress where I will be safe.

³You are my rock and my fortress. For the honor of your name, lead me out of this danger. ⁴Pull me from the trap my enemies set for me, for I find protection in you alone. ⁵I entrust my spirit into your hand. Rescue me, LORD, for you are a faithful God.

⁶I hate those who worship worthless idols. I trust in the LORD. ⁷I will be glad and rejoice in your unfailing love, for you have seen my troubles, and you care about the anguish of my soul. ⁸You have not handed me over to my enemies but have set me in a safe place.

Psalm 31:2-8

Confessing your sin doesn't mean you'll never sin again

Psalm 32 is one of a group of psalms known as "the seven psalms" that concentrates on confessing sin. Psalm 52, where David confesses his sin with Bathsheba, is the most well known of the seven. This story of David is probably also the background to Psalm 32.

[1]Oh, what joy for those whose disobedience is forgiven, whose sin is put out of sight! [2]Yes, what joy for those whose record the LORD has cleared of guilt, whose lives are lived in complete honesty!

[3]When I refused to confess my sin, my body wasted away, and I groaned all day long. [4]Day and night your hand of discipline was heavy on me. My strength evaporated like water in the summer heat.

[5]Finally, I confessed all my sins to you and stopped trying to hide my guilt. I said to myself, "I will confess my rebellion to the LORD." And you forgave me! All my guilt is gone.

[6]Therefore, let all the godly pray to you while there is still time, that they may not drown in the floodwaters of judgment. [7]For you are my hiding place; you protect me from trouble. You surround me with songs of victory.

Psalm 32:1-7

Praise God alone

To truly live is to praise God, and to praise God is to live. If we praise anything else or anyone besides God it will disrupt, and eventually destroy, our lives. Therefore, know this: The words that we use to praise God mold the world that we live in every day.

¹Let the godly sing for joy to the LORD; it is fitting for the pure to praise him. ²Praise the LORD with melodies on the lyre; make music for him on the ten-stringed harp. ³Sing a new song of praise to him; play skillfully on the harp, and sing with joy.

⁴For the word of the LORD holds true, and we can trust everything he does. ⁵He loves whatever is just and good; the unfailing love of the LORD fills the earth.

⁶The LORD merely spoke, and the heavens were created. He breathed the word, and all the stars were born. ⁷He assigned the sea its boundaries and locked the oceans in vast reservoirs. ⁸Let the whole world fear the LORD, and let everyone stand in awe of him. ⁹For when he spoke, the world began! It appeared at his command.

²²Let your unfailing love surround us, LORD, for our hope is in you alone.

Psalm 33:1-9, 22

God's direction
is the best direction

This is a psalm of wisdom that speaks directly to people about God — unlike other psalms that talk to God directly. The Hebrew word for "trust" (vv. 3, 5) literally means "roll." In other words, you "roll" your life up in God's hands. This is good advice to follow.

¹Don't worry about the wicked or envy those who do wrong. ²For like grass, they soon fade away. Like spring flowers, they soon wither.

³Trust in the LORD and do good. Then you will live safely in the land and prosper. ⁴Take delight in the LORD, and he will give you your heart's desires.

⁵Commit everything you do to the LORD. Trust him, and he will help you. ⁶He will make your innocence radiate like the dawn, and the justice of your cause will shine like the noonday sun.

²³The LORD directs the steps of the godly. He delights in every detail of their lives. ²⁴Though they stumble, they will never fall, for the LORD holds them by the hand.

Psalm 37:1-6, 23-24

Clues for when you have the blues

The psalmist of Psalm 42 probably had a bad case of the blues. He felt like he was talking to a wall instead of with the living God. This is not really true, because God is always with us – even when it doesn't feel like it. When we look back we see that we are always connected to God 24/7.

[2]I thirst for God, the living God. When can I go and stand before him? [3]Day and night I have only tears for food, while my enemies continually taunt me, saying, "Where is this God of yours?"

[4]My heart is breaking as I remember how it used to be: I walked among the crowds of worshipers, leading a great procession to the house of God, singing for joy and giving thanks amid the sound of a great celebration!

[5]Why am I discouraged? Why is my heart so sad? I will put my hope in God! I will praise him again—my Savior and [6]my God! Now I am deeply discouraged, but I will remember you—even from distant Mount Hermon, the source of the Jordan, from the land of Mount Mizar. [7]I hear the tumult of the raging seas as your waves and surging tides sweep over me.

Psalm 42:2-7

Be still and experience God

We desperately need to become still, otherwise we race through life and miss both big and small joys of life! This psalm is there to help us to come to a standstill. Whenever fear wants to get the upper hand, it will help us to pray these words, "Be still, and know that I am God."

¹God is our refuge and strength, always ready to help in times of trouble. ²So we will not fear when earthquakes come and the mountains crumble into the sea. ³Let the oceans roar and foam. Let the mountains tremble as the waters surge!

⁴A river brings joy to the city of our God, the sacred home of the Most High. ⁵God dwells in that city; it cannot be destroyed. From the very break of day, God will protect it. ⁶The nations are in chaos, and their kingdoms crumble! God's voice thunders, and the earth melts! ⁷The LORD of Heaven's Armies is here among us; the God of Israel is our fortress.

⁸Come, see the glorious works of the LORD: See how he brings destruction upon the world. ⁹He causes wars to end throughout the earth. He breaks the bow and snaps the spear; he burns the shields with fire.

¹⁰"Be still, and know that I am God! I will be honored by every nation. I will be honored throughout the world."

¹¹The LORD of Heaven's Armies is here among us; the God of Israel is our fortress.

Psalm 46:1-11

Open your eyes to God

Psalm 48 is a song for the pilgrims on their way to Zion. For us reading it today it sounds a bit strange and we don't understand everything in it. But you can replace "Zion" with "the kingdom of God" and "Jerusalem" with "church" whenever you pray this psalm.

¹How great is the LORD, how deserving of praise, in the city of our God, which sits on his holy mountain! ²It is high and magnificent; the whole earth rejoices to see it! Mount Zion, the holy mountain, is the city of the great King! ³God himself is in Jerusalem's towers, revealing himself as its defender.

⁴The kings of the earth joined forces and advanced against the city.

⁹O God, we meditate on your unfailing love as we worship in your Temple. ¹⁰As your name deserves, O God, you will be praised to the ends of the earth. Your strong right hand is filled with victory.

¹⁴For that is what God is like. He is our God forever and ever, and he will guide us until we die.

Psalm 48:1-4, 9-10, 14

The only makeover that actually works

David asked God on the grounds of His grace (I deserve nothing), His faithful love (I belong to You) and great compassion (His gentleness) to wipe away his sins (like a person wipes a board clean) and to make him clean (I am like dirty laundry), so that David could be pure again (Christians are not perfect, just forgiven).

[1] Have mercy on me, O God, because of your unfailing love. Because of your great compassion, blot out the stain of my sins. [2] Wash me clean from my guilt. Purify me from my sin. [3] For I recognize my rebellion; it haunts me day and night.

[4] Against you, and you alone, have I sinned; I have done what is evil in your sight. You will be proved right in what you say, and your judgment against me is just. [5] For I was born a sinner—yes, from the moment my mother conceived me. [6] But you desire honesty from the womb, teaching me wisdom even there.

[7] Purify me from my sins, and I will be clean; wash me, and I will be whiter than snow. [8] Oh, give me back my joy again; you have broken me—now let me rejoice. [9] Don't keep looking at my sins. Remove the stain of my guilt. [10] Create in me a clean heart, O God. Renew a loyal spirit within me. [11] Do not banish me from your presence, and don't take your Holy Spirit from me.

[12] Restore to me the joy of your salvation, and make me willing to obey you.

Psalm 51:1-12

Cut your wings and face your troubles

God did not give us wings so that we could fly away at the first sign of trouble, but rather He gave us courage to face things. Where do we get courage? David's advice is to call on God morning, noon and night. Talk to Him and discover godly courage!

²Please listen and answer me, for I am overwhelmed by my troubles. ³My enemies shout at me, making loud and wicked threats. They bring trouble on me and angrily hunt me down.

⁴My heart pounds in my chest. The terror of death assaults me. ⁵Fear and trembling overwhelm me, and I can't stop shaking. ⁶Oh, that I had wings like a dove; then I would fly away and rest! ⁷I would fly far away to the quiet of the wilderness.

⁸How quickly I would escape—far from this wild storm of hatred.

¹⁷Morning, noon, and night I cry out in my distress, and the LORD hears my voice. ¹⁸He ransoms me and keeps me safe from the battle waged against me, though many still oppose me.

Psalm 55:2-8, 17-18

God's promises

Three times in the psalm, once in verse 4 and twice in verse 10, the psalmist says, "Praise God." The Word is the answer that God gives to His children whenever they pour out their problems before Him. "Don't be afraid, I am with you." God holds you close because He promises to do so in His Word.

³But when I am afraid, I will put my trust in you. ⁴I praise God for what he has promised. I trust in God, so why should I be afraid? What can mere mortals do to me? ⁵They are always twisting what I say; they spend their days plotting to harm me.

¹⁰I praise God for what he has promised; Yes, I praise the LORD for what he has promised. ¹¹I trust in God, so why should I be afraid? What can mere mortals do to me?

¹²I will fulfill my vows to you, O God, and will offer a sacrifice of thanks for your help. ¹³For you have rescued me from death; you have kept my feet from slipping. So now I can walk in your presence, O God, in your life-giving light.

Psalm 56:3-5, 10-13

April

Trust in God ALONE

Psalm 62 is one of the most gripping declarations of trust in God in the Bible. The word that jumps out is *alone*. And to emphasize the psalmist's point to trust in God alone, verses 9 and 10 state who you *shouldn't* trust: We shouldn't put our trust in people or in our own strength or in riches. No, we must trust in God alone.

5Let all that I am wait quietly before God, for my hope is in him. 6He alone is my rock and my salvation, my fortress where I will not be shaken. 7My victory and honor come from God alone. He is my refuge, a rock where no enemy can reach me. 8O my people, trust in him at all times. Pour out your heart to him, for God is our refuge.

9Common people are as worthless as a puff of wind, and the powerful are not what they appear to be. If you weigh them on the scales, together they are lighter than a breath of air.

10Don't make your living by extortion or put your hope in stealing. And if your wealth increases, don't make it the center of your life.

11God has spoken plainly, and I have heard it many times: Power, O God, belongs to you; 12unfailing love, O Lord, is yours. Surely you repay all people according to what they have done.

Psalm 62:5-12

Simply the best in this life

In Psalm 63 there are four facts that we can hold on to:

1. In times of need, go to God (v. 1).
2. His love is worth more than life (v. 3).
3. His hand holds us always (v. 8).
4. Our main purpose in life is to glorify God and enjoy Him forever (v. 4).

[1]O God, you are my God; I earnestly search for you. My soul thirsts for you; my whole body longs for you in this parched and weary land where there is no water.

[2]I have seen you in your sanctuary and gazed upon your power and glory. [3]Your unfailing love is better than life itself; how I praise you!

[4]I will praise you as long as I live, lifting up my hands to you in prayer. [5]You satisfy me more than the richest feast. I will praise you with songs of joy.

[6]I lie awake thinking of you, meditating on you through the night. [7]Because you are my helper, I sing for joy in the shadow of your wings. [8]I cling to you; your strong right hand holds me securely.

Psalm 63:1-8

Focus on God and life will have a richer meaning

Psalm 73:25 is one of the most beautiful confessions of faith in the Bible. The Westminster Catechism's first answer is almost a paraphrase of this verse: "Man's chief and highest end is to glorify God, and fully to enjoy Him forever."

¹Truly God is good to Israel, to those whose hearts are pure. ²But as for me, I almost lost my footing. My feet were slipping, and I was almost gone. ³For I envied the proud when I saw them prosper despite their wickedness.

¹⁶So I tried to understand why the wicked prosper. But what a difficult task it is! ¹⁷Then I went into your sanctuary, O God, and I finally understood the destiny of the wicked. ¹⁸Truly, you put them on a slippery path and send them sliding over the cliff to destruction.

²²I was so foolish and ignorant—I must have seemed like a senseless animal to you. ²³Yet I still belong to you; you hold my right hand. ²⁴You guide me with your counsel, leading me to a glorious destiny. ²⁵Whom have I in heaven but you? I desire you more than anything on earth. ²⁶My health may fail, and my spirit may grow weak, but God remains the strength of my heart; he is mine forever.

Psalm 73:1-3, 16-18, 22-26

The psalmist would rather be a gatekeeper in God's house (v. 10). A gatekeeper or door steward greets people at church and makes them feel welcome. Only when people feel loved by God's children, will they begin to believe that God is Love.

[1]How lovely is your dwelling place, O LORD of Heaven's Armies. [2]I long, yes, I faint with longing to enter the courts of the LORD. With my whole being, body and soul, I will shout joyfully to the living God.

[3]Even the sparrow finds a home, and the swallow builds her nest and raises her young at a place near your altar, O LORD of Heaven's Armies, my King and my God! [4]What joy for those who can live in your house, always singing your praises.

[10]A single day in your courts is better than a thousand anywhere else! I would rather be a gatekeeper in the house of my God than live the good life in the homes of the wicked.

[11]For the LORD God is our sun and our shield. He gives us grace and glory. The LORD will withhold no good thing from those who do what is right. [12]O LORD of Heaven's Armies, what joy for those who trust in you.

Psalm 84:1-4, 10-12

Imitate Christ to others

Psalm 85 says if we let God control our lives, then love and truth embrace, and righteousness and peace kiss each other. No wonder a pope once said that there would be no heathens if Christians just lived like the Lord tells us to.

¹LORD, you poured out blessings on your land! You restored the fortunes of Israel. ²You forgave the guilt of your people—yes, you covered all their sins.

³You held back your fury. You kept back your blazing anger.

⁴Now restore us again, O God of our salvation. Put aside your anger against us once more. ⁵Will you be angry with us always? Will you prolong your wrath to all generations? ⁶Won't you revive us again, so your people can rejoice in you? ⁷Show us your unfailing love, O LORD, and grant us your salvation.

¹⁰Unfailing love and truth have met together. Righteousness and peace have kissed! ¹¹Truth springs up from the earth, and righteousness smiles down from heaven. ¹²Yes, the LORD pours down his blessings. Our land will yield its bountiful harvest.

¹³Righteousness goes as a herald before him, preparing the way for his steps.

Psalm 85:1-7, 10-13

We advertise God's grace

The are many requests in Psalm 86. But one single petition sums it all up, "Grant me purity of heart, so that I may honor You" (v. 11). Like a harpoon with many hooks but one sharp point, prayer can have many requests, but they're all aimed in the same direction – God's direction.

¹Bend down, O LORD, and hear my prayer; answer me, for I need your help. ²Protect me, for I am devoted to you. Save me, for I serve you and trust you. You are my God. ³Be merciful to me, O Lord, for I am calling on you constantly.

⁴Give me happiness, O Lord, for I give myself to you. ⁵O Lord, you are so good, so ready to forgive, so full of unfailing love for all who ask for your help. ⁶Listen closely to my prayer, O LORD; hear my urgent cry. ⁷I will call to you whenever I'm in trouble, and you will answer me.

⁸No pagan god is like you, O Lord. None can do what you do! ⁹All the nations you made will come and bow before you, Lord; they will praise your holy name. ¹⁰For you are great and perform wonderful deeds. You alone are God.

¹¹Teach me your ways, O LORD, that I may live according to your truth! Grant me purity of heart, so that I may honor you. ¹²With all my heart I will praise you, O Lord my God. I will give glory to your name forever, ¹³for your love for me is very great. You have rescued me from the depths of death.

Psalm 86:1-13

Spend some time with God

The Jewish people have two words for a place where people live: *Bajit* (house), and *mahoon* (home). The word *house* makes a person think of a building. The word *home* makes you think of a fireplace, dining together and talking. Isn't it wonderful that the psalmist uses the word *home* to describe God?

¹Lord, through all the generations you have been our home! ²Before the mountains were born, before you gave birth to the earth and the world, from beginning to end, you are God.

³You turn people back to dust, saying, "Return to dust, you mortals!" ⁴For you, a thousand years are as a passing day, as brief as a few night hours. ⁵You sweep people away like dreams that disappear. They are like grass that springs up in the morning. ⁶In the morning it blooms and flourishes, but by evening it is dry and withered. ⁷We wither beneath your anger; we are overwhelmed by your fury. ⁸You spread out our sins before you—our secret sins—and you see them all.

¹⁴Satisfy us each morning with your unfailing love, so we may sing for joy to the end of our lives. ¹⁵Give us gladness in proportion to our former misery! Replace the evil years with good. ¹⁶Let us, your servants, see you work again; let our children see your glory. ¹⁷And may the Lord our God show us his approval and make our efforts successful. Yes, make our efforts successful!

Psalm 90:1-8, 14-17

God saves us because
He loves us

God will never forget you. Psalm 91 emphasizes this through God's words: "I rescue, I protect, I answer, I will be with you, I will honor you, I will reward you." But it assumes there is a deep relationship between God and us. God describes such a relationship like this: "Love Me, know Me, call on Me." Let's live like this!

¹Those who live in the shelter of the Most High will find rest in the shadow of the Almighty. ²This I declare about the LORD: He alone is my refuge, my place of safety; he is my God, and I trust him. ³For he will rescue you from every trap and protect you from deadly disease.

⁹If you make the LORD your refuge, if you make the Most High your shelter, ¹⁰no evil will conquer you; no plague will come near your home. ¹¹For he will order his angels to protect you wherever you go. ¹²They will hold you up with their hands so you won't even hurt your foot on a stone. ¹³You will trample upon lions and cobras; you will crush fierce lions and serpents under your feet!

¹⁴The LORD says, "I will rescue those who love me. I will protect those who trust in my name. ¹⁵When they call on me, I will answer; I will be with them in trouble. I will rescue and honor them. ¹⁶I will reward them with a long life and give them my salvation."

Psalm 91:1-3, 9-16

Never stop growing

The palm and cedar are two exceptional types of trees and are known as the two kings of all trees. They are especially known for their unbelievable vitality. Palm trees can grow to be two centuries old and cedars even older, and yet they continue to be green, healthy and useful. Incidentally the cedar is the tree that is most mentioned in the Bible.

¹It is good to give thanks to the LORD, to sing praises to the Most High. ²It is good to proclaim your unfailing love in the morning, your faithfulness in the evening, ³accompanied by the ten-stringed harp and the melody of the lyre.

⁴You thrill me, LORD, with all you have done for me! I sing for joy because of what you have done. ⁵O LORD, what great works you do! And how deep are your thoughts. ⁶Only a simpleton would not know, and only a fool would not understand this: ⁷Though the wicked sprout like weeds and evildoers flourish, they will be destroyed forever.

¹²But the godly will flourish like palm trees and grow strong like the cedars of Lebanon. ¹³For they are transplanted to the LORD's own house. They flourish in the courts of our God. ¹⁴Even in old age they will still produce fruit; they will remain vital and green. ¹⁵They will declare, "The LORD is just! He is my rock! There is no evil in him!"

Psalm 92:1-7, 12-15

it's all about God

This is a great psalm where the psalmist bubbles over with thankfulness. The psalm is filled with thanksgiving to God, who made us and will love us forever. Verse 3 reminds us that our identity begins and ends with God.

¹Shout with joy to the LORD, all the earth! ²Worship the LORD with gladness. Come before him, singing with joy.

³Acknowledge that the LORD is God! He made us, and we are his. We are his people, the sheep of his pasture. ⁴Enter his gates with thanksgiving; go into his courts with praise. Give thanks to him and praise his name.

⁵For the LORD is good. His unfailing love continues forever, and his faithfulness continues to each generation.

Psalm 100:1-5

God has enough grace for the whole world

God always forgives you. You don't have to walk around with a guilty conscience ever again. If you confess your sins the Lord removes them as far as the east is from the west (sunrise from sunset). How far is that? Immeasurable! Your forgiven sins can never be found again.

[1]Let all that I am praise the LORD; with my whole heart, I will praise his holy name. [2]Let all that I am praise the LORD; may I never forget the good things he does for me. [3]He forgives all my sins and heals all my diseases. [4]He redeems me from death and crowns me with love and tender mercies. [5]He fills my life with good things. My youth is renewed like the eagle's!

[10]He does not punish us for all our sins; he does not deal harshly with us, as we deserve. [11]For his unfailing love toward those who fear him is as great as the height of the heavens above the earth. [12]He has removed our sins as far from us as the east is from the west. [13]The LORD is like a father to his children, tender and compassionate to those who fear him.

[14]For he knows how weak we are; he remembers we are only dust. [15]Our days on earth are like grass; like wildflowers, we bloom and die. [16]The wind blows, and we are gone—as though we had never been here. [17]But the love of the LORD remains forever with those who fear him. His salvation extends to the children's children [18]of those who are faithful to his covenant, of those who obey his commandments!

Psalm 103:1-5, 10-18

God's wonderful color palette

In Psalm 104 the psalmist realizes that every-thing in the world is woven together and con-nected. He doesn't just see animals and plants and rivers; he sees the Creator. He sees the Painter sitting behind the painting of the whole universe. He praises God for His greatness.

¹Let all that I am praise the LORD. O LORD my God, how great you are! You are robed with honor and majesty.

³⁰When you give them your breath, life is created, and you renew the face of the earth.

³¹May the glory of the LORD continue forever! The LORD takes pleasure in all he has made! ³²The earth trembles at his glance; the mountains smoke at his touch.

³³I will sing to the LORD as long as I live. I will praise my God to my last breath! ³⁴May all my thoughts be pleasing to him, for I rejoice in the LORD. ³⁵Let all sinners vanish from the face of the earth; let the wicked disappear forever. Let all that I am praise the LORD. Praise the LORD!

Psalm 104:1, 30-35

Wake the sleeping sun

David was so excited about what he learned from God that he wanted to wake the dawn with music. Usually this works the other way around – the sunrise wakes us up. But, if you are truly excited about God, such excitement turns everything upside-down!

¹My heart is confident in you, O God; no wonder I can sing your praises with all my heart!

²Wake up, lyre and harp! I will wake the dawn with my song. ³I will thank you, LORD, among all the people. I will sing your praises among the nations. ⁴For your unfailing love is higher than the heavens. Your faithfulness reaches to the clouds.

⁵Be exalted, O God, above the highest heavens. May your glory shine over all the earth.

Psalm 108:1-5

Wisdom is ...

Psalm 111 says that wisdom is noticing what God does, and letting that inspire you to serve Him. What does God do? He performs His miracles in people and gives us His law (how we should live) in order for us to be His living miracles, His hallelujahs, in the world.

¹Praise the LORD! I will thank the LORD with all my heart as I meet with his godly people. ²How amazing are the deeds of the LORD! All who delight in him should ponder them.

³Everything he does reveals his glory and majesty. His righteousness never fails. ⁴He causes us to remember his wonderful works. How gracious and merciful is our LORD!

⁵He gives food to those who fear him; he always remembers his covenant. ⁶He has shown his great power to his people by giving them the lands of other nations. ⁷All he does is just and good, and all his commandments are trustworthy. ⁸They are forever true, to be obeyed faithfully and with integrity.

⁹He has paid a full ransom for his people. He has guaranteed his covenant with them forever. What a holy, awe-inspiring name he has! ¹⁰Fear of the LORD is the foundation of true wisdom. All who obey his commandments will grow in wisdom. Praise him forever!

Psalm 111:1-10

God's goodness has no end

Psalm 113-118 were sung during the Passover meal. The first two psalms were sung before the meal and the rest were sung afterward. Verse 29 of Psalm 118 was probably the last thing that Jesus sung before He went to the Garden of Gethsemane and was eventually crucified for us.

¹Give thanks to the LORD, for he is good! His faithful love endures forever.

⁵In my distress I prayed to the LORD, and the LORD answered me and set me free.

⁸It is better to take refuge in the LORD than to trust in people. ⁹It is better to take refuge in the LORD than to trust in princes.

²⁴This is the day the LORD has made. We will rejoice and be glad in it. ²⁵Please, LORD, please save us. Please, LORD, please give us success. ²⁶Bless the one who comes in the name of the LORD. We bless you from the house of the LORD. ²⁷The LORD is God, shining upon us. Take the sacrifice and bind it with cords on the altar. ²⁸You are my God, and I will praise you! You are my God, and I will exalt you!

²⁹Give thanks to the LORD, for he is good! His faithful love endures forever.

Psalm 118:1, 5, 8-9, 24-29

God is available 24/7 –
He never sleeps

Psalm 121 was written for those traveling to or from the temple in Jerusalem for one of the big feasts. The road to and from Jerusalem was not very safe for travelers. Wild animals and robbers sometimes hid in the hilly landscape. But even in danger believers know that God is their help.

[1]I look up to the mountains—does my help come from there? [2]My help comes from the LORD, who made heaven and earth!

[3]He will not let you stumble; the one who watches over you will not slumber. [4]Indeed, he who watches over Israel never slumbers or sleeps.

[5]The LORD himself watches over you! The LORD stands beside you as your protective shade. [6]The sun will not harm you by day, nor the moon at night.

[7]The LORD keeps you from all harm and watches over your life. [8]The LORD keeps watch over you as you come and go, both now and forever.

Psalm 121:1-8

Joy shouldn't be kept a secret

What is the secret to the joy in Psalm 126? The secret is found in two words: *remember* and *hope*. We must think back on what God has done, we must read the Bible – God's photo album. And we must look ahead to what that same God is still going to do. If this does not fill you with joy, then you have missed the point.

¹When the LORD brought back his exiles to Jerusalem, it was like a dream!

²We were filled with laughter, and we sang for joy. And the other nations said, "What amazing things the LORD has done for them." ³Yes, the LORD has done amazing things for us! What joy!

⁴Restore our fortunes, LORD, as streams renew the desert. ⁵Those who plant in tears will harvest with shouts of joy. ⁶They weep as they go to plant their seed, but they sing as they return with the harvest.

Psalm 126:1-6

The secret to a meaningful life

Psalm 127 points out a few important things: Take God seriously, make Him the Builder of your life, follow His ways and you will have a meaningful life. This psalm teaches us that a meaningful life is not made up of our possessions or what we have, but how much love we have for others.

[1]Unless the LORD builds a house, the work of the builders is wasted. Unless the LORD protects a city, guarding it with sentries will do no good.

[2]It is useless for you to work so hard from early morning until late at night, anxiously working for food to eat; for God gives rest to his loved ones.

[3]Children are a gift from the LORD; they are a reward from him. [4]Children born to a young man are like arrows in a warrior's hands. [5]How joyful is the man whose quiver is full of them! He will not be put to shame when he confronts his accusers at the city gates.

Psalm 127:1-5

Wait ... watch ...
God is coming

There is a wall of remembrance in Dachau, Germany, where a concentration camp used to be. The first five verses of Psalm 130 are inscribed there. Remember that we can count on God in any and every situation, even in a concentration camp.

¹From the depths of despair, O LORD, I call for your help. ²Hear my cry, O Lord. Pay attention to my prayer.

³LORD, if you kept a record of our sins, who, O Lord, could ever survive? ⁴But you offer forgiveness, that we might learn to fear you.

⁵I am counting on the LORD; yes, I am counting on him. I have put my hope in his word. ⁶I long for the Lord more than sentries long for the dawn, yes, more than sentries long for the dawn.

⁷O Israel, hope in the LORD; for with the LORD there is unfailing love. His redemption overflows. ⁸He himself will redeem Israel from every kind of sin.

Psalm 130:1-8

A short psalm that takes long to learn

Psalm 131 helps us to fight one of the oldest sins we know – pride. Pride was the reason Adam and Eve were banished from the Garden of Eden – and pride needs to be overcome by humility. Being proud is when you think you are god, and being humble is when you know without a doubt that there is a Savior.

¹LORD, my heart is not proud; my eyes are not haughty. I don't concern myself with matters too great or too awesome for me to grasp.

²Instead, I have calmed and quieted myself, like a weaned child who no longer cries for its mother's milk. Yes, like a weaned child is my soul within me.

³O Israel, put your hope in the LORD—now and always.

Psalm 131:1-3

Without God's blessing, no one can survive

The chief focus of Psalm 134 is the word "bless" in verse 3. What does "the Lord will bless you" mean? Many people confuse this with having lots of possessions. Actually, it refers to what God does for us: He promises us a relationship with Himself and promises to never leave us. We share in His love, peace and light.

¹Oh, praise the LORD, all you servants of the LORD, you who serve at night in the house of the LORD.

²Lift up holy hands in prayer, and praise the LORD.

³May the LORD, who made heaven and earth, bless you from Jerusalem.

Psalm 134:1-3

There is no end to God's love for us

"His faithful love endures forever" is repeated twenty-six times in Psalm 136. It's as if the psalmist is trying to make us sensitive to God's love. In this way we will stay focused on God, the central point of our lives, and then thankfulness to Him will become our lifestyle 24/7.

¹Give thanks to the Lord, for he is good! *His faithful love endures forever.* ²Give thanks to the God of gods. *His faithful love endures forever.* ³Give thanks to the Lord of lords. *His faithful love endures forever.*

⁴Give thanks to him who alone does mighty miracles. *His faithful love endures forever.* ⁵Give thanks to him who made the heavens so skillfully. *His faithful love endures forever.* ⁶Give thanks to him who placed the earth among the waters. *His faithful love endures forever.*

⁷Give thanks to him who made the heavenly lights—*His faithful love endures forever.* ⁸the sun to rule the day, *His faithful love endures forever.* ⁹and the moon and stars to rule the night. *His faithful love endures forever.*

²³He remembered us in our weakness. *His faithful love endures forever.* ²⁴He saved us from our enemies. *His faithful love endures forever.* ²⁵He gives food to every living thing. *His faithful love endures forever.* ²⁶Give thanks to the God of heaven. *His faithful love endures forever.*

Psalm 136:1-9, 23-26

Wow!
God made you!

Every person has, in his or her own body, enough reasons to be thankful to God. People display God's skill. You are not an accident. You are not a mistake. God decided the world would be a poorer place without you; therefore He created you! You are a miracle!

¹O LORD, you have examined my heart and know everything about me. ²You know when I sit down or stand up. You know my thoughts even when I'm far away. ³You see me when I travel and when I rest at home. You know everything I do. ⁴You know what I am going to say even before I say it, LORD.

⁵You go before me and follow me. You place your hand of blessing on my head. ⁶Such knowledge is too wonderful for me, too great for me to understand!

¹³You made all the delicate, inner parts of my body and knit me together in my mother's womb. ¹⁴Thank you for making me so wonderfully complex! Your workmanship is marvelous—how well I know it. ¹⁵You watched me as I was being formed in utter seclusion, as I was woven together in the dark of the womb.

¹⁶You saw me before I was born. Every day of my life was recorded in your book. Every moment was laid out before a single day had passed.

Psalm 139:1-6, 13-16

Put a guard, no, an army, before my mouth!

The Jewish wise man, Ben Sirah, made this true statement, "Many have fallen by the edge of the sword; but not so many as have fallen by the tongue." Therefore we should pray verse 3 every day so that only constructive, godly words come out of our mouths.

¹O LORD, I am calling to you. Please hurry! Listen when I cry to you for help! ²Accept my prayer as incense offered to you, and my upraised hands as an evening offering.

³Take control of what I say, O LORD, and guard my lips. ⁴Don't let me drift toward evil or take part in acts of wickedness. Don't let me share in the delicacies of those who do wrong.

⁹Keep me from the traps they have set for me, from the snares of those who do wrong. ¹⁰Let the wicked fall into their own nets, but let me escape.

Psalm 141:1-4, 9-10

Hallelujah!

Five joy-filled praise psalms bring the book of Psalms (1-150) to an end. In the original Hebrew text every single one of these psalms began and ended with the word *Hallelujah*, which means, "Praise the Lord." What a good way to start and end the day!

¹Praise the LORD! Let all that I am praise the LORD. ²I will praise the LORD as long as I live. I will sing praises to my God with my dying breath.

³Don't put your confidence in powerful people; there is no help for you there. ⁴When they breathe their last, they return to the earth, and all their plans die with them. ⁵But joyful are those who have the God of Israel as their helper, whose hope is in the LORD their God.

⁶He made heaven and earth, the sea, and everything in them. He keeps every promise forever. ⁷He gives justice to the oppressed and food to the hungry. The LORD frees the prisoners. ⁸The LORD opens the eyes of the blind. The LORD lifts up those who are weighed down. The LORD loves the godly. ⁹The LORD protects the foreigners among us. He cares for the orphans and widows, but he frustrates the plans of the wicked. ¹⁰The LORD will reign forever. He will be your God, O Jerusalem, throughout the generations. Praise the LORD!

Psalm 146:1-10

Make your whole life a symphony of praise

Psalm 150 invites the whole of humankind, creation and the heavens to praise God. Because it's God who should be praised, it's not necessary to give a single reason for it. It is enough to say, "Let everything that has breath praise the Lord." That's what we'll do one day – forever.

¹Praise the LORD! Praise God in his sanctuary; praise him in his mighty heaven! ²Praise him for his mighty works; praise his unequaled greatness!

³Praise him with a blast of the ram's horn; praise him with the lyre and harp! ⁴Praise him with the tambourine and dancing; praise him with strings and flutes! ⁵Praise him with a clash of cymbals; praise him with loud clanging cymbals. ⁶Let everything that breathes sing praises to the LORD! Praise the LORD!

Psalm 150:1-6

Live and learn

The Hebrew word that we translate as "ask God what His will is" means that you are aware of Him all the time and are constantly in meaningful contact with God so that His approval can be on your life. Therefore Proverbs 3:7 emphasizes that you can never sit back in life and think you know it all, you must always be open to learning new things.

¹My child, never forget the things I have taught you. Store my commands in your heart. ²If you do this, you will live many years, and your life will be satisfying.

³Never let loyalty and kindness leave you! Tie them around your neck as a reminder. Write them deep within your heart. ⁴Then you will find favor with both God and people, and you will earn a good reputation.

⁵Trust in the LORD with all your heart; do not depend on your own understanding. ⁶Seek his will in all you do, and he will show you which path to take.

⁷Don't be impressed with your own wisdom. Instead, fear the LORD and turn away from evil. ⁸Then you will have healing for your body and strength for your bones.

Proverbs 3:1-8

The heart,
your control center

The word "heart" (v. 23) is used here as an image of who you are as a person (and does not refer to the human organ that pumps blood). That is why the writer of Proverbs warns us about what we allow into our hearts, because it impacts how you live your life.

[18]The way of the righteous is like the first gleam of dawn, which shines ever brighter until the full light of day. [19]But the way of the wicked is like total darkness. They have no idea what they are stumbling over.

[20]My child, pay attention to what I say. Listen carefully to my words. [21]Don't lose sight of them. Let them penetrate deep into your heart, [22]for they bring life to those who find them, and healing to their whole body.

[23]Guard your heart above all else, for it determines the course of your life.

[24]Avoid all perverse talk; stay away from corrupt speech.

[25]Look straight ahead, and fix your eyes on what lies before you. [26]Mark out a straight path for your feet; stay on the safe path. [27]Don't get sidetracked; keep your feet from following evil.

Proverbs 4:18-27

Learn a lesson from the ants!

If you study ants you will learn that each ant colony has at least one queen who their lives revolve around. Let your life revolve around Jesus! Faithful believers will stay away from the seven things that God hates. Believers should be like ants who are hardworking and full of life and don't even know what laziness is.

⁶Take a lesson from the ants, you lazybones. Learn from their ways and become wise! ⁷Though they have no prince or governor or ruler to make them work, ⁸they labor hard all summer, gathering food for the winter.

⁹But you, lazybones, how long will you sleep? When will you wake up? ¹⁰A little extra sleep, a little more slumber, a little folding of the hands to rest—¹¹then poverty will pounce on you like a bandit; scarcity will attack you like an armed robber.

¹⁶There are six things the LORD hates—no, seven things he detests: ¹⁷haughty eyes, a lying tongue, hands that kill the innocent, ¹⁸a heart that plots evil, feet that race to do wrong, ¹⁹a false witness who pours out lies, a person who sows discord in a family.

Proverbs 6:6-11, 16-19

Tracks to heaven

Our lives should leave tracks that lead to heaven. Therefore the following verses will help you to watch your words and not to harm others by what you say. Act in such a way that people will want to be around you because your words are like a fountain of goodness and love that enriches and inspires others.

⁶The godly are showered with blessings; the words of the wicked conceal violent intentions.

⁷We have happy memories of the godly, but the name of a wicked person rots away.

⁸The wise are glad to be instructed, but babbling fools fall flat on their faces.

⁹People with integrity walk safely, but those who follow crooked paths will slip and fall.

¹⁰People who wink at wrong cause trouble, but a bold reproof promotes peace.

¹¹The words of the godly are a life-giving fountain; the words of the wicked conceal violent intentions.

¹²Hatred stirs up quarrels, but love makes up for all offenses.

¹⁸Hiding hatred makes you a liar; slandering others makes you a fool.

¹⁹Too much talk leads to sin. Be sensible and keep your mouth shut.

²⁰The words of the godly are like sterling silver; the heart of a fool is worthless.

²¹The words of the godly encourage many, but fools are destroyed by their lack of common sense.

Proverbs 10:6-12, 18-21

May

Think before you speak

Differences are a part of life. People rub each other up the wrong way sometimes, which causes conflict. When there are differences between people it is easy to let words just slip out. But the verses in Proverbs 13 give advice for this. Keep your mouth shut and listen. First try to understand before you expect to be understood.

²Wise words will win you a good meal, but treacherous people have an appetite for violence.

³Those who control their tongue will have a long life; opening your mouth can ruin everything.

⁴Lazy people want much but get little, but those who work hard will prosper.

⁵The godly hate lies; the wicked cause shame and disgrace.

⁶Godliness guards the path of the blameless, but the evil are misled by sin.

⁷Some who are poor pretend to be rich; others who are rich pretend to be poor.

⁸The rich can pay a ransom for their lives, but the poor won't even get threatened.

⁹The life of the godly is full of light and joy, but the light of the wicked will be snuffed out.

¹⁰Pride leads to conflict; those who take advice are wise.

Proverbs 13:2-10

Make life a celebration

Proverbs 15:3 shows how great God really is. He's so great that He is everywhere and sees everything. He is so great that the heavens cannot hold Him, but so humble that He lives inside you. That's why we, as His children, must live in such a way that we make life a celebration for others; and then life will be a celebration for us too!

[1]A gentle answer deflects anger, but harsh words make tempers flare.

[2]The tongue of the wise makes knowledge appealing, but the mouth of a fool belches out foolishness.

[3]The LORD is watching everywhere, keeping his eye on both the evil and the good.

[4]Gentle words are a tree of life; a deceitful tongue crushes the spirit.

[13]A glad heart makes a happy face; a broken heart crushes the spirit.

[14]A wise person is hungry for knowledge, while the fool feeds on trash.

[15]For the despondent, every day brings trouble; for the happy heart, life is a continual feast.

[16]Better to have little, with fear for the LORD, than to have great treasure and inner turmoil.

[17]A bowl of vegetables with someone you love is better than steak with someone you hate.

[18]A hot-tempered person starts fights; a cool-tempered person stops them.

[19]A lazy person's way is blocked with briers, but the path of the upright is an open highway.

Proverbs 15:1-4, 13-19

What happens in this life echoes in the afterlife

We either rely on luck – hoping for the best – or we hope in God. To hope in God is the best and safest and makes a big difference. Remember, your faith gives you direction – you are on the road to heaven. It also gives you purpose – you must love God and your fellow man.

[1]We can make our own plans, but the LORD gives the right answer.

[2]People may be pure in their own eyes, but the LORD examines their motives.

[3]Commit your actions to the LORD, and your plans will succeed.

[4]The LORD has made everything for his own purposes, even the wicked for a day of disaster.

[5]The LORD detests the proud; they will surely be punished.

[6]Unfailing love and faithfulness make atonement for sin. By fearing the LORD, people avoid evil.

[7]When people's lives please the LORD, even their enemies are at peace with them.

[8]Better to have little, with godliness, than to be rich and dishonest.

[9]We can make our plans, but the LORD determines our steps.

Proverbs 16:1-9

Proverbs 17:1 asks that we live a life of simplicity. What does that mean? Simplicity means to look around you and realize that there is more to God and His creation than you realized!

¹Better a dry crust eaten in peace than a house filled with feasting—and conflict.

²A wise servant will rule over the master's disgraceful son and will share the inheritance of the master's children.

³Fire tests the purity of silver and gold, but the Lord tests the heart.

⁴Wrongdoers eagerly listen to gossip; liars pay close attention to slander.

⁵Those who mock the poor insult their Maker; those who rejoice at the misfortune of others will be punished.

⁶Grandchildren are the crowning glory of the aged; parents are the pride of their children.

⁷Eloquent words are not fitting for a fool; even less are lies fitting for a ruler.

⁸A bribe is like a lucky charm; whoever gives one will prosper!

⁹Love prospers when a fault is forgiven, but dwelling on it separates close friends.

Proverbs 17:1-9

Treasure your good reputation

Proverbs 22:1 does not say that money is bad, but it emphasizes that nothing is worth more than a good name. A person's name – his reputation and what he stands for – is the most precious treasure. A good reputation is the most difficult thing in the world to get, and the easiest thing in the world to lose.

¹Choose a good reputation over great riches; being held in high esteem is better than silver or gold.

²The rich and poor have this in common: The LORD made them both.

³A prudent person foresees danger and takes precautions. The simpleton goes blindly on and suffers the consequences.

⁴True humility and fear of the LORD lead to riches, honor, and long life. ⁵Corrupt people walk a thorny, treacherous road; whoever values life will avoid it.

⁶Direct your children onto the right path, and when they are older, they will not leave it.

⁷Just as the rich rule the poor, so the borrower is servant to the lender.

⁸Those who plant injustice will harvest disaster, and their reign of terror will come to an end.

⁹Blessed are those who are generous, because they feed the poor.

¹⁰Throw out the mocker, and fighting goes, too. Quarrels and insults will disappear.

¹¹Whoever loves a pure heart and gracious speech will have the king as a friend. ¹²The LORD preserves those with knowledge, but he ruins the plans of the treacherous.

Proverbs 22:1-12

Small in stature, but very wise

Ants teach us to focus on our work and not be lazy. Rock rabbits teach us that our strength and safety does not lie with us, but in God who shelters us. Locusts teach us that together we are strong. And lizards teach us about fearlessness.

¹⁸There are three things that amaze me—no, four things that I don't understand: ¹⁹how an eagle glides through the sky, how a snake slithers on a rock, how a ship navigates the ocean, how a man loves a woman.

²⁰An adulterous woman consumes a man, then wipes her mouth and says, "What's wrong with that?"

²¹There are three things that make the earth tremble—no, four it cannot endure: ²²a slave who becomes a king, an overbearing fool who prospers, ²³a bitter woman who finally gets a husband, a servant girl who supplants her mistress.

²⁴There are four things on earth that are small but unusually wise: ²⁵Ants—they aren't strong, but they store up food all summer. ²⁶Hyraxes—they aren't powerful, but they make their homes among the rocks. ²⁷Locusts—they have no king, but they march in formation. ²⁸Lizards—they are easy to catch, but they are found even in kings' palaces.

Proverbs 30:18-28

Without God everything is meaningless

You cannot survive or live with any meaning until you start where it matters, because, according to Ecclesiastes, everything under the sun is like chasing after the wind. Where do you start? In a manner of speaking "above the sun"; with God of course.

2"Everything is meaningless," says the Teacher, "completely meaningless!"

3What do people get for all their hard work under the sun? 4Generations come and generations go, but the earth never changes. 5The sun rises and the sun sets, then hurries around to rise again. 6The wind blows south, and then turns north. Around and around it goes, blowing in circles. 7Rivers run into the sea, but the sea is never full. Then the water returns again to the rivers and flows out again to the sea. 8Everything is wearisome beyond description. No matter how much we see, we are never satisfied. No matter how much we hear, we are not content.

9History merely repeats itself. It has all been done before. Nothing under the sun is truly new. 10Sometimes people say, "Here is something new!" But actually it is old; nothing is ever truly new. 11We don't remember what happened in the past, and in future generations, no one will remember what we are doing now.

12I, the Teacher, was king of Israel, and I lived in Jerusalem. 13I devoted myself to search for understanding and to explore by wisdom everything being done under heaven. I soon discovered that God has dealt a tragic existence to the human race. 14I observed everything going on under the sun, and really, it is all meaningless—like chasing the wind.

Ecclesiastes 1:2-14

Use your time wisely

Time is precious! Cherish every moment you have so that every moment can become a "heaven on earth" moment. Always remember what Betty Smith said about time: "Look at everything as though you were seeing it either for the first or last time. Then your time on earth will be filled with glory."

¹For everything there is a season, a time for every activity under heaven.

²A time to be born and a time to die. A time to plant and a time to harvest. ³A time to kill and a time to heal. A time to tear down and a time to build up. ⁴A time to cry and a time to laugh. A time to grieve and a time to dance. ⁵A time to scatter stones and a time to gather stones. A time to embrace and a time to turn away. ⁶A time to search and a time to quit searching. A time to keep and a time to throw away. ⁷A time to tear and a time to mend. A time to be quiet and a time to speak. ⁸A time to love and a time to hate. A time for war and a time for peace.

⁹What do people really get for all their hard work? ¹⁰I have seen the burden God has placed on us all. ¹¹Yet God has made everything beautiful for its own time. He has planted eternity in the human heart, but even so, people cannot see the whole scope of God's work from beginning to end. ¹²So I concluded there is nothing better than to be happy and enjoy ourselves as long as we can. ¹³And people should eat and drink and enjoy the fruits of their labor, for these are gifts from God.

Ecclesiastes 3:1-13

The three-stranded cord

We were not created to be alone, but to be with other people – because together we are strong. The three-stranded cord in Ecclesiastes 4:12 means that people who are united in God are stronger together than they are alone.

⁹Two people are better off than one, for they can help each other succeed. ¹⁰If one person falls, the other can reach out and help. But someone who falls alone is in real trouble.

¹¹Likewise, two people lying close together can keep each other warm. But how can one be warm alone?

¹²A person standing alone can be attacked and defeated, but two can stand back-to-back and conquer. Three are even better, for a triple-braided cord is not easily broken.

Ecclesiastes 4:9-12

Keep your promises

Ecclesiastes warns us not to make rash promises to God. To promise something was a very serious matter for the Jews; you could promise whatever you wanted but you could not break that promise. Remember: a promise you make is a promise you keep.

[1]As you enter the house of God, keep your ears open and your mouth shut. It is evil to make mindless offerings to God. [2]Don't make rash promises, and don't be hasty in bringing matters before God. After all, God is in heaven, and you are here on earth. So let your words be few.

[3]Too much activity gives you restless dreams; too many words make you a fool.

[4]When you make a promise to God, don't delay in following through, for God takes no pleasure in fools. Keep all the promises you make to him. [5]It is better to say nothing than to make a promise and not keep it. [6]Don't let your mouth make you sin. And don't defend yourself by telling the Temple messenger that the promise you made was a mistake. That would make God angry, and he might wipe out everything you have achieved.

[7]Talk is cheap, like daydreams and other useless activities. Fear God instead.

Ecclesiastes 5:1-7

Beware of the "good old days"

It's easy to long for the good old days when you are having a hard time in the present. But usually people only remember the good things and they forget the bad things. Don't cling to the past; make the best of today. You must live for the future, and learn from the past.

[8]Finishing is better than starting. Patience is better than pride.

[9]Control your temper, for anger labels you a fool.

[10]Don't long for "the good old days." This is not wise.

[11]Wisdom is even better when you have money. Both are a benefit as you go through life. [12]Wisdom and money can get you almost anything, but only wisdom can save your life.

[13]Accept the way God does things, for who can straighten what he has made crooked?

[14]Enjoy prosperity while you can, but when hard times strike, realize that both come from God. Remember that nothing is certain in this life.

Ecclesiastes 7:8-14

Enjoy life!

Ecclesiastes is not filled with advice for the dead, but for the living. Life is a gift from God and is to be enjoyed. We must do everything to the best of our abilities! Everyone dies, but to live with enthusiasm every day is a challenge. We don't have to fear death, because Jesus conquered death through His resurrection.

⁴There is hope only for the living. As they say, "It's better to be a live dog than a dead lion!"

⁵The living at least know they will die, but the dead know nothing. They have no further reward, nor are they remembered. ⁶Whatever they did in their lifetime—loving, hating, envying—is all long gone. They no longer play a part in anything here on earth. ⁷So go ahead. Eat your food with joy, and drink your wine with a happy heart, for God approves of this! ⁸Wear fine clothes, with a splash of cologne!

⁹Live happily with the woman you love through all the meaningless days of life that God has given you under the sun. The wife God gives you is your reward for all your earthly toil. ¹⁰Whatever you do, do well. For when you go to the grave, there will be no work or planning or knowledge or wisdom.

Ecclesiastes 9:4-10

To see the Son

Live every day like you are on vacation, but remember that no one stays young forever. So don't do anything now that will prevent you from enjoying life when you are older. Here's a tip: Look at the Son. Jesus is the Source of your happiness and He is with you both when you are young and when you are old.

11[7]Light is sweet; how pleasant to see a new day dawning. [9]It's wonderful to be young! Do everything you want to do; take it all in. But remember that you must give an account to God for everything you do. [10]So refuse to worry. But remember that youth, with a whole life before you, is meaningless.

12[1]Don't let the excitement of youth cause you to forget your Creator. Honor him in your youth before you grow old and say, "Life is not pleasant anymore." [3]Remember him before your legs—the guards of your house—start to tremble; and before your shoulders—the strong men—stoop. Remember him before your teeth—your few remaining servants—stop grinding; and before your eyes—the women looking through the windows—see dimly.

[6]Yes, remember your Creator now while you are young, before the silver cord of life snaps and the golden bowl is broken. [7]For then the dust will return to the earth, and the spirit will return to God who gave it.

Ecclesiastes 11:7, 9-12:1-3, 6-7

A warning

In today's Scripture, we are given a warning. We are cautioned not to be foolish, but to become wise and live honorable lives that are pleasing to God. Parties and laziness do not get a person anywhere. If you want to make something out of your life, you have to work hard at it.

[1]As dead flies cause even a bottle of perfume to stink,
   so a little foolishness spoils great wisdom and honor.
[2]A wise person chooses the right road;
   a fool takes the wrong one.
[3]You can identify fools
   just by the way they walk down the street!
[4]If your boss is angry at you, don't quit!
   A quiet spirit can overcome even great mistakes.
[17]Happy is the land whose king is a noble leader
   and whose leaders feast at the proper time
   to gain strength for their work, not to get drunk.
[18]Laziness leads to a sagging roof;
   idleness leads to a leaky house.

Ecclesiastes 10:1-4, 17-18

Love brings
out the poet in you

The Hebrew for Songs of Songs means "the most beautiful song." This Bible book is a celebration of the love between a man and a woman. Love is God's gift to His people, but it is also something to protect and keep safe until you meet the person you intend to marry.

⁴Promise me, O women of Jerusalem,
   not to awaken love until the time is right.
Place me like a seal over your heart,
   like a seal on your arm.
⁶For love is as strong as death,
   its jealousy as enduring as the grave.
Love flashes like fire,
   the brightest kind of flame.
⁷Many waters cannot quench love,
   nor can rivers drown it.
If a man tried to buy love
   with all his wealth,
   his offer would be utterly scorned.

Songs of Songs 8:4, 6-7

Learn to do good

These Scripture verses impress upon us to turn from our sin and learn to do good, not just to "earn" points with God, but to reflect God's love to the world because we love Him and want to be His hands and feet in this world.

[17]"Learn to do good. Seek justice. Help the oppressed.
Defend the cause of orphans.
Fight for the rights of widows.
[18]"Come now, let's settle this," says the Lord.
"Though your sins are like scarlet,
I will make them as white as snow.
Though they are red like crimson,
I will make them as white as wool.
[19]If you will only obey me,
you will have plenty to eat.
[20]But if you turn away and refuse to listen,
you will be devoured by the sword of your enemies.
I, the Lord, have spoken!"

Isaiah 1:17-20

God's grace makes you new

Our sins are like scarlet. Sin stands out for all to see. Only God can make His children's lives clean again. Out of thankfulness for His wonderful grace we must be obedient and do good.

²Listen, O heavens! Pay attention, earth! This is what the Lord says: "The children I raised and cared for have rebelled against me.

³Even an ox knows its owner, and a donkey recognizes its master's care – but Israel doesn't know its master. My people don't recognize my care for them."

¹²When you come to worship me, who asked you to parade through my courts with all your ceremony?

¹³Stop bringing me your meaningless gifts; the incense of your offerings disgusts me!

As for your celebrations of the new moon and the Sabbath and your special days for fasting – they are all sinful and false. I want no more of your pious meetings.

¹⁴I hate your new moon celebrations and your annual festivals. They are a burden to me. I cannot stand them!

¹⁵When you lift up your hands in prayer, I will not look. Though you offer many prayers, I will not listen, for your hands are covered with the blood of innocent victims.

Isaiah 1:2-3, 12-15

Bitter grapes

God Himself sings a beautiful song when He compares His relationship with His children to a farmer and a vineyard. The farmer put his all into the vineyard but all it produced was bitter grapes. What a disappointment! The Lord wants our lives to be sweet. But they are bitter if His children are not filled with love for others.

¹Now I will sing for the one I love a song about his vineyard: My beloved had a vineyard on a rich and fertile hill. ²He plowed the land, cleared its stones, and planted it with the best vines. In the middle he built a watchtower and carved a winepress in the nearby rocks. Then he waited for a harvest of sweet grapes, but the grapes that grew were bitter.

³Now, you people of Jerusalem and Judah, you judge between me and my vineyard. ⁴What more could I have done for my vineyard that I have not already done? When I expected sweet grapes, why did my vineyard give me bitter grapes?

⁵Now let me tell you what I will do to my vineyard: I will tear down its hedges and let it be destroyed. I will break down its walls and let the animals trample it. ⁶I will make it a wild place where the vines are not pruned and the ground is not hoed, a place overgrown with briers and thorns. I will command the clouds to drop no rain on it.

⁷The nation of Israel is the vineyard of the LORD of Heaven's Armies. The people of Judah are his pleasant garden. He expected a crop of justice, but instead he found oppression. He expected to find righteousness, but instead he heard cries of violence.

Isaiah 5:1-7

Never the same again!

This encounter that Isaiah had with God took his breath away. He realized God is holy. *Holy* is repeated three times. This emphasizes how almighty, unique and omnipresent God is. Isaiah felt he was not worthy to be in God's company. But God changed him and sent him to work for Him.

¹It was in the year King Uzziah died that I saw the Lord. He was sitting on a lofty throne, and the train of his robe filled the Temple. ²Attending him were mighty seraphim, each having six wings. With two wings they covered their faces, with two they covered their feet, and with two they flew. ³They were calling out to each other, "Holy, holy, holy is the LORD of Heaven's Armies! The whole earth is filled with his glory!"

⁴Their voices shook the Temple to its foundations, and the entire building was filled with smoke.

⁵Then I said, "It's all over! I am doomed, for I am a sinful man. I have filthy lips, and I live among a people with filthy lips. Yet I have seen the King, the LORD of Heaven's Armies."

⁶Then one of the seraphim flew to me with a burning coal he had taken from the altar with a pair of tongs. ⁷He touched my lips with it and said, "See, this coal has touched your lips. Now your guilt is removed, and your sins are forgiven."

⁸Then I heard the Lord asking, "Whom should I send as a messenger to this people? Who will go for us?"

I said, "Here I am. Send me."

Isaiah 6:1-8

This Baby is the King of the universe

Matthew quoted Isaiah 7:14 to show that Jesus is Immanuel, which means "God is with us." Isaiah gives the titles of this Immanuel Baby in Isaiah 9:6 (believers connect this name with Jesus Christ). These titles are better than all the titles of worldly kings.

7 ¹⁴The Lord himself will give you the sign. Look! The virgin will conceive a child! She will give birth to a son and will call him Immanuel (which means 'God is with us').

9 ¹Nevertheless, that time of darkness and despair will not go on forever. There will be a time in the future when Galilee of the Gentiles will be filled with glory.

²The people who walk in darkness will see a great light. For those who live in a land of deep darkness, a light will shine. ³You will enlarge the nation of Israel, and its people will rejoice. They will rejoice before you as people rejoice at the harvest and like warriors dividing the plunder. ⁴For you will break the yoke of their slavery and lift the heavy burden from their shoulders. You will break the oppressor's rod, just as you did when you destroyed the army of Midian. ⁵The boots of the warrior and the uniforms bloodstained by war will all be burned. They will be fuel for the fire.

⁶For a child is born to us, a son is given to us. The government will rest on his shoulders. And he will be called: Wonderful Counselor, Mighty God, Everlasting Father, Prince of Peace.

⁷His government and its peace will never end. He will rule with fairness and justice from the throne of His ancestor David for all eternity. The passionate commitment of the Lord of Heaven's Armies will make this happen!

Isaiah 7:14; 9:1-7

God's everlasting summer

When the Messiah comes (the special Savior who we know as Jesus) there will be a total turnaround in relationships: enemies will become friends and opposites will attract. One day, when Jesus comes back, there will be everlasting life. When enemies become friends it is a sign that God's summer is on the way.

¹Out of the stump of David's family will grow a shoot—yes, a new Branch bearing fruit from the old root. ²And the Spirit of the LORD will rest on him—the Spirit of wisdom and understanding, the Spirit of counsel and might, the Spirit of knowledge and the fear of the LORD.

³He will delight in obeying the LORD. He will not judge by appearance nor make a decision based on hearsay. ⁴He will give justice to the poor and make fair decisions for the exploited. The earth will shake at the force of his word, and one breath from his mouth will destroy the wicked. ⁵He will wear righteousness like a belt and truth like an undergarment.

⁶In that day the wolf and the lamb will live together; the leopard will lie down with the baby goat. The calf and the yearling will be safe with the lion, and a little child will lead them all. ⁷The cow will graze near the bear. The cub and the calf will lie down together. The lion will eat hay like a cow. ⁸The baby will play safely near the hole of a cobra. Yes, a little child will put its hand in a nest of deadly snakes without harm.

⁹Nothing will hurt or destroy in all my holy mountain, for as the waters fill the sea, so the earth will be filled with people who know the LORD.

Isaiah 11:1-9

First class or second class?

Dwight L. Moody said: A person can travel to heaven with a first-class or a second-class ticket. On the second-class ticket it is written: "Every time I am afraid, I will trust." But on the first-class ticket is written Isaiah 12:2, "I will trust in God and not be afraid." First-class looks the best!

¹In that day you will sing: "I will praise you, O LORD! You were angry with me, but not any more. Now you comfort me. ²See, God has come to save me. I will trust in him and not be afraid. The LORD GOD is my strength and my song; he has given me victory."

³With joy you will drink deeply from the fountain of salvation! ⁴In that wonderful day you will sing: "Thank the LORD! Praise his name! Tell the nations what he has done. Let them know how mighty he is! ⁵Sing to the LORD, for he has done wonderful things. Make known his praise around the world. ⁶Let all the people of Jerusalem shout his praise with joy! For great is the Holy One of Israel who lives among you."

Isaiah 12:1-6

The best dining opportunity ever

Dining at an expensive restaurant with delicious-smelling food is a wonderful experience. And when the bill is paid for you it becomes an unforgettable experience! These verses in Isaiah 25 make us think of this because they say that one day we will be permanently in God's presence and will celebrate for eternity with Him for free.

⁶In Jerusalem, the LORD of Heaven's Armies will spread a wonderful feast for all the people of the world. It will be a delicious banquet with clear, well-aged wine and choice meat.

⁷There he will remove the cloud of gloom, the shadow of death that hangs over the earth. ⁸He will swallow up death forever! The Sovereign LORD will wipe away all tears. He will remove forever all insults and mockery against his land and people. The LORD has spoken!

⁹In that day the people will proclaim, "This is our God! We trusted in him, and he saved us! This is the LORD, in whom we trusted. Let us rejoice in the salvation he brings!"

Isaiah 25:6-9

A colorful flower paradise

One of the most beautiful sights to behold is when Namakwaland in South Africa is transformed into a paradise of colorful flowers. It is the type of image that Isaiah uses to show how God's salvation changes people's lives. With God in your life you will bloom like never before.

¹Even the wilderness and desert will be glad in those days. The wasteland will rejoice and blossom with spring crocuses. ²Yes, there will be an abundance of flowers and singing and joy! The deserts will become as green as the mountains of Lebanon, as lovely as Mount Carmel or the plain of Sharon. There the LORD will display his glory, the splendor of our God.

⁵And when he comes, he will open the eyes of the blind and unplug the ears of the deaf. ⁶The lame will leap like a deer, and those who cannot speak will sing for joy! Springs will gush forth in the wilderness, and streams will water the wasteland. ⁷The parched ground will become a pool, and springs of water will satisfy the thirsty land. Marsh grass and reeds and rushes will flourish where desert jackals once lived.

⁸And a great road will go through that once deserted land. It will be named the Highway of Holiness. Evil-minded people will never travel on it. It will be only for those who walk in God's ways; fools will never walk there. ⁹Lions will not lurk along its course, nor any other ferocious beasts. There will be no other dangers. Only the redeemed will walk on it. ¹⁰Those who have been ransomed by the LORD will return. They will enter Jerusalem singing, crowned with everlasting joy. Sorrow and mourning will disappear, and they will be filled with joy and gladness.

Isaiah 35:1-2, 5-10

Incomparable

Who can compare with God? He is incomparably great. That is why we must follow Him, because we will get power – not just any kind of power, but God's power – to help us deal with problems and be filled with energy to continue on our journey through life.

[25]"To whom will you compare me? Who is my equal?" asks the Holy One.

[26]Look up into the heavens. Who created all the stars? He brings them out like an army, one after another, calling each by its name. Because of his great power and incomparable strength, not a single one is missing.

[27]O Jacob, how can you say the LORD does not see your troubles? O Israel, how can you say God ignores your rights? [28]Have you never heard? Have you never understood? The LORD is the everlasting God, the Creator of all the earth. He never grows weak or weary. No one can measure the depths of his understanding. [29]He gives power to the weak and strength to the powerless. [30]Even youths will become weak and tired, and young men will fall in exhaustion.

[31]But those who trust in the LORD will find new strength. They will soar high on wings like eagles. They will run and not grow weary. They will walk and not faint.

Isaiah 40:25-31

A promise to hold on to

What a promise! God won't crush the weakest reed (our broken, messed-up lives). No, He will call us, hold us tight and protect us, because He wants us to make a difference in this world. You can be sure of one thing: If a believer is down and out, God's hand is near to help him up.

¹"Look at my servant, whom I strengthen. He is my chosen one, who pleases me. I have put my Spirit upon him. He will bring justice to the nations. ²He will not shout or raise his voice in public. ³He will not crush the weakest reed or put out a flickering candle. He will bring justice to all who have been wronged. ⁴He will not falter or lose heart until justice prevails throughout the earth. Even distant lands beyond the sea will wait for his instruction."

⁵God, the LORD, created the heavens and stretched them out. He created the earth and everything in it. He gives breath to everyone, life to everyone who walks the earth. And it is he who says, ⁶"I, the LORD, have called you to demonstrate my righteousness. I will take you by the hand and guard you, and I will give you to my people, Israel, as a symbol of my covenant with them. And you will be a light to guide the nations. ⁷You will open the eyes of the blind. You will free the captives from prison, releasing those who sit in dark dungeons.

⁸"I am the LORD; that is my name! I will not give my glory to anyone else, nor share my praise with carved idols. ⁹Everything I prophesied has come true, and now I will prophesy again. I will tell you the future before it happens."

Isaiah 42:1-9

God knows you by name

God will never leave you. You are special to Him. He knows you inside and out. You are not just a number to Him. Nope, He knows you by name. Doesn't that thought take your breath away? God knows you and the rest of the billions of people on this earth by name. What a great God we serve!

¹The one who formed you says, "Do not be afraid, for I have ransomed you. I have called you by name; you are mine. ²When you go through deep waters, I will be with you. When you walk through the fire of oppression, you will not be burned up. ³For I am the LORD, your God, the Holy One of Israel, your Savior. I gave Egypt as a ransom for your freedom; I gave Ethiopia and Seba in your place. ⁴I traded their lives for yours because you are precious to me. You are honored, and I love you.

⁵"Do not be afraid, for I am with you. I will gather you and your children from east and west. ⁶I will say to the north and south, 'Bring my sons and daughters back to Israel from the distant corners of the earth. ⁷Bring all who claim me as their God, for I have made them for my glory. It was I who created them.'"

⁸Bring out the people who have eyes but are blind, who have ears but are deaf. ⁹Gather the nations together! Which of their idols has ever foretold such things? Which can predict what will happen tomorrow? Who can verify that they spoke the truth?

¹¹"I, yes I, am the LORD, and there is no other Savior. ¹²First I predicted your rescue, then I saved you and proclaimed it to the world. No foreign god has ever done this. You are witnesses that I am the only God," says the LORD. ¹³"From eternity to eternity I am God. No one can snatch anyone out of my hand. No one can undo what I have done."

Isaiah 43:1-9, 11-13

God is like ...

Sometimes people wonder if God has forgotten about them. In Isaiah 49 the prophet uses four images to show the opposite is true. God is like a mother (v. 15). God is like a person whose love is engraved on His palms (v. 16). God is like a guard on a wall (v. 16). God is like a jeweler who adorns you with the most beautiful jewels (v. 18).

¹³Sing for joy, O heavens! Rejoice, O earth! Burst into song, O mountains! For the LORD has comforted his people and will have compassion on them in their suffering.

¹⁴Yet Jerusalem says, "The LORD has deserted us; the Lord has forgotten us."

¹⁵"Never! Can a mother forget her nursing child? Can she feel no love for the child she has borne? But even if that were possible, I would not forget you! ¹⁶See, I have written your name on the palms of my hands. Always in my mind is a picture of Jerusalem's walls in ruins.

¹⁷"Soon your descendants will come back, and all who are trying to destroy you will go away. ¹⁸Look around you and see, for all your children will come back to you. As surely as I live," says the LORD, "they will be like jewels or bridal ornaments for you to display."

Isaiah 49:13-18

The gentle Healer reveals His own wounds

The prophecies in Isaiah 53 were realized through Jesus in the New Testament. If you read it with Jesus in mind, you can see His life before you and you will realize how much God loves us. His wounds permanently healed our wounds!

²My servant grew up in the LORD's presence like a tender green shoot, like a root in dry ground. There was nothing beautiful or majestic about his appearance, nothing to attract us to him. ³He was despised and rejected—a man of sorrows, acquainted with deepest grief. We turned our backs on him and looked the other way. He was despised, and we did not care.

⁴Yet it was our weaknesses he carried; it was our sorrows that weighed him down. And we thought his troubles were a punishment from God, a punishment for his own sins!

⁷He was oppressed and treated harshly, yet he never said a word. He was led like a lamb to the slaughter. And as a sheep is silent before the shearers, he did not open his mouth. ⁸Unjustly condemned, he was led away. No one cared that he died without descendants, that his life was cut short in midstream. But he was struck down for the rebellion of my people. ⁹He had done no wrong and had never deceived anyone. But he was buried like a criminal; he was put in a rich man's grave.

¹⁰But it was the LORD's good plan to crush him and cause him grief. Yet when his life is made an offering for sin, he will have many descendants. He will enjoy a long life, and the LORD's good plan will prosper in his hands. ¹¹When he sees all that is accomplished by his anguish, he will be satisfied. And because of his experience, my righteous servant will make it possible for many to be counted righteous, for he will bear all their sins.

Isaiah 53:2-4, 7-11

Grace is so costly – it must be for free!

You cannot pay for God's grace. It is way too expensive. That's why God gives it to His children for free – and He is not stingy about it. Nope, God works on a principle of abundance: He pours out His grace on His children till it overflows.

[1]"Is anyone thirsty? Come and drink—even if you have no money! Come, take your choice of wine or milk—it's all free! [2]Why spend your money on food that does not give you strength? Why pay for food that does you no good? Listen to me, and you will eat what is good. You will enjoy the finest food.

[3]"Come to me with your ears wide open. Listen, and you will find life. I will make an everlasting covenant with you. I will give you all the unfailing love I promised to David.

[8]"My thoughts are nothing like your thoughts," says the LORD. "And my ways are far beyond anything you could imagine. [9]For just as the heavens are higher than the earth, so my ways are higher than your ways and my thoughts higher than your thoughts.

[10]"The rain and snow come down from the heavens and stay on the ground to water the earth. They cause the grain to grow, producing seed for the farmer and bread for the hungry. [11]It is the same with my word. I send it out, and it always produces fruit. It will accomplish all I want it to, and it will prosper everywhere I send it. [12]You will live in joy and peace. The mountains and hills will burst into song, and the trees of the field will clap their hands! [13]Where once there were thorns, cypress trees will grow. Where nettles grew, myrtles will sprout up. These events will bring great honor to the LORD's name; they will be an everlasting sign of his power and love."

Isaiah 55:1-3, 8-13

God hears and
gladly helps us

Isaiah 59:1 says that God's arm is never too weak to save and His ears are never too deaf to hear. Therefore He expects His children to reach for His hand and to call on Him when life deals them a blow. Then they will experience joy like never before because they made God happy!

58⁵You humble yourselves by going through the motions of penance, bowing your heads like reeds bending in the wind. You dress in burlap and cover yourselves with ashes. Is this what you call fasting? Do you really think this will please the LORD?

⁶"No, this is the kind of fasting I want: Free those who are wrongly imprisoned; lighten the burden of those who work for you. Let the oppressed go free, and remove the chains that bind people. ⁷Share your food with the hungry, and give shelter to the homeless. Give clothes to those who need them, and do not hide from relatives who need your help.

⁹"Then when you call, the LORD will answer. 'Yes, I am here,' he will quickly reply. Remove the heavy yoke of oppression. Stop pointing your finger and spreading vicious rumors!

¹⁰"Feed the hungry, and help those in trouble. Then your light will shine out from the darkness, and the darkness around you will be as bright as noon. ¹¹The LORD will guide you continually, giving you water when you are dry and restoring your strength.

¹⁴"Then the LORD will be your delight. I will give you great honor and satisfy you with the inheritance I promised to your ancestor Jacob. I, the LORD, have spoken!"

59¹Listen! The LORD's arm is not too weak to save you, nor is his ear too deaf to hear you call.

Isaiah 58:5-7, 9-11, 14; 59:1

June

About this
you can be certain

You can be certain of this! What can we be so certain of, Isaiah? That the Lord loves you. With the Lord is where you belong. The Lord cares for you. The Lord rejoices over you.

¹Because I love Zion, I will not keep still. Because my heart yearns for Jerusalem, I cannot remain silent. I will not stop praying for her until her righteousness shines like the dawn, and her salvation blazes like a burning torch. ²The nations will see your righteousness. World leaders will be blinded by your glory. And you will be given a new name by the LORD's own mouth.

³The LORD will hold you in his hand for all to see—a splendid crown in the hand of God. ⁴Never again will you be called "The Forsaken City" or "The Desolate Land." Your new name will be "The City of God's Delight" and "The Bride of God," for the LORD delights in you and will claim you as his bride. ⁵Your children will commit themselves to you, O Jerusalem, just as a young man commits himself to his bride. Then God will rejoice over you as a bridegroom rejoices over his bride.

⁶O Jerusalem, I have posted watchmen on your walls; they will pray day and night, continually. Take no rest, all you who pray to the LORD. ⁷Give the LORD no rest until he completes his work, until he makes Jerusalem the pride of the earth.

¹¹The LORD has sent this message to every land: "Tell the people of Israel, 'Look, your Savior is coming. See, he brings his reward with him as he comes.'" ¹²They will be called "The Holy People" and "The People Redeemed by the LORD." And Jerusalem will be known as "The Desirable Place" and "The City No Longer Forsaken."

Isaiah 62:1-7, 11-12

A new heaven and earth

Isaiah 65 is not about the old earth being destroyed, but about God creating a totally new beginning for His people. It will be characterized by joy (vv. 18-19), life like God intended it (v. 20), prosperity (vv. 21-24), and peace and harmony (v. 25).

17"Look! I am creating new heavens and a new earth, and no one will even think about the old ones anymore. 18Be glad; rejoice forever in my creation! And look! I will create Jerusalem as a place of happiness. Her people will be a source of joy. 19I will rejoice over Jerusalem and delight in my people. And the sound of weeping and crying will be heard in it no more.

20"No longer will babies die when only a few days old. No longer will adults die before they have lived a full life. No longer will people be considered old at one hundred! Only the cursed will die that young! 21In those days people will live in the houses they build and eat the fruit of their own vineyards. 22Unlike the past, invaders will not take their houses and confiscate their vineyards. For my people will live as long as trees, and my chosen ones will have time to enjoy their hard-won gains.

23"They will not work in vain, and their children will not be doomed to misfortune. For they are people blessed by the LORD, and their children, too, will be blessed. 24I will answer them before they even call to me. While they are still talking about their needs, I will go ahead and answer their prayers!

25"The wolf and the lamb will feed together. The lion will eat hay like a cow. But the snakes will eat dust. In those days no one will be hurt or destroyed on my holy mountain. I, the LORD, have spoken!"

Isaiah 65:17-25

My "I" against God's "I"

Our "I" cannot stand against God's "I." God answers Jeremiah's "I-excuses," like "I can't speak well," or "I am too young" with His own "I-answers," like "I am sending you," or "Don't be afraid, I am with you," or "I will put My words in your mouth." Against this no person can resist.

⁴The LORD gave me this message: ⁵"I knew you before I formed you in your mother's womb. Before you were born I set you apart and appointed you as my prophet to the nations."

⁶"O Sovereign LORD," I said, "I can't speak for you! I'm too young!"

⁷The LORD replied, "Don't say, 'I'm too young,' for you must go wherever I send you and say whatever I tell you. ⁸And don't be afraid of the people, for I will be with you and will protect you. I, the LORD, have spoken!"

⁹Then the LORD reached out and touched my mouth and said, "Look, I have put my words in your mouth! ¹⁰Today I appoint you to stand up against nations and kingdoms. Some you must uproot and tear down, destroy and overthrow. Others you must build up and plant."

Jeremiah 1:4-10

A terrible disease

66

Children of God can suffer from a terrible disease: they can forget. Not silly things like forgetting where they put their keys, but they can forget about God. They forget that their security lies in God. This happened in Jeremiah's time and it still happens today.

2"I remember how eager you were to please me as a young bride long ago, how you loved me and followed me even through the barren wilderness. 3In those days Israel was holy to the Lord, the first of his children. All who harmed his people were declared guilty, and disaster fell on them. I, the Lord, have spoken!"

5This is what the Lord says: "What did your ancestors find wrong with me that led them to stray so far from me? They worshiped worthless idols, only to become worthless themselves.

8"The priests did not ask, 'Where is the Lord?' Those who taught my word ignored me, the rulers turned against me, and the prophets spoke in the name of Baal, wasting their time on worthless idols. 9Therefore, I will bring my case against you," says the Lord. "I will even bring charges against your children's children in the years to come.

11"Has any nation ever traded its gods for new ones, even though they are not gods at all? Yet my people have exchanged their glorious God for worthless idols! 12The heavens are shocked at such a thing and shrink back in horror and dismay," says the Lord. 13"For my people have done two evil things: They have abandoned me—the fountain of living water. And they have dug for themselves cracked cisterns that can hold no water at all!"

A grace-balm for sinful lives

Jeremiah saw the sins and evil of the people that couldn't be put right. It was a disease that all the miracle balm and gifted doctors in Gilead couldn't heal. But there is always a solution – the grace-balm of Gilead. There is only one Doctor who can make us whole – God.

8 ¹⁸My grief is beyond healing; my heart is broken. ¹⁹Listen to the weeping of my people; it can be heard all across the land. "Has the LORD abandoned Jerusalem?" the people ask. "Is her King no longer there?"

"Oh, why have they provoked my anger with their carved idols and their worthless foreign gods?" says the LORD.

²⁰"The harvest is finished, and the summer is gone," the people cry, "yet we are not saved!"

²¹I hurt with the hurt of my people. I mourn and am overcome with grief. ²²Is there no medicine in Gilead? Is there no physician there? Why is there no healing for the wounds of my people?

9 ¹If only my head were a pool of water and my eyes a fountain of tears, I would weep day and night for all my people who have been slaughtered.

Jeremiah 8:18-9:1

Two types of people

According to Jeremiah there are two types of people: unbelievers, who put their trust in everything except God; and believers, who place all their trust in God. One is like a stunted shrub in the desert and the other is like a tree that is planted by a river. Which one are you?

[5]This is what the LORD says: "Cursed are those who put their trust in mere humans, who rely on human strength and turn their hearts away from the LORD. [6]They are like stunted shrubs in the desert, with no hope for the future. They will live in the barren wilderness, in an uninhabited salty land.

[7]"But blessed are those who trust in the LORD and have made the LORD their hope and confidence. [8]They are like trees planted along a riverbank, with roots that reach deep into the water. Such trees are not bothered by the heat or worried by long months of drought. Their leaves stay green, and they never stop producing fruit.

[9]"The human heart is the most deceitful of all things, and desperately wicked. Who really knows how bad it is? [10]But I, the LORD, search all hearts and examine secret motives. I give all people their due rewards, according to what their actions deserve."

[11]Like a partridge that hatches eggs she has not laid, so are those who get their wealth by unjust means. At midlife they will lose their riches; in the end, they will become poor old fools. [12]But we worship at your throne—eternal, high, and glorious! [13]O LORD, the hope of Israel, all who turn away from you will be disgraced. They will be buried in the dust of the earth, for they have abandoned the LORD, the fountain of living water.

Jeremiah 17:5-13

Clay in the Potter's hand

After a certain believer read Jeremiah 18:1-11, his reaction was, "God will not try to mend or fix me. He will totally re-make me!" In spite of all the mistakes he had made in his life, he knew he was still on the Potter's wheel. God only stops molding you when you die. Until then you are like clay in His hands!

[1]The LORD gave another message to Jeremiah. He said, [2]"Go down to the potter's shop, and I will speak to you there." [3]So I did as he told me and found the potter working at his wheel. [4]But the jar he was making did not turn out as he had hoped, so he crushed it into a lump of clay again and started over.

[5]Then the LORD gave me this message: [6]"O Israel, can I not do to you as this potter has done to his clay? As the clay is in the potter's hand, so are you in my hand. [7]If I announce that a certain nation or kingdom is to be uprooted, torn down, and destroyed, [8]but then that nation renounces its evil ways, I will not destroy it as I had planned. [9]And if I announce that I will plant and build up a certain nation or kingdom, [10]but then that nation turns to evil and refuses to obey me, I will not bless it as I said I would.

[11]"Therefore, Jeremiah, go and warn all Judah and Jerusalem. Say to them, 'This is what the LORD says: I am planning disaster for you instead of good. So turn from your evil ways, each of you, and do what is right.'"

Jeremiah 18:1-11

Half-hearted or wholehearted?

Jeremiah spoke of the promises of the new covenant. You don't need to live half-heartedly – you can live wholeheartedly. You can live fully! A life without faith is half dead and half-hearted, but a life with God is wholehearted.

27"The day is coming," says the LORD, "when I will greatly increase the human population and the number of animals here in Israel and Judah. 28In the past I deliberately uprooted and tore down this nation. I overthrew it, destroyed it, and brought disaster upon it. But in the future I will just as deliberately plant it and build it up. I, the LORD, have spoken!

31"The day is coming," says the LORD, "when I will make a new covenant with the people of Israel and Judah. 32This covenant will not be like the one I made with their ancestors when I took them by the hand and brought them out of the land of Egypt. They broke that covenant, though I loved them as a husband loves his wife," says the LORD.

33"But this is the new covenant I will make with the people of Israel on that day," says the LORD. "I will put my instructions deep within them, and I will write them on their hearts. I will be their God, and they will be my people. 34And they will not need to teach their neighbors, nor will they need to teach their relatives, saying, 'You should know the LORD.' For everyone, from the least to the greatest, will know me already," says the LORD. "And I will forgive their wickedness, and I will never again remember their sins."

Jeremiah 31:27-28, 31-34

Buy that field in Anathoth

Jeremiah realized that God wanted to use the field in Anathoth, where the Babylonian army was camping, to bring His promise to pass. Build your hope on God's promises – because a promise that He makes is one He will keep!

⁶At that time the Lᴏʀᴅ sent me a message. He said, ⁷"Your cousin Hanamel son of Shallum will come and say to you, 'Buy my field at Anathoth. By law you have the right to buy it before it is offered to anyone else.'"

⁸Then, just as the Lᴏʀᴅ had said he would, my cousin Hanamel came and visited me in the prison. He said, "Please buy my field at Anathoth in the land of Benjamin. By law you have the right to buy it before it is offered to anyone else, so buy it for yourself." Then I knew that the message I had heard was from the Lᴏʀᴅ.

⁹So I bought the field at Anathoth, paying Hanamel seventeen pieces of silver for it. ¹⁰I signed and sealed the deed of purchase before witnesses, weighed out the silver, and paid him. ¹¹Then I took the sealed deed and an unsealed copy of the deed, which contained the terms and conditions of the purchase, ¹²and I handed them to Baruch son of Neriah and grandson of Mahseiah.

¹³Then I said to Baruch, ¹⁴"This is what the Lᴏʀᴅ of Heaven's Armies, the God of Israel, says: 'Take both this sealed deed and the unsealed copy, and put them into a pottery jar to preserve them for a long time.' ¹⁵For this is what the Lᴏʀᴅ of Heaven's Armies, the God of Israel, says: 'Someday people will again own property here in this land and will buy and sell houses and vineyards and fields.'"

Jeremiah 32:6-15

The best word:
Thanks

Our best word is *thanks*. Lamentations 3 will help you to say thanks to God in difficult times – because it gives you a new perspective on everything – God's perspective. Here are the reasons from Lamentations why we should thank God:

1. God's love is unchanging, therefore we can count on it.
2. There is no end to His care for us.
3. He is our life, therefore we hope in Him.

¹⁸I cry out, "My splendor is gone! Everything I had hoped for from the LORD is lost!"

¹⁹The thought of my suffering and homelessness is bitter beyond words. ²⁰I will never forget this awful time, as I grieve over my loss. ²¹Yet I still dare to hope when I remember this:

²²The faithful love of the LORD never ends! His mercies never cease. ²³Great is his faithfulness; his mercies begin afresh each morning. ²⁴I say to myself, "The LORD is my inheritance; therefore, I will hope in him!"

²⁵The LORD is good to those who depend on him, to those who search for him. ²⁶So it is good to wait quietly for salvation from the LORD. ²⁷And it is good for people to submit at an early age to the yoke of his discipline:

²⁸Let them sit alone in silence beneath the LORD'S demands. ²⁹Let them lie face down in the dust, for there may be hope at last. ³⁰Let them turn the other cheek to those who strike them and accept the insults of their enemies. ³¹For no one is abandoned by the Lord forever. ³²Though he brings grief, he also shows compassion because of the greatness of his unfailing love. ³³For he does not enjoy hurting people or causing them sorrow.

Lamentations 3:18-33

Eat the Book

People will easily eat a juicy hamburger, but that's not what Ezekiel had to eat. He had to eat a Book! It wasn't just any old book, though; it was the Word of God. You can't be a witness for God if you don't first "eat" God's Book. Luckily for Ezekiel and us it tastes like honey and is good for you!

¹The voice said to me, "Son of man, eat what I am giving you—eat this scroll! Then go and give its message to the people of Israel." ²So I opened my mouth, and he fed me the scroll. ³"Fill your stomach with this," he said. And when I ate it, it tasted as sweet as honey in my mouth.

⁴Then he said, "Son of man, go to the people of Israel and give them my messages. ⁵I am not sending you to a foreign people whose language you cannot understand. ⁶No, I am not sending you to people with strange and difficult speech. If I did, they would listen! ⁷But the people of Israel won't listen to you any more than they listen to me! For the whole lot of them are hard-hearted and stubborn. ⁸But look, I have made you as obstinate and hard-hearted as they are. ⁹I have made your forehead as hard as the hardest rock! So don't be afraid of them or fear their angry looks, even though they are rebels."

¹⁰Then he added, "Son of man, let all my words sink deep into your own heart first. Listen to them carefully for yourself. ¹¹Then go to your people in exile and say to them, 'This is what the Sovereign LORD says!' Do this whether they listen to you or not."

Ezekiel 3:1-11

Shepherds vs. the Shepherd

In Ezekiel 34 shepherds are compared to leaders. Some leaders only have their own interests at heart. A true leader, however, is there to serve and watch over the others. God is such a Leader and He expects all His leaders to be like this.

¹Then this message came to me from the LORD: ²"Son of man, prophesy against the shepherds, the leaders of Israel. Give them this message from the Sovereign LORD: What sorrow awaits you shepherds who feed yourselves instead of your flocks. ³You drink the milk, wear the wool, and butcher the best animals, but you let your flocks starve. ⁴You have not taken care of the weak. You have not tended the sick or bound up the injured. You have not gone looking for those who have wandered away and are lost. ⁵So my sheep have been scattered without a shepherd, and they are easy prey for any wild animal. ⁶They have wandered through all the mountains and all the hills, yet no one has gone to search for them.

¹¹"For this is what the Sovereign LORD says: I myself will search and find my sheep. ¹²I will find my sheep and rescue them from all the places where they were scattered on that dark and cloudy day. ¹³I will bring them back home to their own land of Israel from among the peoples and nations. I will feed them on the mountains of Israel and by the rivers and in all the places where people live. ¹⁴Yes, I will give them good pastureland on the high hills of Israel. ¹⁵I myself will tend my sheep and give them a place to lie down in peace, says the Sovereign LORD. ¹⁶I will search for my lost ones who strayed away, and I will bring them safely home again. But I will destroy those who are fat and powerful. I will feed them, yes—feed them justice!"

Ezekiel 34:1-6, 11-16

The first heart transplant

Chris Barnard was not the first person to perform a heart transplant in the Groote Schuur hospital in Cape Town – God had already done it! He gives His believers a new heart (lifestyle) and spirit (attitude) as well as the Holy Spirit. Then you become a brand-new person!

[22]"Therefore, give the people of Israel this message from the Sovereign LORD: I am bringing you back, but not because you deserve it. I am doing it to protect my holy name, on which you brought shame while you were scattered among the nations. [23]I will show how holy my great name is—the name on which you brought shame among the nations. And when I reveal my holiness through you before their very eyes, says the Sovereign LORD, then the nations will know that I am the LORD. [24]For I will gather you up from all the nations and bring you home again to your land.

[25]"Then I will sprinkle clean water on you, and you will be clean. Your filth will be washed away, and you will no longer worship idols. [26]And I will give you a new heart, and I will put a new spirit in you. I will take out your stony, stubborn heart and give you a tender, responsive heart. [27]And I will put my Spirit in you so that you will follow my decrees and be careful to obey my regulations.

[28]"And you will live in Israel, the land I gave your ancestors long ago. You will be my people, and I will be your God."

Ezekiel 36:22-28

God has a plan

Ezekiel 37 says that God has a plan. Even though there is chaos in the world, God has a salvation plan for the world that does work! As believers we need to remember this. Everything is right, even though it looks wrong.

¹The LORD took hold of me, and I was carried away by the Spirit of the LORD to a valley filled with bones.

³Then he asked me, "Son of man, can these bones become living people again?"

"O Sovereign LORD," I replied, "you alone know the answer to that."

⁴Then he said to me, "Speak a prophetic message to these bones and say, 'Dry bones, listen to the word of the LORD! ⁵This is what the Sovereign LORD says: Look! I am going to put breath into you and make you live again! ⁶I will put flesh and muscles on you and cover you with skin. I will put breath into you, and you will come to life. Then you will know that I am the LORD.'"

⁷So I spoke this message, just as he told me. The bones of each body came together and attached themselves as complete skeletons. ⁸Muscles and flesh formed over the bones. Then skin formed to cover their bodies, but they still had no breath in them.

⁹Then he said to me, "Speak a prophetic message to the winds, son of man. Speak a prophetic message and say, 'This is what the Sovereign LORD says: Come, O breath, from the four winds! Breathe into these dead bodies so they may live again.'"

¹⁰So I spoke the message as he commanded me, and breath came into their bodies.

Be different

The changing of Daniel and his friends' names was an attempt to distance them from their Jewish identity. Their old Jewish names referred to God. Their new names referred to the Babylonian gods. Daniel and his friends lived differently — they stood up and stood out for God.

⁶Daniel, Hananiah, Mishael, and Azariah were four of the young men chosen, all from the tribe of Judah. ⁷The chief of staff renamed them with these Babylonian names: Daniel was called Belteshazzar. Hananiah was called Shadrach. Mishael was called Meshach. Azariah was called Abednego.

⁸But Daniel was determined not to defile himself by eating the food and wine given to them by the king. He asked the chief of staff for permission not to eat these unacceptable foods.

¹¹Daniel spoke with the attendant who had been appointed by the chief of staff to look after Daniel, Hananiah, Mishael, and Azariah. ¹²"Please test us for ten days on a diet of vegetables and water," Daniel said. ¹³"At the end of the ten days, see how we look compared to the other young men who are eating the king's food. Then make your decision in light of what you see." ¹⁴The attendant agreed to Daniel's suggestion and tested them for ten days.

¹⁵At the end of the ten days, Daniel and his three friends looked healthier and better nourished than the young men who had been eating the food assigned by the king. ¹⁶So after that, the attendant fed them only vegetables instead of the food and wine provided for the others.

¹⁷God gave these four young men an unusual aptitude for understanding every aspect of literature and wisdom.

Daniel 1:6-8, 11-17

In fiery situations

Two things stand out from the passage below: Firstly, Daniel's friends were thrown into the furnace because they refused to deny God. They stood strong in their faith. Secondly, even in the "hottest' situations believers are never alone – God is always there.

[14]Nebuchadnezzar said to them, "Is it true, Shadrach, Meshach, and Abednego, that you refuse to serve my gods or to worship the gold statue I have set up? [15]I will give you one more chance to bow down and worship the statue I have made. But if you refuse, you will be thrown immediately into the blazing furnace."

[16]Shadrach, Meshach, and Abednego replied, [17]"If we are thrown into the blazing furnace, the God whom we serve is able to save us. He will rescue us from your power, Your Majesty. [18]But even if he doesn't, we want to make it clear to you, Your Majesty, that we will never serve your gods or worship the gold statue you have set up."

[19]Nebuchadnezzar commanded that the furnace be heated seven times hotter than usual. [20]Then he ordered some of the strongest men of his army to bind Shadrach, Meshach, and Abednego and throw them into the blazing furnace.

[24]Suddenly, Nebuchadnezzar jumped up in amazement and exclaimed, "Didn't we tie up three men and throw them into the furnace?" "Yes, Your Majesty, we certainly did," they replied. [25]"Look!" Nebuchadnezzar shouted. "I see four men, unbound, walking around in the fire unharmed! And the fourth looks like a god!"

[26]Then Nebuchadnezzar shouted: "Shadrach, Meshach, and Abednego, servants of the Most High God, come out!"

Daniel 3:14-20, 24-26

The writing
is on the wall

Whenever you are deaf to God and try to play god yourself, the writing's on the wall. King Belshazzar used the cups from the temple in Jerusalem to honor other gods. God does not allow anyone to mess with Him like that.

[1]Many years later King Belshazzar gave a great feast for his nobles, and he drank wine with them. [2]He gave orders to bring in the gold and silver cups that Nebuchadnezzar had taken from the Temple in Jerusalem. [4]While they drank from them they praised their idols.

[5]Suddenly, they saw the fingers of a human hand writing on the plaster wall of the king's palace. The king himself saw the hand as it wrote, [6]and his face turned pale with fright. His knees knocked together in fear and his legs gave way beneath him.

[17]Daniel answered the king, "I will tell you what the writing means. [23]For you have proudly defied the Lord of heaven and have had these cups from his Temple brought before you. You and your nobles and your wives and concubines have been drinking wine from them while praising gods of silver, gold, bronze, iron, wood, and stone—gods that neither see nor hear nor know anything at all. But you have not honored the God who gives you the breath of life and controls your destiny!

[25]"This is the message that was written: MENE, MENE, TEKEL, and PARSIN. [26]*Mene* means 'numbered'—God has numbered the days of your reign and has brought it to an end. [27]*Tekel* means 'weighed'—you have been weighed on the balances and have not measured up. [28]*Parsin* means 'divided'—your kingdom has been divided and given to the Medes and Persians."

[30]That very night Belshazzar was killed.

Daniel 5:1-2, 4-6, 17, 23, 25-28, 30

Don't ever compromise your faith, no matter how big the danger. Remember that the God of Daniel is still our God today. If God could protect Daniel by closing the lions' mouths, just think what He can do for you today. Be faithful to Him!

[12]So they went straight to the king and reminded him about his law. "Did you not sign a law that for the next thirty days any person who prays to anyone, divine or human—except to you, Your Majesty—will be thrown into the den of lions?"

"Yes," the king replied.

[13]Then they told the king, "That man Daniel, one of the captives from Judah, is ignoring you and your law. He still prays to his God three times a day."

[14]Hearing this, the king was deeply troubled, and he tried to think of a way to save Daniel.

[17]A stone was brought and placed over the mouth of the den. The king sealed the stone with his own royal seal and the seals of his nobles, so that no one could rescue Daniel. [18]Then the king returned to his palace and spent the night fasting.

[19]Very early the next morning, the king got up and hurried out to the lions' den. [20]When he got there, he called out in anguish, "Daniel, servant of the living God! Was your God, whom you serve so faithfully, able to rescue you from the lions?"

[21]Daniel answered, "Long live the king! [22]My God sent his angel to shut the lions' mouths so that they would not hurt me, for I have been found innocent in his sight."

[23]The king was overjoyed and ordered that Daniel be lifted from the den. Not a scratch was found on him, for he had trusted in his God.

Daniel 6:12-14, 17-23

The champion pray-er's prayer guidelines

Daniel gives us a good framework for prayer: He starts his prayer with who God is and what He does. Then he confesses his sins and those of God's people. He closes his prayer with a request and a rededication to God.

⁴I prayed to the LORD my God and confessed: "O Lord, you are a great and awesome God! You always fulfill your covenant and keep your promises of unfailing love to those who love you and obey your commands. ⁵But we have sinned and done wrong. We have rebelled against you and scorned your commands and regulations.

⁹"But the Lord our God is merciful and forgiving, even though we have rebelled against him. ¹⁰We have not obeyed the LORD our God, for we have not followed the instructions he gave us through his servants the prophets. ¹¹All Israel has disobeyed your instruction and turned away, refusing to listen to your voice.

¹⁵"O Lord our God, you brought lasting honor to your name by rescuing your people from Egypt in a great display of power. But we have sinned and are full of wickedness.

¹⁷"O our God, hear your servant's prayer! Listen as I plead. For your own sake, Lord, smile again on your desolate sanctuary.

¹⁸"O my God, lean down and listen to me. Open your eyes and see our despair. See how your city—the city that bears your name—lies in ruins. We make this plea, not because we deserve help, but because of your mercy.

¹⁹"O Lord, hear. O Lord, forgive. O Lord, listen and act! For your own sake, do not delay, O my God, for your people and your city bear your name."

Daniel 9:4-5, 9-11, 15, 17-19

God's grace always wins

The names of Hosea's three children tell a story of God's judgment. The first one indicates political judgment, the second name indicates God removing His love and faithfulness, and the last concerns God's covenant with Israel. In Hosea 1:10 God turns His words of judgment into words of grace in a surprising way. Yes, God's grace always wins!

²When the LORD first began speaking to Israel through Hosea, he said to him, "Go and marry a prostitute, so that some of her children will be conceived in prostitution. This will illustrate how Israel has acted like a prostitute by turning against the LORD and worshiping other gods."

³So Hosea married Gomer, the daughter of Diblaim, and she became pregnant and gave Hosea a son. ⁴And the LORD said, "Name the child Jezreel, for I am about to punish King Jehu's dynasty to avenge the murders he committed at Jezreel."

⁶Soon Gomer became pregnant again and gave birth to a daughter. And the LORD said to Hosea, "Name your daughter Lo-ruhamah—'Not loved'—for I will no longer show love to the people of Israel or forgive them."

⁸After Gomer had weaned Lo-ruhamah, she again became pregnant and gave birth to a second son. ⁹And the LORD said, "Name him Lo-ammi—'Not my people'—for Israel is not my people, and I am not their God.

¹⁰"Yet the time will come when Israel's people will be like the sands of the seashore—too many to count! Then, at the place where they were told, 'You are not my people,' it will be said, 'You are children of the living God.'"

Hosea 1:2-4, 6, 8-10

Dead-end streets become streets of hope

The Valley of Achor is where Achan and his whole family were stoned as they entered Canaan because he stole God's possessions. The Valley of Achor was Israel's valley of trouble. Then God declared that He was going to make a door of hope there. This means that God can make a door of hope in every dead-end situation.

[14]"But then I will win her back once again. I will lead her into the desert and speak tenderly to her there. [15]I will return her vineyards to her and transform the Valley of Trouble into a gateway of hope. She will give herself to me there, as she did long ago when she was young, when I freed her from her captivity in Egypt. [16]When that day comes," says the LORD, "you will call me 'my husband' instead of 'my master.'

[17]"O Israel, I will wipe the many names of Baal from your lips, and you will never mention them again. [18]On that day I will make a covenant with all the wild animals and the birds of the sky and the animals that scurry along the ground so they will not harm you. I will remove all weapons of war from the land, all swords and bows, so you can live unafraid in peace and safety. [19]I will make you my wife forever, showing you righteousness and justice, unfailing love and compassion. [20]I will be faithful to you and make you mine, and you will finally know me as the LORD.

[21]"In that day, I will answer," says the LORD. "I will answer the sky as it pleads for clouds. And the sky will answer the earth with rain. [22]Then the earth will answer the thirsty cries of the grain, the grapevines, and the olive trees. And they in turn will answer, 'Jezreel'—'God plants!'"

Hosea 2:14-22

God's unexpected grace

The words of Hosea 11 are filled with the surprise of God's grace and can be summed up with the words: "Oh, how can I give you up, Israel? How can I let you go? How can I destroy you like Admah or demolish you like Zeboiim? My heart is torn within Me, and My compassion overflows." God is gentle and compassionate, therefore He surprises us constantly with His unexpected grace.

¹"When Israel was a child, I loved him, and I called my son out of Egypt. ²But the more I called to him, the farther he moved from me, offering sacrifices to the images of Baal and burning incense to idols.

³"I myself taught Israel how to walk, leading him along by the hand. But he doesn't know or even care that it was I who took care of him. ⁴I led Israel along with my ropes of kindness and love. I lifted the yoke from his neck, and I myself stooped to feed him.

⁵"But since my people refuse to return to me, they will return to Egypt and will be forced to serve Assyria. ⁶War will swirl through their cities; their enemies will crash through their gates. They will destroy them, trapping them in their own evil plans.

⁸"Oh, how can I give you up, Israel? How can I let you go? How can I destroy you like Admah or demolish you like Zeboiim? My heart is torn within me, and my compassion overflows. ⁹No, I will not unleash my fierce anger. I will not completely destroy Israel, for I am God and not a mere mortal. I am the Holy One living among you, and I will not come to destroy."

Hosea 11:1-6, 8-9

God waits for you with open arms

God will definitely look for you if you wander off (Jesus spoke about this in Luke 15). He promises to be your God. How will you know God is looking for you? Look for the Person with open arms!

¹²That is why the LORD says, "Turn to me now, while there is time. Give me your hearts. Come with fasting, weeping, and mourning. ¹³Don't tear your clothing in your grief, but tear your hearts instead." Return to the LORD your God, for he is merciful and compassionate, slow to get angry and filled with unfailing love. He is eager to relent and not punish. ¹⁴Who knows? Perhaps he will give you a reprieve, sending you a blessing instead of this curse. Perhaps you will be able to offer grain and wine to the LORD your God as before.

¹⁵Blow the ram's horn in Jerusalem! Announce a time of fasting; call the people together for a solemn meeting. ¹⁶Gather all the people—the elders, the children, and even the babies. Call the bridegroom from his quarters and the bride from her private room.

¹⁷Let the priests, who minister in the LORD's presence, stand and weep between the entry room to the Temple and the altar. Let them pray, "Spare your people, LORD! Don't let your special possession become an object of mockery. Don't let them become a joke for unbelieving foreigners who say, 'Has the God of Israel left them?'"

¹⁸Then the LORD will pity his people and jealously guard the honor of his land.

Joel 2:12-18

All children of God
have the Spirit

Peter quoted Joel 2:25-32 on the day of Pentecost to confirm that a new era had dawned when the Holy Spirit had been poured out on everybody. In Old Testament times people believed that the Spirit was given to only a few special people. To Jesus we are all special; therefore we all receive the Spirit.

25The LORD says, "I will give you back what you lost to the swarming locusts, the hopping locusts, the stripping locusts, and the cutting locusts. It was I who sent this great destroying army against you. 26Once again you will have all the food you want, and you will praise the LORD your God, who does these miracles for you. Never again will my people be disgraced. 27Then you will know that I am among my people Israel, that I am the LORD your God, and there is no other. Never again will my people be disgraced.

28"Then, after doing all those things, I will pour out my Spirit upon all people. Your sons and daughters will prophesy. Your old men will dream dreams, and your young men will see visions. 29In those days I will pour out my Spirit even on servants—men and women alike. 30And I will cause wonders in the heavens and on the earth—blood and fire and columns of smoke. 31The sun will become dark, and the moon will turn blood red before that great and terrible day of the LORD arrives. 32But everyone who calls on the name of the LORD will be saved, for some on Mount Zion in Jerusalem will escape, just as the LORD has said. These will be among the survivors whom the LORD has called.

Joel 2:25-32

The Bible is
our plumb line tool

When God uses His plumb line tool, He wants to bind together everybody who lives from His grace, and judge those who have forgotten His grace. The Bible helps us to live in grace and not to forget it. Why did those specific places in Amos 7:9 have to be destroyed? Because those places were where God's grace was abused and His law ignored.

7He showed me another vision. I saw the Lord standing beside a wall that had been built using a plumb line. He was using a plumb line to see if it was still straight. 8And the LORD said to me, "Amos, what do you see?" I answered, "A plumb line."

And the Lord replied, "I will test my people with this plumb line. I will no longer ignore all their sins. 9The pagan shrines of your ancestors will be ruined, and the temples of Israel will be destroyed; I will bring the dynasty of King Jeroboam to a sudden end."

10Then Amaziah, the priest of Bethel, sent a message to Jeroboam, king of Israel: "Amos is hatching a plot against you right here on your very doorstep! What he is saying is intolerable. 11He is saying, 'Jeroboam will soon be killed, and the people of Israel will be sent away into exile.'"

12Then Amaziah sent orders to Amos: "Get out of here, you prophet! Go on back to the land of Judah, and earn your living by prophesying there! 13Don't bother us with your prophecies here in Bethel. This is the king's sanctuary and the national place of worship!"

14But Amos replied, "I'm not a professional prophet. I'm just a shepherd. 15But the LORD called me away from my flock and told me, 'Go and prophesy to my people in Israel.'"

Amos 7:7-15

Your soul dies long before your body

There are two important messages in Amos 8. 1) Self-satisfaction is one of the mortal enemies of your faith. 2) To care for and love others is a sure sign of a living faith. The people in Amos's time lived number 1 and not number 2 – their souls were dead. God does not accept this.

¹Then the Sovereign LORD showed me another vision. In it I saw a basket filled with ripe fruit. ²"What do you see, Amos?" he asked. I replied, "A basket full of ripe fruit."

Then the LORD said, "Like this fruit, Israel is ripe for punishment! I will not delay their punishment again. ³In that day the singing in the Temple will turn to wailing. Dead bodies will be scattered everywhere. They will be carried out of the city in silence. I, the Sovereign LORD, have spoken!"

⁴Listen to this, you who rob the poor and trample down the needy! ⁵You can't wait for the Sabbath day to be over and the religious festivals to end so you can get back to cheating the helpless. You measure out grain with dishonest measures and cheat the buyer with dishonest scales. ⁶And you mix the grain you sell with chaff swept from the floor. Then you enslave poor people for one piece of silver or a pair of sandals.

⁹"In that day," says the Sovereign LORD, "I will make the sun go down at noon and darken the earth while it is still day. ¹⁰I will turn your celebrations into times of mourning and your singing into weeping. You will wear funeral clothes and shave your heads to show your sorrow. How very bitter that day will be! ¹¹The time is surely coming," says the Sovereign LORD, "when I will send a famine on the land—not a famine of bread or water but of hearing the words of the LORD."

Amos 8:1-6, 9-11

Nothing is ever completely lost

There is an expression, "It's not over till the fat lady sings." This applies to believers in another way. We so easily forget that nothing is completely lost, because God is always there. He wants to be your lifesaver – so let Him.

[11]"When they were invaded, you stood aloof, refusing to help them. Foreign invaders carried off their wealth and cast lots to divide up Jerusalem, but you acted like one of Israel's enemies.

[12]"You should not have gloated when they exiled your relatives to distant lands. You should not have rejoiced when the people of Judah suffered such misfortune. You should not have spoken arrogantly in that terrible time of trouble. [13]You should not have plundered the land of Israel when they were suffering such calamity. You should not have gloated over their destruction when they were suffering such calamity. You should not have seized their wealth when they were suffering such calamity. [14]You should not have stood at the crossroads, killing those who tried to escape. You should not have captured the survivors and handed them over in their terrible time of trouble.

[15]"The day is near when I, the LORD, will judge all godless nations! As you have done to Israel, so it will be done to you. All your evil deeds will fall back on your own heads. [16]Just as you swallowed up my people on my holy mountain, so you and the surrounding nations will swallow the punishment I pour out on you. Yes, all you nations will drink and stagger and disappear from history.

[17]"But Jerusalem will become a refuge for those who escape; it will be a holy place. And the people of Israel will come back to reclaim their inheritance."

Obadiah 11-17

I am not going to Sin City

The Assyrians were known to be a brutal nation. No wonder Jonah didn't want to go to Nineveh. Jonah learned, however, that it's impossible to run away from God. No one can ever run that far!

¹The LORD gave this message to Jonah son of Amittai: ²"Get up and go to the great city of Nineveh. Announce my judgment against it because I have seen how wicked its nation are."

³But Jonah got up and went in the opposite direction to get away from the LORD. He went down to the port of Joppa, where he found a ship leaving for Tarshish. He bought a ticket and went on board, hoping to escape from the LORD.

⁴But the LORD hurled a powerful wind over the sea, causing a violent storm that threatened to break the ship apart. ⁵Fearing for their lives, the desperate sailors shouted to their gods for help. ⁷Then the crew cast lots to see which of them had offended the gods and caused the terrible storm. When they did this, the lots identified Jonah as the culprit. ⁸"Why has this awful storm come down on us?" they demanded. "Who are you? What is your line of work? What country are you from? What is your nationality?" ⁹Jonah answered, "I am a Hebrew, and I worship the LORD, the God of heaven, who made the sea and the land."

¹⁰The sailors were terrified when they heard this, for he had already told them he was running away from the LORD. ¹⁵Then the sailors picked Jonah up and threw him into the raging sea, and the storm stopped at once!

¹⁷Now the LORD had arranged for a great fish to swallow Jonah. And Jonah was inside the fish for three days and three nights.

Jonah 1:1-5, 7-10, 15, 17

The runaway discovers how God feels about His people

What kind of fish it was that swallowed Jonah, is not as important as what happened inside the fish – Jonah prayed! Remember that whenever you are in trouble, pray – prayer opens your eyes up to do God's will. That's how you can get out of trouble.

¹Then Jonah prayed to the LORD his God from inside the fish. ²He said, "I cried out to the LORD in my great trouble, and he answered me. I called to you from the land of the dead, and LORD, you heard me! ³You threw me into the ocean depths, and I sank down to the heart of the sea. The mighty waters engulfed me; I was buried beneath your wild and stormy waves. ⁴Then I said, 'O LORD, you have driven me from your presence. Yet I will look once more toward your holy Temple.'

⁵"I sank beneath the waves, and the waters closed over me. Seaweed wrapped itself around my head. ⁶I sank down to the very roots of the mountains. I was imprisoned in the earth, whose gates lock shut forever. But you, O LORD my God, snatched me from the jaws of death!

⁷"As my life was slipping away, I remembered the LORD. And my earnest prayer went out to you in your holy Temple. ⁸Those who worship false gods turn their backs on all God's mercies. ⁹But I will offer sacrifices to you with songs of praise, and I will fulfill all my vows. For my salvation comes from the LORD alone."

¹⁰Then the LORD ordered the fish to spit Jonah out onto the beach.

Jonah 2:1-10

A change of plans

Finally Jonah went to the great city of Nineveh. There he walked around for a day and preached the shortest sermon imaginable: "In 40 days Nineveh will be destroyed!" The effect of Jonah's words was astounding: The whole city turned back to God. When God saw the sincerity of their repentance, He changed His plan.

¹Then the LORD spoke to Jonah a second time: ²"Get up and go to the great city of Nineveh, and deliver the message I have given you."

³This time Jonah obeyed the LORD's command and went to Nineveh, a city so large that it took three days to see it all. ⁴On the day Jonah entered the city, he shouted to the crowds: "Forty days from now Nineveh will be destroyed!" ⁵The people believed God's message, and from the greatest to the least, they declared a fast and put on burlap to show their sorrow.

⁶When the king of Nineveh heard what Jonah was saying, he stepped down from his throne and took off his royal robes. He dressed himself in burlap and sat on a heap of ashes. ⁷Then the king and his nobles sent this decree throughout the city: "No one, not even the animals from your herds and flocks, may eat or drink anything at all. ⁸People and animals alike must wear garments of mourning, and everyone must pray earnestly to God. They must turn from their evil ways and stop all their violence. ⁹Who can tell? Perhaps even yet God will change his mind and hold back his fierce anger from destroying us."

¹⁰When God saw what they had done and how they had put a stop to their evil ways, he changed his mind and did not carry out the destruction he had threatened.

Jonah 3:1-10

July

How God loves us

Jonah knew that God is full of grace, but he didn't realize He had so much grace! Jonah thought that God was supposed to wipe out the evil people of Nineveh. But just like Jonah we must learn to look at others through God's eyes and be gracious.

²So he complained to the LORD about it: "Didn't I say before I left home that you would do this, LORD? That is why I ran away to Tarshish! I knew that you are a merciful and compassionate God, slow to get angry and filled with unfailing love. You are eager to turn back from destroying people. ³Just kill me now, LORD! I'd rather be dead than alive if what I predicted will not happen."

⁵Then Jonah went out to the east side of the city and made a shelter to sit under as he waited to see what would happen to the city. ⁶And the LORD God arranged for a leafy plant to grow there, and soon it spread its broad leaves over Jonah's head, shading him from the sun. This eased his discomfort, and Jonah was very grateful for the plant.

⁷But God also arranged for a worm! The next morning at dawn the worm ate through the stem of the plant so that it withered away. ⁸And as the sun grew hot, God arranged for a scorching east wind to blow on Jonah. The sun beat down on his head until he grew faint and wished to die.

¹⁰Then the LORD said, "You feel sorry about the plant, though you did nothing to put it there. It came quickly and died quickly. ¹¹But Nineveh has more than 120,000 people living in spiritual darkness, not to mention all the animals. Shouldn't I feel sorry for such a great city?"

Jonah 4:2-3, 5-8, 10-11

Less is always more
with God

Micah 5:2-7 is a prophesy of the birth of Jesus. Bethlehem, an insignificant little town, was where David was born and where Micah predicted that the Messiah, the Savior of the world, would be born. God can turn a humble beginning into a miracle.

²But you, O Bethlehem Ephrathah, are only a small village among all the people of Judah. Yet a ruler of Israel will come from you, one whose origins are from the distant past. ³The people of Israel will be abandoned to their enemies until the woman in labor gives birth. Then at last his fellow countrymen will return from exile to their own land. ⁴And he will stand to lead his flock with the LORD'S strength, in the majesty of the name of the LORD his God. Then his people will live there undisturbed, for he will be highly honored around the world.

⁵And he will be the source of peace. When the Assyrians invade our land and break through our defenses, we will appoint seven rulers to watch over us, eight princes to lead us. ⁶They will rule Assyria with drawn swords and enter the gates of the land of Nimrod. He will rescue us from the Assyrians when they pour over the borders to invade our land.

⁷Then the remnant left in Israel will take their place among the nations. They will be like dew sent by the LORD or like rain falling on the grass, which no one can hold back and no one can restrain.

Micah 5:2-7

it's simple:
it's what God wants

God asks His children to live out their faith in all their relationships. Therefore it is good to follow the advice in Micah. A child summarized this Scripture like this: "Play fair, be nice and put your hand in God's hand."

[1]Listen to what the LORD is saying: "Stand up and state your case against me. Let the mountains and hills be called to witness your complaints. [2]And now, O mountains, listen to the LORD's complaint! He has a case against his people. He will bring charges against Israel.

[3]"O my people, what have I done to you? What have I done to make you tired of me? Answer me! [4]For I brought you out of Egypt and redeemed you from slavery. I sent Moses, Aaron, and Miriam to help you. [5]Don't you remember, my people, how King Balak of Moab tried to have you cursed and how Balaam son of Beor blessed you instead? And remember your journey from Acacia Grove to Gilgal, when I, the LORD, did everything I could to teach you about my faithfulness."

[6]What can we bring to the LORD? What kind of offerings should we give him? Should we bow before God with offerings of yearling calves? [7]Should we offer him thousands of rams and ten thousand rivers of olive oil? Should we sacrifice our first-born children to pay for our sins?

[8]No, O people, the LORD has told you what is good, and this is what he requires of you: to do what is right, to love mercy, and to walk humbly with your God.

Micah 6:1-8

No fishing allowed!

The oldest advice in the book is: Trust in God alone, because He will never leave you nor forsake you. He is the gracious One who throws your sins in the deepest sea and then puts up a sign with the words: No fishing allowed. Because He knows that we will try to fish them out again. Forget them, you are forgiven, so start again. You can trust God!

[5]Don't trust anyone—not your best friend or even your wife! [6]For the son despises his father. The daughter defies her mother. The daughter-in-law defies her mother-in-law. Your enemies are right in your own household!

[7]As for me, I look to the LORD for help. I wait confidently for God to save me, and my God will certainly hear me.

[18]Where is another God like you, who pardons the guilt of the remnant, overlooking the sins of his special people? You will not stay angry with your people forever, because you delight in showing unfailing love.

[19]Once again you will have compassion on us. You will trample our sins under your feet and throw them into the depths of the ocean! [20]You will show us your faithfulness and unfailing love as you promised to our ancestors Abraham and Jacob long ago.

Micah 7:5-7, 18-20

A fountain of goodness

Remember, in times of crisis God is our hiding place. He will look after us. He doesn't do it because we are so good; He does it because He is the fountain of all that is good. From this fountain flows a goodness that refreshes like cold water on a hot day.

¹This message concerning Nineveh came as a vision to Nahum, who lived in Elkosh.

²The LORD is a jealous God, filled with vengeance and rage. He takes revenge on all who oppose him and continues to rage against his enemies! ³The LORD is slow to get angry, but his power is great, and he never lets the guilty go unpunished. He displays his power in the whirlwind and the storm. The billowing clouds are the dust beneath his feet.

⁴At his command the oceans dry up, and the rivers disappear. The lush pastures of Bashan and Carmel fade, and the green forests of Lebanon wither. ⁵In his presence the mountains quake, and the hills melt away; the earth trembles, and its people are destroyed. ⁶Who can stand before his fierce anger? Who can survive his burning fury? His rage blazes forth like fire, and the mountains crumble to dust in his presence.

⁷The LORD is good, a strong refuge when trouble comes. He is close to those who trust in him.

Nahum 1:1-7

Sometimes people feel like things have gone on for long enough and nothing is happening, so they decide to take matters into their own hands. God warns us against this. He says to wait, and while you wait, have faith. You will be surprised at what happens. In the meantime don't forget that God's presence is with you 24/7.

¹I will climb up to my watchtower and stand at my guardpost. There I will wait to see what the LORD says and how he will answer my complaint.

²Then the LORD said to me, "Write my answer plainly on tablets, so that a runner can carry the correct message to others. ³This vision is for a future time. It describes the end, and it will be fulfilled. If it seems slow in coming, wait patiently, for it will surely take place. It will not be delayed.

⁴"Look at the proud! They trust in themselves, and their lives are crooked. But the righteous will live by their faithfulness to God.

¹⁸"What good is an idol carved by man, or a cast image that deceives you? How foolish to trust in your own creation—a god that can't even talk! ¹⁹What sorrow awaits you who say to wooden idols, 'Wake up and save us!' To speechless stone images you say, 'Rise up and teach us!' Can an idol tell you what to do? They may be overlaid with gold and silver, but they are lifeless inside. ²⁰But the LORD is in his holy Temple. Let all the earth be silent before him."

Habakkuk 2:1-4, 18-20

Do math when it's dark

"When a train goes through a tunnel and it gets dark, you don't throw away the ticket and jump off. You sit still and trust the engineer" (Corrie ten Boom). In dark times do some math – count your blessings one by one. You'll be surprised at how much God loves you!

[2]I have heard all about you, LORD. I am filled with awe by your amazing works. In this time of our deep need, help us again as you did in years gone by. And in your anger, remember your mercy.

[3]I see God moving across the deserts from Edom, the Holy One coming from Mount Paran. His brilliant splendor fills the heavens, and the earth is filled with his praise.

[6]When he stops, the earth shakes. When he looks, the nations tremble. He shatters the everlasting mountains and levels the eternal hills. He is the Eternal One!

[17]Even though the fig trees have no blossoms, and there are no grapes on the vines; even though the olive crop fails, and the fields lie empty and barren; even though the flocks die in the fields, and the cattle barns are empty, [18]yet I will rejoice in the LORD! I will be joyful in the God of my salvation! [19]The Sovereign LORD is my strength! He makes me as surefooted as a deer, able to tread upon the heights.

Habakkuk 3:2-3, 6, 17-19

Choose now, choose right

Judgment Day (in the original Hebrew, "The day of the Lord") is a terrible day for some and a wonderful day for others. Whether it will be terrible or wonderful depends on what side you are on – are you for or against God? You can't make the choice on Judgment Day – you have to make it now. Choose wisely!

1 ⁷Stand in silence in the presence of the Sovereign LORD, for the awesome day of the LORD's judgment is near. The LORD has prepared his people for a great slaughter and has chosen their executioners.

2 ¹Gather together—yes, gather together, you shameless nation. ²Gather before judgment begins, before your time to repent is blown away like chaff. Act now, before the fierce fury of the LORD falls and the terrible day of the LORD's anger begins.

³Seek the LORD, all who are humble, and follow his commands. Seek to do what is right and to live humbly. Perhaps even yet the LORD will protect you—protect you from his anger on that day of destruction. Judgment against Philistia ⁴Gaza and Ashkelon will be abandoned, Ashdod and Ekron torn down.

Zephaniah 1:7; 2:1-4

This is how God feels about you

If you ever doubt how God feels about you, read Zephaniah 3:17 over and over … God promises that these comforting words are still true – even when His children disappoint Him. He speaks about their punishment, but then He changes His topic to His forgiveness and presence. God's grace always triumphs over His wrath.

¹⁴Sing, O daughter of Zion; shout aloud, O Israel! Be glad and rejoice with all your heart, O daughter of Jerusalem! ¹⁵For the LORD will remove his hand of judgment and will disperse the armies of your enemy. And the LORD himself, the King of Israel, will live among you! At last your troubles will be over, and you will never again fear disaster.

¹⁶On that day the announcement to Jerusalem will be, "Cheer up, Zion! Don't be afraid! ¹⁷For the LORD your God is living among you. He is a mighty savior. He will take delight in you with gladness. With his love, he will calm all your fears. He will rejoice over you with joyful songs.

¹⁸"I will gather you who mourn for the appointed festivals; you will be disgraced no more.

¹⁹"And I will deal severely with all who have oppressed you. I will save the weak and helpless ones; I will bring together those who were chased away. I will give glory and fame to my former exiles, wherever they have been mocked and shamed.

²⁰"On that day I will gather you together and bring you home again. I will give you a good name, a name of distinction, among all the nations of the earth, as I restore your fortunes before their very eyes. I, the LORD, have spoken!"

Zephaniah 3:14-20

Get your priorities straight

Johann Wolgang von Goethe said, "Things which matter most, must never be at the mercy of things which matter least." In Haggai we clearly see that God must be your top priority. In everything you do others should be able to see that God is number one in your life. What or Who do people see in your life?

1²"This is what the LORD of Heaven's Armies says: The people are saying, 'The time has not yet come to rebuild the house of the LORD.'"

³Then the LORD sent this message through the prophet Haggai: ⁴"Why are you living in luxurious houses while my house lies in ruins? ⁵This is what the LORD of Heaven's Armies says: Look at what's happening to you! ⁶You have planted much but harvest little. You eat but are not satisfied. You drink but are still thirsty. You put on clothes but cannot keep warm. Your wages disappear as though you were putting them in pockets filled with holes!

⁷"This is what the LORD of Heaven's Armies says: Look at what's happening to you! ⁸Now go up into the hills, bring down timber, and rebuild my house. Then I will take pleasure in it and be honored, says the LORD."

2⁴"But now the LORD says: Be strong, Zerubbabel. Be strong, Jeshua son of Jehozadak, the high priest. Be strong, all you people still left in the land. And now get to work, for I am with you, says the LORD of Heaven's Armies. ⁵My Spirit remains among you, just as I promised when you came out of Egypt. So do not be afraid.'"

Haggai 1:2-8; 2:4-5

A single day

Forgiven sinners, that's what believers are, get new instructions: to distribute grace and share about the day when all their sins were removed. Golgotha is the one day that proves that our sin does not have the last say in our lives and that relationships between people can be restored (v. 10).

¹Then the angel showed me Jeshua the high priest standing before the angel of the LORD. The Accuser, Satan, was there at the angel's right hand, making accusations against Jeshua. ²And the LORD said to Satan, "I, the LORD, reject your accusations, Satan. This man is like a burning stick that has been snatched from the fire."

³Jeshua's clothing was filthy as he stood there before the angel. ⁴So the angel said to the others standing there, "Take off his filthy clothes." And turning to Jeshua he said, "See, I have taken away your sins, and now I am giving you these fine new clothes." ⁶Then the angel of the LORD spoke very solemnly to Jeshua and said, ⁷"This is what the LORD of Heaven's Armies says: If you follow my ways and carefully serve me, then you will be given authority over my Temple and its courtyards. ⁸"Listen to me, O Jeshua the high priest, and all you other priests. You are symbols of things to come. Soon I am going to bring my servant, the Branch. ⁹Now look at the jewel I have set before Jeshua, a single stone with seven facets. I will engrave an inscription on it, says the LORD of Heaven's Armies, and I will remove the sins of this land in a single day.

¹⁰"And on that day, says the LORD of Heaven's Armies, each of you will invite your neighbor to sit with you peacefully under your own grapevine and fig tree."

Zechariah 3:1-4, 6-10

Bigger isn't always better

Two things are important:

1. No one is a self-made person but rather a God-made person. See all your success in this light.
2. We live in a world where we believe "bigger is better." But Zechariah reminds us that God is also in the small, everyday things and we should celebrate these too!

[6]Then he said to me, "This is what the LORD says to Zerubbabel: It is not by force nor by strength, but by my Spirit, says the LORD of Heaven's Armies. [7]Nothing, not even a mighty mountain, will stand in Zerubbabel's way; it will become a level plain before him! And when Zerubbabel sets the final stone of the Temple in place, the people will shout: 'May God bless it! May God bless it!'"

[8]Then another message came to me from the LORD: [9]"Zerubbabel is the one who laid the foundation of this Temple, and he will complete it. Then you will know that the LORD of Heaven's Armies has sent me. [10]Do not despise these small beginnings, for the LORD rejoices to see the work begin, to see the plumb line in Zerubbabel's hand." (The seven lamps represent the eyes of the LORD that search all around the world.)

Zechariah 4:6-10

Wells, not walls!

"Don't build walls ... We propose a better and more biblical way ... sink wells," someone once suggested. The bad thing about a wall is that it keeps people both in and out! The good thing about a well is that it doesn't shut anyone out. Jesus is our "well". If we always live with Him as the center of everything then Zechariah 8:23 will become true.

³"And now the LORD says: I am returning to Mount Zion, and I will live in Jerusalem. Then Jerusalem will be called the Faithful City; the mountain of the LORD of Heaven's Armies will be called the Holy Mountain.

⁴"This is what the LORD of Heaven's Armies says: Once again old men and women will walk Jerusalem's streets with their canes and will sit together in the city squares. ⁵And the streets of the city will be filled with boys and girls at play.

⁶"This is what the LORD of Heaven's Armies says: All this may seem impossible to you now, a small remnant of God's people. But is it impossible for me? says the LORD of Heaven's Armies.

²⁰"This is what the LORD of Heaven's Armies says: People from nations and cities around the world will travel to Jerusalem. ²¹The people of one city will say to the people of another, 'Come with us to Jerusalem to ask the LORD to bless us. Let's worship the LORD of Heaven's Armies. I'm determined to go.'

²³"This is what the LORD of Heaven's Armies says: In those days ten men from different nations and languages of the world will clutch at the sleeve of one Jew. And they will say, 'Please let us walk with you, for we have heard that God is with you.'"

Zechariah 8:3-6, 20-21, 23

God did not create weapons of mass destruction. He also didn't put people in concentration camps or try to eradicate them. People did that. So is it reasonable for us to blame God for the chaos in the world and ask: Is God a God of love? Rather, what does it say about us?

²"I have always loved you," says the LORD. But you retort, "Really? How have you loved us?" And the LORD replies, "This is how I showed my love for you: I loved your ancestor Jacob, ³but I rejected his brother, Esau, and devastated his hill country."

⁴Esau's descendants in Edom may say, "We have been shattered, but we will rebuild the ruins." But the LORD of Heaven's Armies replies, "They may try to rebuild, but I will demolish them again."

⁶The LORD of Heaven's Armies says to the priests: "A son honors his father, and a servant respects his master. If I am your father and master, where are the honor and respect I deserve? You have shown contempt for my name! "But you ask, 'How have we ever shown contempt for your name?'

⁷"You have shown contempt by offering defiled sacrifices on my altar. Then you ask, 'How have we defiled the sacrifices?' You defile them by saying the altar of the LORD deserves no respect. ⁸Isn't it wrong to offer animals that are crippled and diseased? Try giving gifts like that to your governor, and see how pleased he is!" says the LORD of Heaven's Armies.

⁹"Go ahead, beg God to be merciful to you! But when you bring that kind of offering, why should he show you any favor at all?" asks the LORD of Heaven's Armies.

Malachi 1:2-4, 6-9

Like refined silver

A silversmith knows that the refining process is only complete when he can see his own reflection in the silver. God will also purify His children so that He can see His Son's reflection shining out from them.

¹"Look! I am sending my messenger, and he will prepare the way before me. Then the Lord you are seeking will suddenly come to his Temple. The messenger of the covenant, whom you look for so eagerly, is surely coming," says the LORD of Heaven's Armies.

²"But who will be able to endure it when he comes? Who will be able to stand and face him when he appears? For he will be like a blazing fire that refines metal, or like a strong soap that bleaches clothes. ³He will sit like a refiner of silver, burning away the dross. He will purify the Levites, refining them like gold and silver, so that they may once again offer acceptable sacrifices to the LORD. ⁴Then once more the LORD will accept the offerings brought to him by the people of Judah and Jerusalem, as he did in the past.

⁵"At that time I will put you on trial. I am eager to witness against all sorcerers and adulterers and liars. I will speak against those who cheat employees of their wages, who oppress widows and orphans, or who deprive the foreigners living among you of justice, for these people do not fear me," says the LORD of Heaven's Armies.

⁶"I am the LORD, and I do not change. That is why you descendants of Jacob are not already destroyed.

Malachi 3:1-6

All or nothing?

Your tithe reveals how much you really care about God. Usually the last thing anyone gives God is his wallet. It's easy to say something is better than nothing, but God says all or nothing. Give God your best.

¹⁰"Bring all the tithes into the storehouse so there will be enough food in my Temple. If you do," says the LORD of Heaven's Armies, "I will open the windows of heaven for you. I will pour out a blessing so great you won't have enough room to take it in! Try it! Put me to the test!

¹²"Then all nations will call you blessed, for your land will be such a delight," says the LORD of Heaven's Armies.

¹³"You have said terrible things about me," says the LORD. "But you say, 'What do you mean? What have we said against you?' ¹⁴You have said, 'What's the use of serving God? What have we gained by obeying his commands or by trying to show the LORD of Heaven's Armies that we are sorry for our sins? ¹⁵From now on we will call the arrogant blessed. For those who do evil get rich, and those who dare God to punish them suffer no harm.'"

¹⁶Then those who feared the LORD spoke with each other, and the LORD listened to what they said. In his presence, a scroll of remembrance was written to record the names of those who feared him and always thought about the honor of his name.

¹⁷"They will be my people," says the LORD of Heaven's Armies. "On the day when I act in judgment, they will be my own special treasure. ¹⁸Then you will again see the difference between the righteous and the wicked, between those who serve God and those who do not."

Malachi 3:10, 12-18

The Sun of Righteousness

Those who serve the Lord share in the healing and wisdom He brings. Malachi 4 can be seen as a bridge between the New and Old Testaments because it hints at the arrival of Jesus, God's Son, who brings healing and joy to the world.

¹The LORD of Heaven's Armies says, "The day of judgment is coming, burning like a furnace. On that day the arrogant and the wicked will be burned up like straw. They will be consumed—roots, branches, and all.

²"But for you who fear my name, the Sun of Righteousness will rise with healing in his wings. And you will go free, leaping with joy like calves let out to pasture. ³On the day when I act, you will tread upon the wicked as if they were dust under your feet," says the LORD of Heaven's Armies.

⁴"Remember to obey the Law of Moses, my servant—all the decrees and regulations that I gave him on Mount Sinai for all Israel.

⁵"Look, I am sending you the prophet Elijah before the great and dreadful day of the LORD arrives. ⁶His preaching will turn the hearts of fathers to their children, and the hearts of children to their fathers. Otherwise I will come and strike the land with a curse."

Malachi 4:1-6

Two names
that can help you

The two names of God's Son, Jesus and Immanuel, give us a new, fresh perspective on life – God's perspective! Jesus means *God who saves*, which means you can be saved from sin. His other name is Immanuel, which means *God with us*. You are never alone – God is with you 24/7.

[18]This is how Jesus the Messiah was born. His mother, Mary, was engaged to be married to Joseph. But before the marriage took place, while she was still a virgin, she became pregnant through the power of the Holy Spirit. [19]Joseph, her fiancé, was a good man and did not want to disgrace her publicly, so he decided to break the engagement quietly.

[20]As he considered this, an angel of the Lord appeared to him in a dream. "Joseph, son of David," the angel said, "do not be afraid to take Mary as your wife. For the child within her was conceived by the Holy Spirit. [21]And she will have a son, and you are to name him Jesus, for he will save his people from their sins."

[22]All of this occurred to fulfill the Lord's message through his prophet: [23]"Look! The virgin will conceive a child! She will give birth to a son, and they will call him Immanuel, which means 'God is with us.'"

[24]When Joseph woke up, he did as the angel of the Lord commanded and took Mary as his wife. [25]But he did not have sexual relations with her until her son was born. And Joseph named him Jesus.

Matthew 1:18-25

A star, expensive gifts and the ultimate Gift

Gold, frankincense and myrrh were not only the most expensive gifts in biblical times, but also the most valuable. But the wise men went home with an even better gift. They had met the King of the universe and nothing would ever be the same for them (and others) again!

¹Jesus was born in Bethlehem in Judea, during the reign of King Herod. About that time some wise men from eastern lands arrived in Jerusalem, asking, ²"Where is the newborn king of the Jews? We saw his star as it rose, and we have come to worship him."

⁴He called a meeting of the leading priests and teachers of religious law and asked, "Where is the Messiah supposed to be born?"

⁵"In Bethlehem in Judea," they said.

⁸Then he told them, "Go to Bethlehem and search carefully for the child. And when you find him, come back and tell me so that I can go and worship him, too!"

⁹After this interview the wise men went their way. And the star they had seen in the east guided them to Bethlehem. It went ahead of them and stopped over the place where the child was.

¹¹They entered the house and saw the child with his mother, Mary, and they bowed down and worshiped him. Then they opened their treasure chests and gave him gifts of gold, frankincense, and myrrh.

¹²When it was time to leave, they returned to their own country by another route, for God had warned them in a dream not to return to Herod.

Matthew 2:1-2, 4-5, 8-9, 11-12

On Temptation Island

The three temptations Jesus faced can be summed up in the following: to be in control; to be spectacular; to be mighty. All three temptations are still relevant today. Your love for Jesus will help you stand strong against temptations.

¹Then Jesus was led by the Spirit into the wilderness to be tempted there by the devil. ²For forty days and forty nights he fasted and became very hungry.

³During that time the devil came and said to him, "If you are the Son of God, tell these stones to become loaves of bread."

⁴But Jesus told him, "No! The Scriptures say, 'People do not live by bread alone, but by every word that comes from the mouth of God.'"

⁵Then the devil took him to the holy city, Jerusalem, to the highest point of the Temple, ⁶and said, "If you are the Son of God, jump off! For the Scriptures say, 'He will order his angels to protect you. And they will hold you up with their hands so you won't even hurt your foot on a stone.'"

⁷Jesus responded, "The Scriptures also say, 'You must not test the Lord your God.'"

⁸Next the devil took him to the peak of a very high mountain and showed him all the kingdoms of the world and their glory. ⁹"I will give it all to you," he said, "if you will kneel down and worship me."

¹⁰"Get out of here, Satan," Jesus told him. "For the Scriptures say, 'You must worship the Lord your God and serve only him.'"

Matthew 4:1-10

Come, be My disciples

How can one refuse such an invitation? Especially from Someone who loves you in spite of who you are and rejoices over you. Of course you will follow Him – for eternity. Will you leave behind what you think is important and make God your first priority?

[18]One day as Jesus was walking along the shore of the Sea of Galilee, he saw two brothers—Simon, also called Peter, and Andrew—throwing a net into the water, for they fished for a living. [19]Jesus called out to them, "Come, follow me, and I will show you how to fish for people!" [20]And they left their nets at once and followed him.

[21]A little farther up the shore he saw two other brothers, James and John, sitting in a boat with their father, Zebedee, repairing their nets. And he called them to come, too. [22]They immediately followed him, leaving the boat and their father behind.

[23]Jesus traveled throughout the region of Galilee, teaching in the synagogues and announcing the Good News about the Kingdom. And he healed every kind of disease and illness. [24]News about him spread as far as Syria, and people soon began bringing to him all who were sick. And whatever their sickness or disease, or if they were demon possessed or epileptic or paralyzed—he healed them all.

[25]Large crowds followed him wherever he went—people from Galilee, the Ten Towns, Jerusalem, from all over Judea, and from east of the Jordan River.

Matthew 4:18-25

The secret to a happy life

The lifestyle that Jesus proposes is different to how people of the world live today. But Jesus' way of life will bring you happiness that is out of this world – a happiness that God intended for us from the beginning. It is a true and genuine happiness.

¹One day as he saw the crowds gathering, Jesus went up on the mountainside and sat down. His disciples gathered around him, ²and he began to teach them.

³"God blesses those who are poor and realize their need for him, for the Kingdom of Heaven is theirs.

⁴"God blesses those who mourn, for they will be comforted.

⁵"God blesses those who are humble, for they will inherit the whole earth.

⁶"God blesses those who hunger and thirst for justice, for they will be satisfied.

⁷"God blesses those who are merciful, for they will be shown mercy.

⁸"God blesses those whose hearts are pure, for they will see God.

⁹"God blesses those who work for peace, for they will be called the children of God.

¹⁰"God blesses those who are persecuted for doing right, for the Kingdom of Heaven is theirs.

¹¹"God blesses you when people mock you and persecute you and lie about you and say all sorts of evil things against you because you are my followers. ¹²Be happy about it! Be very glad! For a great reward awaits you in heaven. And remember, the ancient prophets were persecuted in the same way."

Matthew 5:1-12

Salt and light

As salt a person should promote purity, preserve good things and flavor each day with godliness. As light a person should reveal all the God-colors in the world. If you are like salt and light then people will see Jesus in you and in the world around them. Then people will begin to sing songs to our heavenly Father.

[13]"You are the salt of the earth. But what good is salt if it has lost its flavor? Can you make it salty again? It will be thrown out and trampled underfoot as worthless.

[14]"You are the light of the world—like a city on a hilltop that cannot be hidden. [15]No one lights a lamp and then puts it under a basket. Instead, a lamp is placed on a stand, where it gives light to everyone in the house. [16]In the same way, let your good deeds shine out for all to see, so that everyone will praise your heavenly Father."

Matthew 5:13-16

Be a promise keeper

There are too many people who break promises. People struggle to keep their promises. If you keep a promise then you are cultivating a Jesus character. Let your yes be yes and your no be no. Be a person of integrity in your thoughts, words and actions.

33"You have also heard that our ancestors were told, 'You must not break your vows; you must carry out the vows you make to the LORD.'

34"But I say, do not make any vows! Do not say, 'By heaven!' because heaven is God's throne. 35And do not say, 'By the earth!' because the earth is his footstool. And do not say, 'By Jerusalem!' for Jerusalem is the city of the great King. 36Do not even say, 'By my head!' for you can't turn one hair white or black. 37Just say a simple, 'Yes, I will,' or 'No, I won't.' Anything beyond this is from the evil one."

Matthew 5:33-37

Retaliate with love

"An eye for an eye" makes the whole world blind. The best revenge is to forgive unconditionally. It catches the person off-guard because he receives grace. Always react to injustice with the power of love.

38"You have heard the law that says the punishment must match the injury: 'An eye for an eye, and a tooth for a tooth.' 39But I say, do not resist an evil person! If someone slaps you on the right cheek, offer the other cheek also. 40If you are sued in court and your shirt is taken from you, give your coat, too. 41If a soldier demands that you carry his gear for a mile, carry it two miles. 42Give to those who ask, and don't turn away from those who want to borrow.

43"You have heard the law that says, 'Love your neighbor' and hate your enemy. 44But I say, love your enemies! Pray for those who persecute you! 45In that way, you will be acting as true children of your Father in heaven. For he gives his sunlight to both the evil and the good, and he sends rain on the just and the unjust alike. 46If you love only those who love you, what reward is there for that? Even corrupt tax collectors do that much. 47If you are kind only to your friends, how are you different from anyone else? Even pagans do that.

48"But you are to be perfect, even as your Father in heaven is perfect."

Matthew 5:38-48

Don't put on a show

Being a believer is not the same as playing a part in a Hollywood movie or a Broadway play. If people clap and cheer for you instead of Jesus, then it is just a show. You should not do something just to be in the spotlight, you should do it because of Jesus' goodness, love and grace.

[1]"Watch out! Don't do your good deeds publicly, to be admired by others, for you will lose the reward from your Father in heaven. [2]When you give to someone in need, don't do as the hypocrites do—blowing trumpets in the synagogues and streets to call attention to their acts of charity! I tell you the truth, they have received all the reward they will ever get. [3]But when you give to someone in need, don't let your left hand know what your right hand is doing. [4]Give your gifts in private, and your Father, who sees everything, will reward you.

[5]"When you pray, don't be like the hypocrites who love to pray publicly on street corners and in the synagogues where everyone can see them. I tell you the truth, that is all the reward they will ever get. [6]But when you pray, go away by yourself, shut the door behind you, and pray to your Father in private. Then your Father, who sees everything, will reward you.

[7]"When you pray, don't babble on and on as people of other religions do. They think their prayers are answered merely by repeating their words again and again. [8]Don't be like them, for your Father knows exactly what you need even before you ask him!"

Matthew 6:1-8

Pray to your Father

Jesus gave us a prayer that broadens our prayer lives. Pray it, but more than that – live it. A faith-filled prayer is a powerful prayer. The word *Abba* means Father, and Jesus teaches us to call God that. So always remember you have a caring Father who hears your prayers.

[9]Pray like this: Our Father in heaven, may your name be kept holy. [10]May your Kingdom come soon. May your will be done on earth, as it is in heaven. [11]Give us today the food we need, [12]and forgive us our sins, as we have forgiven those who sin against us. [13]And don't let us yield to temptation, but rescue us from the evil one.

[14]"If you forgive those who sin against you, your heavenly Father will forgive you. [15]But if you refuse to forgive others, your Father will not forgive your sins."

Matthew 6:9-15

Who's your boss?

Your treasure reveals your heart's priorities. Let your life's goal always be in harmony with your "Jesus priorities". If you have Jesus as the number one priority in your life then you will keep your eyes focused on the right things and you will work for the right Boss – God.

¹⁹"Don't store up treasures here on earth, where moths eat them and rust destroys them, and where thieves break in and steal. ²⁰Store your treasures in heaven, where moths and rust cannot destroy, and thieves do not break in and steal. ²¹Wherever your treasure is, there the desires of your heart will also be.

²²"Your eye is a lamp that provides light for your body. When your eye is good, your whole body is filled with light. ²³But when your eye is bad, your whole body is filled with darkness. And if the light you think you have is actually darkness, how deep that darkness is!

²⁴"No one can serve two masters. For you will hate one and love the other; you will be devoted to one and despise the other. You cannot serve both God and money."

Matthew 6:19-24

Don't be a worrywart

Worry is like a treadmill. It keeps you busy but you don't get anywhere. Trusting in God allows you to enjoy life to the full because you know that your Father (Abba) cares for you. Your life is in His hands, all you have to do is to roll up your sleeves and give 100% for God. Then you will get somewhere!

25"That is why I tell you not to worry about everyday life—whether you have enough food and drink, or enough clothes to wear. Isn't life more than food, and your body more than clothing?

26"Look at the birds. They don't plant or harvest or store food in barns, for your heavenly Father feeds them. And aren't you far more valuable to him than they are? 27Can all your worries add a single moment to your life?

28"And why worry about your clothing? Look at the lilies of the field and how they grow. They don't work or make their clothing, 29yet Solomon in all his glory was not dressed as beautifully as they are. 30And if God cares so wonderfully for wildflowers that are here today and thrown into the fire tomorrow, he will certainly care for you. Why do you have so little faith?"

Matthew 6:25-30

Don't criticize –
rather encourage

Negative, destructive criticism can hurt and destroy someone. It makes you blind to the positive things in other people. Critical words become a log in your own eye that makes you unable to see God's image in others. Rather choose to appreciate someone than criticize them.

¹"Do not judge others, and you will not be judged. ²For you will be treated as you treat others. The standard you use in judging is the standard by which you will be judged.

³"And why worry about a speck in your friend's eye when you have a log in your own? ⁴How can you think of saying to your friend, 'Let me help you get rid of that speck in your eye,' when you can't see past the log in your own eye? ⁵Hypocrite! First get rid of the log in your own eye; then you will see well enough to deal with the speck in your friend's eye.

⁶"Don't waste what is holy on people who are unholy. Don't throw your pearls to pigs! They will trample the pearls, then turn and attack you."

Matthew 7:1-6

Healthy trees and strong foundations

People who follow Jesus and do what He says are like healthy trees; they begin to show good fruit when they build their lives on the right foundation. The more you read the Word and live according to it, the stronger your foundation will be and the more fruit you will produce.

[15]"Beware of false prophets who come disguised as harmless sheep but are really vicious wolves. [16]You can identify them by their fruit, that is, by the way they act. Can you pick grapes from thornbushes, or figs from thistles? [17]A good tree produces good fruit, and a bad tree produces bad fruit.

[20]"Yes, just as you can identify a tree by its fruit, so you can identify people by their actions.

[21]"Not everyone who calls out to me, 'Lord! Lord!' will enter the Kingdom of Heaven. Only those who actually do the will of my Father in heaven will enter. [22]On judgment day many will say to me, 'Lord! Lord! We prophesied in your name and cast out demons in your name and performed many miracles in your name.' [23]But I will reply, 'I never knew you. Get away from me, you who break God's laws.'

[24]"Anyone who listens to my teaching and follows it is wise, like a person who builds a house on solid rock. [25]Though the rain comes in torrents and the floodwaters rise and the winds beat against that house, it won't collapse because it is built on bedrock. [26]But anyone who hears my teaching and doesn't obey it is foolish, like a person who builds a house on sand. [27]When the rains and floods come and the winds beat against that house, it will collapse with a mighty crash."

Matthew 7:15-17, 20-27

August

Trust God in everything

Do we care enough to really follow Jesus? Or do we have all sorts of excuses, like the people in today's Scripture reading. Jesus looks for people who love Him so much that they are prepared to give up everything for Him and give 100% to Him. You can always trust God – even in the storms of life.

[18]When Jesus saw the crowd around him, he instructed his disciples to cross to the other side of the lake.

[19]Then one of the teachers of religious law said to him, "Teacher, I will follow you wherever you go."

[20]But Jesus replied, "Foxes have dens to live in, and birds have nests, but the Son of Man has no place even to lay his head."

[21]Another of his disciples said, "Lord, first let me return home and bury my father."

[22]But Jesus told him, "Follow now. Let the spiritually dead bury their own dead."

[23]Then Jesus got into the boat and started across the lake with his disciples. [24]Suddenly, a fierce storm struck the lake, with waves breaking into the boat. But Jesus was sleeping. [25]The disciples went and woke him up, shouting, "Lord, save us! We're going to drown!"

[26]Jesus responded, "Why are you afraid? You have so little faith!" Then he got up and rebuked the wind and waves, and suddenly there was a great calm.

Matthew 8:18-26

This new wine is for everyone!

Everyone is called to follow Jesus, even the outsiders of society who no one likes. Jesus asks His followers to have compassion on such people. So show that your life is a new wineskin that holds the new wine that Jesus has poured into you.

⁹As Jesus was walking along, he saw a man named Matthew sitting at his tax collector's booth. "Follow me and be my disciple," Jesus said to him. So Matthew got up and followed him.

¹⁰Later, Matthew invited Jesus and his disciples to his home as dinner guests, along with many tax collectors and other disreputable sinners. ¹¹But when the Pharisees saw this, they asked his disciples, "Why does your teacher eat with such scum?"

¹²When Jesus heard this, he said, "Healthy people don't need a doctor—sick people do." ¹³Then he added, "Now go and learn the meaning of this Scripture: 'I want you to show mercy, not offer sacrifices.' For I have come to call not those who think they are righteous, but those who know they are sinners."

¹⁴One day the disciples of John the Baptist came to Jesus and asked him, "Why don't your disciples fast like we do and the Pharisees do?" ¹⁵Jesus replied, "Do wedding guests mourn while celebrating with the groom? Of course not. But someday the groom will be taken away from them, and then they will fast. ¹⁶Besides, who would patch old clothing with new cloth? For the new patch would shrink and rip away from the old cloth, leaving an even bigger tear than before.

¹⁷"And no one puts new wine into old wineskins. For the old skins would burst from the pressure, spilling the wine and ruining the skins. New wine is stored in new wineskins so that both are preserved."

Matthew 9:9-17

Wanted:
Workers for Jesus

The harvest is great, because people are looking for Jesus. Therefore Jesus looks for people who can show His kind of love to others. He searches for normal people, like the disciples who were fishermen, a tax collector and other everyday people. Follow Jesus and He will make you more than capable of bringing in the harvest.

9 [27] After Jesus left the girl's home, two blind men followed along behind him, shouting, "Son of David, have mercy on us!"

[28] They went right into the house where he was staying, and Jesus asked them, "Do you believe I can make you see?"

"Yes, Lord," they told him, "we do."

[29] Then he touched their eyes and said, "Because of your faith, it will happen." [30] Then their eyes were opened, and they could see! Jesus sternly warned them, "Don't tell anyone about this."

[36] When he saw the crowds, he had compassion on them because they were confused and helpless, like sheep without a shepherd. [37] He said to his disciples, "The harvest is great, but the workers are few. [38] So pray to the Lord who is in charge of the harvest; ask him to send more workers into his fields."

10 [1] Jesus called his twelve disciples together and gave them authority to cast out evil spirits and to heal every kind of disease and illness.

Matthew 9:27-30, 36-10:1

Jesus knows the number of hairs on your head

Jesus-followers are thrown to the wolves. But don't be scared, because the Lord knows the number of hairs on your head. He knows about you personally just like He knows the sparrows! In other words, He provides the best protection. Be shrewd like a snake and harmless like a dove – that is Jesus' advice.

¹⁶"Look, I am sending you out as sheep among wolves. So be as shrewd as snakes and harmless as doves.

¹⁸"You will stand trial before governors and kings because you are my followers. But this will be your opportunity to tell the rulers and other unbelievers about me. ¹⁹When you are arrested, don't worry about how to respond or what to say. God will give you the right words at the right time. ²⁰For it is not you who will be speaking—it will be the Spirit of your Father speaking through you.

²¹"A brother will betray his brother to death, a father will betray his own child, and children will rebel against their parents and cause them to be killed. ²²And all nations will hate you because you are my followers. But everyone who endures to the end will be saved. ²³When you are persecuted in one town, flee to the next. I tell you the truth, the Son of Man will return before you have reached all the towns of Israel.

²⁹"What is the price of two sparrows—one copper coin? But not a single sparrow can fall to the ground without your Father knowing it. ³⁰And the very hairs on your head are all numbered. ³¹So don't be afraid; you are more valuable to God than a whole flock of sparrows."

Matthew 10:16, 18-23, 29-31

A peace like no other

The peace Jesus promises doesn't mean that you won't have any problems or crises in your life. Nope, it's a peace that you experience in the middle of all the drama of your life. Peace means knowing that you can rest in God. Jesus promises this and you can believe what He says.

25At that time Jesus prayed this prayer: "O Father, Lord of heaven and earth, thank you for hiding these things from those who think themselves wise and clever, and for revealing them to the childlike. 26Yes, Father, it pleased you to do it this way!

27"My Father has entrusted everything to me. No one truly knows the Son except the Father, and no one truly knows the Father except the Son and those to whom the Son chooses to reveal him."

28Then Jesus said, "Come to me, all of you who are weary and carry heavy burdens, and I will give you rest. 29Take my yoke upon you. Let me teach you, because I am humble and gentle at heart, and you will find rest for your souls. 30For my yoke is easy to bear, and the burden I give you is light."

Matthew 11:25-30

Good soil

God is like a farmer who sowed His Word like a pack of seeds. But the result was not entirely successful. Birds ate some of the seeds, the sun wilted a few, and others fell among weeds. Fortunately some of the seeds fell on good soil.

3"Listen! A farmer went out to plant some seeds. 4As he scattered them across his field, some seeds fell on a footpath, and the birds came and ate them. 5Other seeds fell on shallow soil with underlying rock. The seeds sprouted quickly because the soil was shallow. 6But the plants soon wilted under the hot sun, and since they didn't have deep roots, they died. 7Other seeds fell among thorns that grew up and choked out the tender plants. 8Still other seeds fell on fertile soil, and they produced a crop that was thirty, sixty, and even a hundred times as much as had been planted!

19"The seed that fell on the footpath represents those who hear the message about the Kingdom and don't understand it. Then the evil one comes and snatches away the seed that was planted in their hearts. 20The seed on the rocky soil represents those who hear the message and immediately receive it with joy. 21But since they don't have deep roots, they don't last long. They fall away as soon as they have problems or are persecuted for believing God's word. 22The seed that fell among the thorns represents those who hear God's word, but all too quickly the message is crowded out by the worries of this life and the lure of wealth, so no fruit is produced. 23The seed that fell on good soil represents those who truly hear and understand God's word and produce a harvest of thirty, sixty, or even a hundred times as much as had been planted!"

Matthew 13:3-8, 19-23

God farms with grace

Weeds began to grow among the farmer's crops but he left them to peacefully grow. He wanted the weeds to grow because when they started growing they looked like wheat. He didn't want His wheat pulled out with the weeds.

24Here is another story Jesus told: "The Kingdom of Heaven is like a farmer who planted good seed in his field. 25But that night as the workers slept, his enemy came and planted weeds among the wheat, then slipped away. 26When the crop began to grow and produce grain, the weeds also grew.

27"The farmer's workers went to him and said, 'Sir, the field where you planted that good seed is full of weeds! Where did they come from?'

28"'An enemy has done this!' the farmer exclaimed.

"'Should we pull out the weeds?' they asked.

29"'No,' he replied, 'you'll uproot the wheat if you do. 30Let both grow together until the harvest. Then I will tell the harvesters to sort out the weeds, tie them into bundles, and burn them, and to put the wheat in the barn.'"

36Then, leaving the crowds outside, Jesus went into the house. His disciples said, "Please explain to us the story of the weeds in the field."

37Jesus replied, "The Son of Man is the farmer who plants the good seed. 38The field is the world, and the good seed represents the people of the Kingdom. The weeds are the people who belong to the evil one. 39The enemy who planted the weeds among the wheat is the devil. The harvest is the end of the world, and the harvesters are the angels."

Matthew 13:24-30, 36-39

Get out of the boat

Jesus walked on water. All His disciples got a big fright – except for Peter! He climbed out of the boat and began walking on water too. But then he became overwhelmed by everything and started to sink. How did Jesus and Peter get back in the boat? Probably by walking on the water!

²²Jesus insisted that his disciples get back into the boat and cross to the other side of the lake, while he sent the people home. ²³After sending them home, he went up into the hills by himself to pray. Night fell while he was there alone.

²⁴Meanwhile, the disciples were in trouble far away from land, for a strong wind had risen, and they were fighting heavy waves. ²⁵About three o'clock in the morning Jesus came toward them, walking on the water. ²⁶When the disciples saw him walking on the water, they were terrified. In their fear, they cried out, "It's a ghost!"

²⁷But Jesus spoke to them at once. "Don't be afraid," he said. "Take courage. I am here!"

²⁸Then Peter called to him, "Lord, if it's really you, tell me to come to you, walking on the water."

²⁹"Yes, come," Jesus said.

So Peter went over the side of the boat and walked on the water toward Jesus. ³⁰But when he saw the strong wind and the waves, he was terrified and began to sink. "Save me, Lord!" he shouted.

³¹Jesus immediately reached out and grabbed him. "You have so little faith," Jesus said. "Why did you doubt me?"

³²When they climbed back into the boat, the wind stopped.

Matthew 14:22-32

Keep forgiving!

70 x 7 was Jesus' way of saying that we mustn't keep a record of wrongs. Believers don't count how many times someone has wronged them, because God doesn't do that. He just forgives!

[21]Peter came to him and asked, "Lord, how often should I forgive someone who sins against me? Seven times?" [22]"No, not seven times," Jesus replied, "but seventy times seven!

[23]"Therefore, the Kingdom of Heaven can be compared to a king who decided to bring his accounts up to date with servants who had borrowed money from him. [24]One of his debtors was brought in who owed him millions of dollars. [25]He couldn't pay, so his master ordered that he be sold—along with his wife, his children, and everything he owned—to pay the debt. [26]But the man fell down before his master and begged him, 'Please, be patient with me, and I will pay it all.' [27]Then his master was filled with pity for him, and he released him and forgave his debt.

[28]"But when the man left the king, he went to a fellow servant who owed him a few thousand dollars. He grabbed him by the throat and demanded instant payment. [29]His fellow servant fell down before him and begged for a little more time. 'Be patient with me, and I will pay it,' he pleaded. [30]But his creditor wouldn't wait. He had the man arrested and put in prison until the debt could be paid in full.

[32]"Then the king called in the man he had forgiven and said, 'You evil servant! I forgave you that tremendous debt because you pleaded with me. [33]Shouldn't you have mercy on your fellow servant, just as I had mercy on you?' [34]Then the angry king sent the man to prison to be tortured until he had paid his entire debt."

Matthew 18:21-30, 32-34

Don't put things off

Jesus shares a story that takes place in every household. A parent asks his child to do something. The child's immediate reaction is, "I don't want to." Later the child decides to do it. Another child might say, "Sure," but he doesn't do anything. Jesus urges us to make sure that disobedience doesn't become a lifestyle.

28"A man with two sons told the older boy, 'Son, go out and work in the vineyard today.' 29The son answered, 'No, I won't go,' but later he changed his mind and went anyway. 30Then the father told the other son, 'You go,' and he said, 'Yes, sir, I will.' But he didn't go.

31"Which of the two obeyed his father?" They replied, "The first." Then Jesus explained his meaning: "I tell you the truth, corrupt tax collectors and prostitutes will get into the Kingdom of God before you do.

32"For John the Baptist came and showed you the right way to live, but you didn't believe him, while tax collectors and prostitutes did. And even when you saw this happening, you refused to believe him and repent of your sins."

Matthew 21:28-32

Be on fire for Jesus

Jesus' parable of the five foolish girls and the five wise girls teaches us to always be prepared. If you aren't ready, then you are going to miss out on important things! Be ready because Jesus could come back at any minute. Make sure your lamp is full of oil so that it can burn for Jesus – that means you are on fire for Jesus!

[1]"Then the Kingdom of Heaven will be like ten bridesmaids who took their lamps and went to meet the bridegroom. [2]Five of them were foolish, and five were wise. [3]The five who were foolish didn't take enough olive oil for their lamps, [4]but the other five were wise enough to take along extra oil. [5]When the bridegroom was delayed, they all became drowsy and fell asleep.

[6]"At midnight they were roused by the shout, 'Look, the bridegroom is coming! Come out and meet him!'

[7]"All the bridesmaids got up and prepared their lamps. [8]Then the five foolish ones asked the others, 'Please give us some of your oil because our lamps are going out.'

[9]"But the others replied, 'We don't have enough for all of us. Go to a shop and buy some for yourselves.'

[10]"But while they were gone to buy oil, the bridegroom came. Then those who were ready went in with him to the marriage feast, and the door was locked. [11]Later, when the other five bridesmaids returned, they stood outside, calling, 'Lord! Lord! Open the door for us!'

[12]"But he called back, 'Believe me, I don't know you!'

[13]"So you, too, must keep watch! For you do not know the day or hour of my return."

Matthew 25:1-13

Do your best

Jesus told a story of three slaves who received five, two and one bags of silver respectively. One day God is going to ask you whether you did the best with what He gave you.

¹⁴"Again, the Kingdom of Heaven can be illustrated by the story of a man going on a long trip. He called together his servants and entrusted his money to them while he was gone. ¹⁵He gave five bags of silver to one, two bags of silver to another, and one bag of silver to the last. He then left on his trip.

¹⁹"After a long time their master returned from his trip and called them to give an account of how they had used his money. ²⁰The servant to whom he had entrusted the five bags of silver came forward with five more and said, 'Master, you gave me five bags of silver to invest, and I have earned five more.' ²¹The master was full of praise. 'Well done, my good and faithful servant. You have been faithful in handling this small amount, so now I will give you many more responsibilities.'

²²"The servant who had received the two bags of silver came forward and said, 'Master, you gave me two bags of silver to invest, and I have earned two more.' ²³The master said, 'Well done, my good and faithful servant. You have been faithful in handling this small amount, so now I will give you many more responsibilities. Let's celebrate together!'

²⁴"Then the servant with the one bag of silver came and said, ²⁵'I was afraid I would lose your money, so I hid it in the earth. Look, here is your money back.'

²⁶"But the master replied, 'You wicked and lazy servant!'

²⁸"Then he ordered, 'Take the money from this servant, and give it to the one with the ten bags of silver.'"

Matthew 25:14-15, 19-26, 28

The eternity test

Just like a shepherd separates the sheep from the goats, God will one day separate the believers from the unbelievers, says Jesus. He will do this by testing us: Did you forget about yourself and love others – especially the unimportant people who crossed your path?

32"All the nations will be gathered in his presence, and he will separate the people as a shepherd separates the sheep from the goats. 33He will place the sheep at his right hand and the goats at his left.

34"Then the King will say to those on his right, 'Come, you who are blessed by my Father, inherit the Kingdom prepared for you from the creation of the world. 35For I was hungry, and you fed me. I was thirsty, and you gave me a drink. I was a stranger, and you invited me into your home. 36I was naked, and you gave me clothing. I was sick, and you cared for me. I was in prison, and you visited me.'

37"Then these righteous ones will reply, 'Lord, when did we ever see you hungry and feed you? Or thirsty and give you something to drink? 38Or a stranger and show you hospitality? Or naked and give you clothing?'

40"And the King will say, 'I tell you the truth, when you did it to one of the least of these my brothers and sisters, you were doing it to me!'

41"Then the King will turn to those on the left and say, 'Away with you, you cursed ones, into the eternal fire prepared for the devil and his demons.'"

Matthew 25:32-38, 40-41

Jesus understands!

Jesus was deeply upset and troubled about what lay before Him. Because of this struggle we know that Jesus also understands what we go through. Through His relationship with His Father, Jesus gained the power to fulfil His purpose on earth. That power is also available to us whenever we are stressed!

[36]Then Jesus went with them to the olive grove called Gethsemane, and he said, "Sit here while I go over there to pray." [37]He took Peter and James and John, and he became anguished and distressed. [38]He told them, "My soul is crushed with grief to the point of death. Stay here and keep watch with me."

[39]He went on a little farther and bowed with his face to the ground, praying, "My Father! If it is possible, let this cup of suffering be taken away from me. Yet I want your will to be done, not mine."

[40]Then he returned to the disciples and found them asleep. He said to Peter, "Couldn't you watch with me even one hour? [41]Keep watch and pray, so that you will not give in to temptation. For the spirit is willing, but the body is weak!"

[42]Then Jesus left them a second time and prayed, "My Father! If this cup cannot be taken away unless I drink it, your will be done." [43]When he returned to them again, he found them sleeping, for they couldn't keep their eyes open.

[44]So he went to pray a third time, saying the same things again. [45]Then he came to the disciples and said, "Go ahead and sleep. Have your rest. But look—the time has come. The Son of Man is betrayed into the hands of sinners. [46]Up, let's be going. Look, my betrayer is here!"

Matthew 26:36-46

His suffering, our gain

Jesus was mocked and humiliated for our sake. His love for us is greater and deeper than we can imagine. He didn't have to be crucified, but He chose to do it because He loves us. If you ever doubt that Jesus loves you, think about Golgotha – it was real, just like His love for you!

[35]After they had nailed him to the cross, the soldiers gambled for his clothes by throwing dice. [37]A sign was fastened above Jesus' head, announcing the charge against him. It read: "This is Jesus, the King of the Jews."

[39]The people passing by shouted abuse, shaking their heads in mockery. [40]"Look at you now!" they yelled at him. "You said you were going to destroy the Temple and rebuild it in three days. Well then, if you are the Son of God, save yourself and come down from the cross!"

[41]The leading priests, the teachers of religious law, and the elders also mocked Jesus. [42]"He saved others," they scoffed, "but he can't save himself! So he is the King of Israel, is he? Let him come down from the cross right now, and we will believe in him! [43]He trusted God, so let God rescue him now if he wants him! For he said, 'I am the Son of God.'"

[45]At noon, darkness fell across the whole land until three o'clock. [46]At about three o'clock, Jesus called out with a loud voice, "Eli, Eli, lema sabachthani?" which means "My God, my God, why have you abandoned me?"

[50]Then Jesus shouted out again, and he released his spirit.

Matthew 27:35, 37, 39-43, 45-46, 50

Resurrection life

The message of the Lord's angel is crystal clear:
We don't need to be afraid of death. Jesus lives
and moves among His people, even now. We must
live with the resurrection always fresh in our
minds because it will give us a positive outlook
on life.

¹Early on Sunday morning, as the new day was dawning, Mary
Magdalene and the other Mary went out to visit the tomb.

²Suddenly there was a great earthquake! For an angel of the
Lord came down from heaven, rolled aside the stone, and sat
on it. ³His face shone like lightning, and his clothing was as white
as snow. ⁴The guards shook with fear when they saw him, and
they fell into a dead faint.

⁵Then the angel spoke to the women. "Don't be afraid!" he
said. "I know you are looking for Jesus, who was crucified. ⁶He
isn't here! He is risen from the dead, just as he said would happen. Come, see where his body was lying. ⁷And now, go quickly
and tell his disciples that he has risen from the dead, and he
is going ahead of you to Galilee. You will see him there. Remember what I have told you."

⁸The women ran quickly from the tomb. They were very fright-
ened but also filled with great joy, and they rushed to give the
disciples the angel's message. ⁹And as they went, Jesus met
them and greeted them. And they ran to him, grasped his feet,
and worshiped him. ¹⁰Then Jesus said to them, "Don't be afraid!
Go tell my brothers to leave for Galilee, and they will see me
there."

Matthew 28:1-10

Share Jesus with others

If one person tells two people about Jesus, and those two people tell another two people, and they also tell another two ... then within twenty days 1 million people will have shared the story of Jesus. Within thirty days 30 million people will know about Jesus. Within thirty-two days the whole world will have heard about Jesus. WOW!

16Then the eleven disciples left for Galilee, going to the mountain where Jesus had told them to go. 17When they saw him, they worshiped him—but some of them doubted!

18Jesus came and told his disciples, "I have been given all authority in heaven and on earth. 19Therefore, go and make disciples of all the nations, baptizing them in the name of the Father and the Son and the Holy Spirit.

20"Teach these new disciples to obey all the commands I have given you. And be sure of this: I am with you always, even to the end of the age."

Matthew 28:16-20

The Greatest Friend

Here we find a miracle before the miracle even took place: God forgave the paralyzed man's sins before the man even asked for forgiveness. Then He also healed the man's body! The man put his mat under his arm and walked away with a spring in his step – free from his sin. God works in surprising ways!

¹When Jesus returned to Capernaum several days later, the news spread quickly that he was back home. ²Soon the house where he was staying was so packed with visitors that there was no more room, even outside the door. While he was preaching God's word to them, ³four men arrived carrying a paralyzed man on a mat. ⁴They couldn't bring him to Jesus because of the crowd, so they dug a hole through the roof above his head. Then they lowered the man on his mat. ⁵Seeing their faith, Jesus said to the paralyzed man, "My child, your sins are forgiven."

⁶But some of the teachers of religious law who were sitting there thought to themselves, ⁷"What is he saying? This is blasphemy! Only God can forgive sins!" ⁸Jesus knew immediately what they were thinking, so he asked them, "Why do you question this in your hearts? ⁹Is it easier to say to the paralyzed man 'Your sins are forgiven,' or 'Stand up, pick up your mat, and walk'? ¹⁰So I will prove to you that the Son of Man has the authority on earth to forgive sins." Then Jesus turned to the paralyzed man and said, ¹¹"Stand up, pick up your mat, and go home!"

¹²And the man jumped up, grabbed his mat, and walked out through the stunned onlookers. They were all amazed and praised God, exclaiming, "We've never seen anything like this before!"

Mark 2:1-12

Part of another family

You have a blood family and you have a spiritual family. The following rule applies to both: They must accept you, even if you don't deserve it. Families must always have an open door, just like God does!

[31] Then Jesus' mother and brothers came to see him. They stood outside and sent word for him to come out and talk with them. [32] There was a crowd sitting around Jesus, and someone said, "Your mother and your brothers are outside asking for you."

[33] Jesus replied, "Who is my mother? Who are my brothers?" [34] Then he looked at those around him and said, "Look, these are my mother and brothers. [35] Anyone who does God's will is my brother and sister and mother."

Mark 3:31-35

Children only

You need to have faith like a child. People either receive God's grace freely, or not at all. Children understand this but adults can't. Don't lose the child in you, because you might just lose eternal life.

¹³One day some parents brought their children to Jesus so he could touch and bless them. But the disciples scolded the parents for bothering him.

¹⁴When Jesus saw what was happening, he was angry with his disciples. He said to them, "Let the children come to me. Don't stop them! For the Kingdom of God belongs to those who are like these children. ¹⁵I tell you the truth, anyone who doesn't receive the Kingdom of God like a child will never enter it." ¹⁶Then he took the children in his arms and placed his hands on their heads and blessed them.

¹⁷As Jesus was starting out on his way to Jerusalem, a man came running up to him, knelt down, and asked, "Good Teacher, what must I do to inherit eternal life?"

¹⁹"To answer your question, you know the commandments: 'You must not murder. You must not steal. You must not testify falsely. You must not cheat anyone. Honor your father and mother.'"

²⁰"Teacher," the man replied, "I've obeyed all these commandments since I was young." ²¹Looking at the man, Jesus felt genuine love for him. "There is still one thing you haven't done," he told him. "Go and sell all your possessions and give the money to the poor, and you will have treasure in heaven. Then come, follow me." ²²At this the man's face fell, and he went away sad, for he had many possessions.

Mark 10:13-17, 19-22

Open your eyes and enjoy life!

As bad as it is to be blind today, it was even worse in Jesus' time. Blind people could only do one thing – beg! Bartimaeus sat year after year at the gates of Jericho and begged. But the fact that he had a relationship with God is seen by his words in Mark 10:47. He just needed Jesus to hear him, and Jesus did! After that Bartimaeus's begging days were over!

⁴⁶Then they reached Jericho, and as Jesus and his disciples left town, a large crowd followed him. A blind beggar named Bartimaeus (son of Timaeus) was sitting beside the road. ⁴⁷When Bartimaeus heard that Jesus of Nazareth was nearby, he began to shout, "Jesus, Son of David, have mercy on me!"

⁴⁸"Be quiet!" many of the people yelled at him. But he only shouted louder, "Son of David, have mercy on me!"

⁴⁹When Jesus heard him, he stopped and said, "Tell him to come here." So they called the blind man. "Cheer up," they said. "Come on, he's calling you!" ⁵⁰Bartimaeus threw aside his coat, jumped up, and came to Jesus.

⁵¹"What do you want me to do for you?" Jesus asked.

"My rabbi," the blind man said, "I want to see!"

⁵²And Jesus said to him, "Go, for your faith has healed you." Instantly the man could see, and he followed Jesus down the road.

Mark 10:46-52

Love makes life blossom

Here is Jesus' advice for a life that will flourish to the end: Love God, love your fellow man and love yourself. If you do this you will live a full and meaningful life. Indeed, "Love makes the world go 'round"!

²⁸One of the teachers of religious law was standing there listening to the debate. He realized that Jesus had answered well, so he asked, "Of all the commandments, which is the most important?"

²⁹Jesus replied, "The most important commandment is this: 'Listen, O Israel! The LORD our God is the one and only LORD. ³⁰And you must love the LORD your God with all your heart, all your soul, all your mind, and all your strength.' ³¹The second is equally important: 'Love your neighbor as yourself.' No other commandment is greater than these."

³²The teacher of religious law replied, "Well said, Teacher. You have spoken the truth by saying that there is only one God and no other. ³³And I know it is important to love him with all my heart and all my understanding and all my strength, and to love my neighbor as myself. This is more important than to offer all of the burnt offerings and sacrifices required in the law."

³⁴Realizing how much the man understood, Jesus said to him, "You are not far from the Kingdom of God." And after that, no one dared to ask him any more questions.

Mark 12:28-34

Hypocrites

In today's Scripture reading Mark places two events next to each other so you can compare them. On the one side he tells of some teachers of the Law who exploit widows – the Never-ready people. And then a poor widow who gave her last little bit of money to God – the Ever-ready person.

[38]Jesus also taught: "Beware of these teachers of religious law! For they like to parade around in flowing robes and receive respectful greetings as they walk in the marketplaces. [39]And how they love the seats of honor in the synagogues and the head table at banquets. [40]Yet they shamelessly cheat widows out of their property and then pretend to be pious by making long prayers in public. Because of this, they will be more severely punished."

[41]Jesus sat down near the collection box in the Temple and watched as the crowds dropped in their money. Many rich people put in large amounts. [42]Then a poor widow came and dropped in two small coins.

[43]Jesus called his disciples to him and said, "I tell you the truth, this poor widow has given more than all the others who are making contributions. [44]For they gave a tiny part of their surplus, but she, poor as she is, has given everything she had to live on."

Mark 12:38-44

The unforgettable gift

In a world of knives and forks, be a spoon! Spoon-people serve others. Consider Mary, who, without even thinking about it, poured her expensive perfume on Jesus' feet. A knife-person, like Judas, would not understand such selfless love.

¹It was now two days before Passover and the Festival of Unleavened Bread. The leading priests and the teachers of religious law were still looking for an opportunity to capture Jesus secretly and kill him. ²"But not during the Passover celebration," they agreed, "or the people may riot."

³Meanwhile, Jesus was in Bethany at the home of Simon, a man who had previously had leprosy. While he was eating, a woman came in with a beautiful alabaster jar of expensive perfume made from essence of nard. She broke open the jar and poured the perfume over his head.

⁴Some of those at the table were indignant. "Why waste such expensive perfume?" they asked. ⁵"It could have been sold for a year's wages and the money given to the poor!" So they scolded her harshly.

⁶But Jesus replied, "Leave her alone. Why criticize her for doing such a good thing to me? ⁷You will always have the poor among you, and you can help them whenever you want to. But you will not always have me. ⁸She has done what she could and has anointed my body for burial ahead of time. ⁹I tell you the truth, wherever the Good News is preached throughout the world, this woman's deed will be remembered and discussed."

Mark 14:1-9

The impossible made possible

Luke 1 tells of the angel's message to Mary, and the world has never been the same since. For God the impossible is indeed possible. Remember, we can do things that are possible, but only God can do the impossible.

²⁶In the sixth month of Elizabeth's pregnancy, God sent the angel Gabriel to Nazareth, a village in Galilee, ²⁷to a virgin named Mary. She was engaged to be married to a man named Joseph, a descendant of King David. ²⁸Gabriel appeared to her and said, "Greetings, favored woman! The Lord is with you!"

³⁰"Don't be afraid, Mary," the angel told her, "for you have found favor with God! ³¹You will conceive and give birth to a son, and you will name him Jesus. ³²He will be very great and will be called the Son of the Most High. The Lord God will give him the throne of his ancestor David. ³³And he will reign over Israel forever; his Kingdom will never end!"

³⁴Mary asked the angel, "But how can this happen? I am a virgin."

³⁵The angel replied, "The Holy Spirit will come upon you, and the power of the Most High will overshadow you. So the baby to be born will be holy, and he will be called the Son of God. ³⁶What's more, your relative Elizabeth has become pregnant in her old age! People used to say she was barren, but she has conceived a son and is now in her sixth month. ³⁷For nothing is impossible with God."

³⁸Mary responded, "I am the Lord's servant. May everything you have said about me come true." And then the angel left her.

Luke 1:26-28, 30-38

God became human

"Yes," said Queen Lucy, "in our world too, a stable once had something inside it that was bigger than our whole world" (from *The Last Battle* by C. S. Lewis, the *Narnia* series). Imagine if God became a baby. That's what happened that night in Bethlehem. The world was never the same again.

¹At that time the Roman emperor, Augustus, decreed that a census should be taken throughout the Roman Empire. ²(This was the first census taken when Quirinius was governor of Syria.)

³All returned to their own ancestral towns to register for this census. ⁴And because Joseph was a descendant of King David, he had to go to Bethlehem in Judea, David's ancient home. He traveled there from the village of Nazareth in Galilee. ⁵He took with him Mary, his fiancée, who was now obviously pregnant.

⁶And while they were there, the time came for her baby to be born. ⁷She gave birth to her first child, a son. She wrapped him snugly in strips of cloth and laid him in a manger, because there was no lodging available for them.

Luke 2:1-7

Heaven visits earth

The night Baby Jesus was born a choir of angels sang and a bright light illuminated them. The shepherds were scared but as soon as the angel spoke to them, they were filled with joy. Who could not be excited after hearing news like that?

[8]That night there were shepherds staying in the fields nearby, guarding their flocks of sheep. [9]Suddenly, an angel of the Lord appeared among them, and the radiance of the Lord's glory surrounded them. They were terrified, [10]but the angel reassured them. "Don't be afraid!" he said. "I bring you good news that will bring great joy to all people. [11]The Savior—yes, the Messiah, the Lord—has been born today in Bethlehem, the city of David! [12]And you will recognize him by this sign: You will find a baby wrapped snugly in strips of cloth, lying in a manger."

[13]Suddenly, the angel was joined by a vast host of others—the armies of heaven—praising God and saying, [14]"Glory to God in highest heaven, and peace on earth to those with whom God is pleased."

[15]When the angels had returned to heaven, the shepherds said to each other, "Let's go to Bethlehem! Let's see this thing that has happened, which the Lord has told us about."

Luke 2:8-15

Shortest message, best response

After the shepherds recovered from the shock of the angel's announcement and the choir's performance, they went to investigate. And sure enough they found the Miracle Baby in a manger. For days afterwards the good news was spread all through Bethlehem.

[15]When the angels had returned to heaven, the shepherds said to each other, "Let's go to Bethlehem! Let's see this thing that has happened, which the Lord has told us about."

[16]They hurried to the village and found Mary and Joseph. And there was the baby, lying in the manger. [17]After seeing him, the shepherds told everyone what had happened and what the angel had said to them about this child. [18]All who heard the shepherds' story were astonished, [19]but Mary kept all these things in her heart and thought about them often.

[20]The shepherds went back to their flocks, glorifying and praising God for all they had heard and seen. It was just as the angel had told them.

Luke 2:15-20

Aim for the bull's eye

One of the most important verses in the Bible is Luke 2:52. Live it out every day because it is your story. Make it your life's goal, your bull's eye to aim at. If you grow like Jesus, then your life will be like it should, because your life will move in the right direction.

⁴¹Every year Jesus' parents went to Jerusalem for the Passover festival. ⁴²When Jesus was twelve years old, they attended the festival as usual. ⁴³After the celebration was over, they started home to Nazareth, but Jesus stayed behind in Jerusalem. His parents didn't miss him at first, ⁴⁴because they assumed he was among the other travelers. But when he didn't show up that evening, they started looking for him among their relatives and friends.

⁴⁵When they couldn't find him, they went back to Jerusalem to search for him there. ⁴⁶Three days later they finally discovered him in the Temple, sitting among the religious teachers, listening to them and asking questions. ⁴⁷All who heard him were amazed at his understanding and his answers.

⁴⁸His parents didn't know what to think. "Son," his mother said to him, "why have you done this to us? Your father and I have been frantic, searching for you everywhere."

⁴⁹"But why did you need to search?" he asked. "Didn't you know that I must be in my Father's house?" ⁵⁰But they didn't understand what he meant.

⁵¹Then he returned to Nazareth with them and was obedient to them. And his mother stored all these things in her heart.

⁵²Jesus grew in wisdom and in stature and in favor with God and all the people.

Luke 2:41-52

A good habit

Jesus made it a habit to go to the synagogue (church). Any habit that was good enough for Jesus is a habit that His followers should definitely learn. To get together regularly with others and worship must be a part of our lives.

¹⁶When he came to the village of Nazareth, his boyhood home, he went as usual to the synagogue on the Sabbath and stood up to read the Scriptures. ¹⁷The scroll of Isaiah the prophet was handed to him. He unrolled the scroll and found the place where this was written:

¹⁸"The Spirit of the LORD is upon me, for he has anointed me to bring Good News to the poor. He has sent me to proclaim that captives will be released, that the blind will see, that the oppressed will be set free, ¹⁹and that the time of the LORD's favor has come."

²⁰He rolled up the scroll, handed it back to the attendant, and sat down. All eyes in the synagogue looked at him intently. ²¹Then he began to speak to them. "The Scripture you've just heard has been fulfilled this very day!"

Luke 4:16-21

Fishing for Jesus

The Greek word for fishing literally means *to catch alive*. Jesus says to each one of us: "Be fishers of people. Catch them, and I will clean them." Catch people with your example rather than your words. The bait? Love!

¹One day as Jesus was preaching on the shore of the Sea of Galilee, great crowds pressed in on him to listen to the word of God. ²He noticed two empty boats at the water's edge, for the fishermen had left them and were washing their nets. ³Stepping into one of the boats, Jesus asked Simon, its owner, to push it out into the water. So he sat in the boat and taught the crowds from there. ⁴When he had finished speaking, he said to Simon, "Now go out where it is deeper, and let down your nets to catch some fish."

⁵"Master," Simon replied, "we worked hard all last night and didn't catch a thing. But if you say so, I'll let the nets down again." ⁶And this time their nets were so full of fish they began to tear! ⁷A shout for help brought their partners in the other boat, and soon both boats were filled with fish and on the verge of sinking.

⁸When Simon Peter realized what had happened, he fell to his knees before Jesus and said, "Oh, Lord, please leave me—I'm too much of a sinner to be around you." ⁹For he was awestruck by the number of fish they had caught, as were the others with him. ¹⁰His partners, James and John, the sons of Zebedee, were also amazed.

Jesus replied to Simon, "Don't be afraid! From now on you'll be fishing for people!" ¹¹And as soon as they landed, they left everything and followed Jesus.

Luke 5:1-11

September

Great faith

In Luke 7:9 as well as Matthew 15:28 Jesus is impressed by a great, strong faith. The Roman officer in today's Scripture reading is not that much different to us because he didn't see Jesus, he sent people on ahead to meet Jesus. The officer just heard Jesus' words and that was enough for him. Jesus was so impressed by this that He declared that He had never seen such great faith.

¹When Jesus had finished saying all this to the people, he returned to Capernaum. ²At that time the highly valued slave of a Roman officer was sick and near death. ³When the officer heard about Jesus, he sent some respected Jewish elders to ask him to come and heal his slave. ⁴So they earnestly begged Jesus to help the man. "If anyone deserves your help, he does," they said, ⁵"for he loves the Jewish people and even built a synagogue for us."

⁶So Jesus went with them. But just before they arrived at the house, the officer sent some friends to say, "Lord, don't trouble yourself by coming to my home, for I am not worthy of such an honor. ⁷I am not even worthy to come and meet you. Just say the word from where you are, and my servant will be healed."

⁹When Jesus heard this, he was amazed. Turning to the crowd that was following him, he said, "I tell you, I haven't seen faith like this in all Israel!" ¹⁰And when the officer's friends returned to his house, they found the slave completely healed.

Luke 7:1-7, 9-10

Love has no boundaries

The question that you must ask every day is not, "Who is my neighbor?" but "Who can I be a neighbor to?" James Finley said, "In loving them, we love Jesus in them. And they, in turn, encounter Him in us in the love we give them."

29The man wanted to justify his actions, so he asked Jesus, "And who is my neighbor?"

30Jesus replied with a story: "A Jewish man was traveling from Jerusalem down to Jericho, and he was attacked by bandits. They stripped him of his clothes, beat him up, and left him half dead beside the road.

31"By chance a priest came along. But when he saw the man lying there, he crossed to the other side of the road and passed him by. 32A Temple assistant walked over and looked at him lying there, but he also passed by on the other side.

33"Then a despised Samaritan came along, and when he saw the man, he felt compassion for him. 34Going over to him, the Samaritan soothed his wounds with olive oil and wine and bandaged them. Then he put the man on his own donkey and took him to an inn, where he took care of him. 35The next day he handed the innkeeper two silver coins, telling him, 'Take care of this man. If his bill runs higher than this, I'll pay you the next time I'm here.'

36"Now which of these three would you say was a neighbor to the man who was attacked by bandits?" Jesus asked.

37The man replied, "The one who showed him mercy." Then Jesus said, "Yes, now go and do the same."

Luke 10:29-37

Only one thing!

In the story of Mary and Martha, the problem is not that Jesus wants Martha to be like Mary, but that Martha rather chooses one thing – to focus on Jesus and therefore achieve a balance between doing and listening. Focus on Jesus and His words, listen to them (Mary) and do them (Martha)!

[38]As Jesus and the disciples continued on their way to Jerusalem, they came to a certain village where a woman named Martha welcomed him into her home.

[39]Her sister, Mary, sat at the Lord's feet, listening to what he taught. [40]But Martha was distracted by the big dinner she was preparing. She came to Jesus and said, "Lord, doesn't it seem unfair to you that my sister just sits here while I do all the work? Tell her to come and help me."

[41]But the Lord said to her, "My dear Martha, you are worried and upset over all these details! [42]There is only one thing worth being concerned about. Mary has discovered it, and it will not be taken away from her."

Luke 10:38-42

Material things are spiritually worthless

Jesus will help us to see ourselves and our success in the right perspective. God is the owner of everything. There is nothing wrong with having possessions, but we must own them, they mustn't own us. Therefore, get your priorities straight. Don't be like the man in today's story who forgot that he would not live forever.

¹³Then someone called from the crowd, "Teacher, please tell my brother to divide our father's estate with me."

¹⁴Jesus replied, "Friend, who made me a judge over you to decide such things as that?" ¹⁵Then he said, "Beware! Guard against every kind of greed. Life is not measured by how much you own."

¹⁶Then he told them a story: "A rich man had a fertile farm that produced fine crops. ¹⁷He said to himself, 'What should I do? I don't have room for all my crops.' ¹⁸Then he said, 'I know! I'll tear down my barns and build bigger ones. Then I'll have room enough to store all my wheat and other goods. ¹⁹And I'll sit back and say to myself, "My friend, you have enough stored away for years to come. Now take it easy! Eat, drink, and be merry!"'

²⁰"But God said to him, 'You fool! You will die this very night. Then who will get everything you worked for?'

²¹"Yes, a person is a fool to store up earthly wealth but not have a rich relationship with God."

Luke 12:13-21

"Ready or not, here i come"

Jesus is coming back one day, suddenly and un-expectedly. Therefore we must always be ready. How do you get ready? Love (Matt. 25:31-46)! The reward for being ready will be great. The Lord will hold a great feast and we will enjoy the most delicious food!

35"Be dressed for service and keep your lamps burning, 36as though you were waiting for your master to return from the wedding feast. Then you will be ready to open the door and let him in the moment he arrives and knocks. 37The servants who are ready and waiting for his return will be rewarded. I tell you the truth, he himself will seat them, put on an apron, and serve them as they sit and eat! 38He may come in the middle of the night or just before dawn. But whenever he comes, he will reward the servants who are ready."

42And the Lord replied, "A faithful, sensible servant is one to whom the master can give the responsibility of managing his other household servants and feeding them. 43If the master returns and finds that the servant has done a good job, there will be a reward. 44I tell you the truth, the master will put that servant in charge of all he owns. 45But what if the servant thinks, 'My master won't be back for a while,' and he begins beating the other servants, partying, and getting drunk? 46The master will return unannounced and unexpected, and he will cut the servant in pieces and banish him with the unfaithful.

48"But someone who does not know, and then does something wrong, will be punished only lightly. When someone has been given much, much will be required in return; and when someone has been entrusted with much, even more will be required."

Luke 12:35-38, 42-46, 48

Grace is expensive!

Grace is free but it's not cheap. It is so expensive that no one can afford it. It cost Jesus a lot! To be proper disciples of Jesus we must think carefully. We must walk as Jesus walked. Anything else will cheapen the costly grace Jesus gave us.

[25]A large crowd was following Jesus. He turned around and said to them, [26]"If you want to be my disciple, you must hate everyone else by comparison—your father and mother, wife and children, brothers and sisters—yes, even your own life. Otherwise, you cannot be my disciple. [27]And if you do not carry your own cross and follow me, you cannot be my disciple.

[28]"But don't begin until you count the cost. For who would begin construction of a building without first calculating the cost to see if there is enough money to finish it? [29]Otherwise, you might complete only the foundation before running out of money, and then everyone would laugh at you. [30]They would say, 'There's the person who started that building and couldn't afford to finish it!'

[31]"Or what king would go to war against another king without first sitting down with his counselors to discuss whether his army of 10,000 could defeat the 20,000 soldiers marching against him? [32]And if he can't, he will send a delegation to discuss terms of peace while the enemy is still far away. [33]So you cannot become my disciple without giving up everything you own."

Luke 14:25-33

The Father with the open arms

We know this story not because we have all heard it many times, but because it is our story too! Will God not give us another chance and listen to us and welcome us back? God's grace surprises us every time. He always waits with open arms.

¹¹"A man had two sons. ¹²The younger son told his father, 'I want my share of your estate now before you die.' So his father agreed to divide his wealth between his sons.

¹³"A few days later this younger son packed all his belongings and moved to a distant land, and there he wasted all his money in wild living. ¹⁴About the time his money ran out, a great famine swept over the land, and he began to starve. ¹⁵He persuaded a local farmer to hire him, and the man sent him into his fields to feed the pigs. ¹⁶The young man became so hungry that even the pods he was feeding the pigs looked good to him.

¹⁷"When he finally came to his senses, he said to himself, 'At home even the hired servants have food enough to spare, and here I am dying of hunger! ¹⁸I will go home to my father and say, "Father, I have sinned against both heaven and you, ¹⁹and I am no longer worthy of being called your son. Please take me on as a hired servant."'

²⁰"So he returned home to his father. And while he was still a long way off, his father saw him coming. Filled with love and compassion, he ran to his son, embraced him, and kissed him.

²²"But his father said to the servants, 'Quick! Bring the finest robe in the house and put it on him. Get a ring for his finger and sandals for his feet. ²³And kill the calf we have been fattening. We must celebrate with a feast, ²⁴for this son of mine was dead and has now returned to life. He was lost, but now he is found.'"

Luke 15:11-20, 22-24

When it's not your party

The older brother in each of us can't understand Susan Yates's lovely words: "Always allow God the privilege of working in another's life differently from the way God has in your own." You can sulk outside or go in and party with everyone else. The one brings bitterness and the other brings joy.

25"Meanwhile, the older son was in the fields working. When he returned home, he heard music and dancing in the house, 26and he asked one of the servants what was going on. 27'Your brother is back,' he was told, 'and your father has killed the fattened calf. We are celebrating because of his safe return.'

28"The older brother was angry and wouldn't go in. His father came out and begged him, 29but he replied, 'All these years I've slaved for you and never once refused to do a single thing you told me to. And in all that time you never gave me even one young goat for a feast with my friends. 30Yet when this son comes back after squandering your money on prostitutes, you celebrate by killing the fattened calf!'

31"His father said to him, 'Look, dear son, you have always stayed by me, and everything I have is yours. 32We had to celebrate this happy day. For your brother was dead and has come back to life! He was lost, but now he is found!'"

Luke 15:25-32

Thank You is enough

In today's story the grateful, healed Samaritan returns to say Thank You to Jesus. Lepers were seen as "dead" people because they were cut off from everyone and everything. Therefore the Jews saw the healing of a leper as equal to a resurrection (see 2 Kings 5:7). No wonder Jesus asked, "Where are the other nine?" Not thanking God runs deeper than we think!

¹²As he entered a village there, ten lepers stood at a distance, ¹³crying out, "Jesus, Master, have mercy on us!"

¹⁴He looked at them and said, "Go show yourselves to the priests." And as they went, they were cleansed of their leprosy.

¹⁵One of them, when he saw that he was healed, came back to Jesus, shouting, "Praise God!" ¹⁶He fell to the ground at Jesus' feet, thanking him for what he had done. This man was a Samaritan.

¹⁷Jesus asked, "Didn't I heal ten men? Where are the other nine? ¹⁸Has no one returned to give glory to God except this foreigner?" ¹⁹And Jesus said to the man, "Stand up and go. Your faith has healed you."

Luke 17:12-19

A down-to-earth person

Only three of Jesus' parables are about prayer. All three are found in Luke – the parable of the friend who shows up at midnight (11:5-8), the parable of the dishonest judge (18:1-8), and the parable of the Pharisee and the tax collector (18:9-14). If you want to appear before God, you must learn to be humble and down-to-earth like the tax collector. This is where prayer begins.

⁹Then Jesus told this story to some who had great confidence in their own righteousness and scorned everyone else:

¹⁰"Two men went to the Temple to pray. One was a Pharisee, and the other was a despised tax collector. ¹¹The Pharisee stood by himself and prayed this prayer: 'I thank you, God, that I am not a sinner like everyone else. For I don't cheat, I don't sin, and I don't commit adultery. I'm certainly not like that tax collector! ¹²I fast twice a week, and I give you a tenth of my income.'

¹³"But the tax collector stood at a distance and dared not even lift his eyes to heaven as he prayed. Instead, he beat his chest in sorrow, saying, 'O God, be merciful to me, for I am a sinner.'

¹⁴"I tell you, this sinner, not the Pharisee, returned home justified before God. For those who exalt themselves will be humbled, and those who humble themselves will be exalted."

Luke 18:9-14

Follow Grace

I don't think anyone will ever understand the mystery of grace. It finds us wherever we are in our lives and calls us to follow. It saves us from our past, changes our today, and gives us direction for the future. It also celebrates with us over our new identity!

¹Jesus entered Jericho and made his way through the town. ²There was a man there named Zacchaeus. He was the chief tax collector in the region, and he had become very rich. ³He tried to get a look at Jesus, but he was too short to see over the crowd. ⁴So he ran ahead and climbed a sycamore-fig tree beside the road, for Jesus was going to pass that way.

⁵When Jesus came by, he looked up at Zacchaeus and called him by name. "Zacchaeus!" he said. "Quick, come down! I must be a guest in your home today." ⁶Zacchaeus quickly climbed down and took Jesus to his house in great excitement and joy. ⁷But the people were displeased. "He has gone to be the guest of a notorious sinner," they grumbled.

⁸Meanwhile, Zacchaeus stood before the Lord and said, "I will give half my wealth to the poor, Lord, and if I have cheated people on their taxes, I will give them back four times as much!"

⁹Jesus responded, "Salvation has come to this home today, for this man has shown himself to be a true son of Abraham. ¹⁰For the Son of Man came to seek and save those who are lost."

Luke 19:1-10

Cheers today, jeers tomorrow

Jesus came into Jerusalem just like Zechariah prophesied ... crowds cheered, they used their cloaks to form a red carpet for Him, and they waved palm branches. They treated Jesus like a king, but a few days later they were not crying *Hosanna* any more, but *Crucify Him*!

[29] As he came to the towns of Bethphage and Bethany on the Mount of Olives, he sent two disciples ahead. [30] "Go into that village over there," he told them. "As you enter it, you will see a young donkey tied there that no one has ever ridden. Untie it and bring it here. [31] If anyone asks, 'Why are you untying that colt?' just say, 'The Lord needs it.'"

[32] So they went and found the colt, just as Jesus had said.

[35] So they brought the colt to Jesus and threw their garments over it for him to ride on.

[36] As he rode along, the crowds spread out their garments on the road ahead of him. [37] When he reached the place where the road started down the Mount of Olives, all of his followers began to shout and sing as they walked along, praising God for all the wonderful miracles they had seen.

[38] "Blessings on the King who comes in the name of the Lord! Peace in heaven, and glory in highest heaven!"

[39] But some of the Pharisees among the crowd said, "Teacher, rebuke your followers for saying things like that!"

[40] He replied, "If they kept quiet, the stones along the road would burst into cheers!"

Luke 19:29-32, 35-40

Be sure of your faith

Being sure of your faith is not to be certain of how strong your faith is, but certain of the God you believe in. We believe that God will never just leave us, even though sometimes we drop Him – like Peter! It doesn't mean that your faith is a failure; it just means that you have failed. There is a big difference! God helps you rise up. You can be certain of this!

[54]So they arrested him and led him to the high priest's home. And Peter followed at a distance. [55]The guards lit a fire in the middle of the courtyard and sat around it, and Peter joined them there. [56]A servant girl noticed him in the firelight and began staring at him. Finally she said, "This man was one of Jesus' followers!" [57]But Peter denied it. "Woman," he said, "I don't even know him!"

[58]After a while someone else looked at him and said, "You must be one of them!" "No, man, I'm not!" Peter retorted.

[59]About an hour later someone else insisted, "This must be one of them, because he is a Galilean, too."

[60]But Peter said, "Man, I don't know what you are talking about." And immediately, while he was still speaking, the rooster crowed.

Luke 22:54-60

More than a moment's grace

The one criminal asked for a breadcrumb of grace: "Remember me please" and he received a bakery: "Today you will be with Me in paradise!" This is a deathbed conversion; on his uncomfortable deathbed of the cross, the man saw the Light!

33When they came to a place called The Skull, they nailed him to the cross. And the criminals were also crucified—one on his right and one on his left.

34Jesus said, "Father, forgive them, for they don't know what they are doing." And the soldiers gambled for his clothes by throwing dice.

35The crowd watched and the leaders scoffed. "He saved others," they said, "let him save himself if he is really God's Messiah, the Chosen One." 36The soldiers mocked him, too, by offering him a drink of sour wine. 37They called out to him, "If you are the King of the Jews, save yourself!" 38A sign was fastened above him with these words: "This is the King of the Jews."

39One of the criminals hanging beside him scoffed, "So you're the Messiah, are you? Prove it by saving yourself—and us, too, while you're at it!"

40But the other criminal protested, "Don't you fear God even when you have been sentenced to die? 41We deserve to die for our crimes, but this man hasn't done anything wrong." 42Then he said, "Jesus, remember me when you come into your Kingdom."

43And Jesus replied, "I assure you, today you will be with me in paradise."

Luke 23:33-43

Your heart burns for the Life

On the way to Emmaus two men were talking about hope, but they agreed that it was dead! Then Jesus joined them and their hearts started to burn with the hope of Jesus. They were so excited by what they experienced that they immediately walked all the way back to Jerusalem.

¹³Two of Jesus' followers were walking to the village of Emmaus, seven miles from Jerusalem. ¹⁵As they talked and discussed these things, Jesus himself suddenly came and began walking with them. ¹⁶But God kept them from recognizing him.

¹⁷He asked them, "What are you discussing so intently as you walk along?"

¹⁹"The things that happened to Jesus, the man from Nazareth," they said. "He was a prophet who did powerful miracles, and he was a mighty teacher in the eyes of God and all the people. ²⁰But our leading priests and other religious leaders crucified him."

²⁵Then Jesus said to them, "You foolish people! ²⁶Wasn't it clearly predicted that the Messiah would have to suffer all these things before entering his glory?" ²⁷Then Jesus took them through the writings of Moses and all the prophets, explaining all the things concerning himself. ²⁹But they begged him, "Stay the night with us." So he went home with them. ³⁰As they sat down to eat, he took the bread and blessed it. Then he broke it and gave it to them. ³¹Suddenly, their eyes were opened, and they recognized him. And at that moment he disappeared!

³²They said to each other, "Didn't our hearts burn within us as he talked with us on the road and explained the Scriptures to us?" ³³And within the hour they were on their way back to Jerusalem.

Luke 24:13, 15-17, 19-20, 25-27, 29-33

Not the average starting point

John begins his gospel at a different point than the other gospel writers. Not with the first Christmas, or with the announcement of Jesus' birth or with Creation, but much earlier – before time even existed. That's why no darkness can put out the light of Jesus.

[1]In the beginning the Word already existed. The Word was with God, and the Word was God. [2]He existed in the beginning with God. [3]God created everything through him, and nothing was created except through him.

[4]The Word gave life to everything that was created, and his life brought light to everyone. [5]The light shines in the darkness, and the darkness can never extinguish it. [6]God sent a man, John the Baptist, [7]to tell about the light so that everyone might believe because of his testimony. [8]John himself was not the light; he was simply a witness to tell about the light. [9]The one who is the true light, who gives light to everyone, was coming into the world.

[10]He came into the very world he created, but the world didn't recognize him. [11]He came to his own people, and even they rejected him. [12]But to all who believed him and accepted him, he gave the right to become children of God. [13]They are reborn—not with a physical birth resulting from human passion or plan, but a birth that comes from God.

[14]So the Word became human and made his home among us. He was full of unfailing love and faithfulness. And we have seen his glory, the glory of the Father's one and only Son.

John 1:1-14

Nazareth?
You must be joking

The Jews looked down on Nazareth because the Roman army was settled there. That's why Nathanael couldn't believe that anything good could come out of Nazareth. Thankfully he realized that Jesus was the True One; a Person to be followed.

⁴³The next day Jesus decided to go to Galilee. He found Philip and said to him, "Come, follow me."

⁴⁵Philip went to look for Nathanael and told him, "We have found the very person Moses and the prophets wrote about! His name is Jesus, the son of Joseph from Nazareth."

⁴⁶"Nazareth!" exclaimed Nathanael. "Can anything good come from Nazareth?"

"Come and see for yourself," Philip replied.

⁴⁷As they approached, Jesus said, "Now here is a genuine son of Israel—a man of complete integrity."

⁴⁸"How do you know about me?" Nathanael asked. Jesus replied, "I could see you under the fig tree before Philip found you."

⁴⁹Then Nathanael exclaimed, "Rabbi, you are the Son of God—the King of Israel!"

⁵⁰Jesus asked him, "Do you believe this just because I told you I had seen you under the fig tree? You will see greater things than this." ⁵¹Then he said, "I tell you the truth, you will all see heaven open and the angels of God going up and down on the Son of Man, the one who is the stairway between heaven and earth."

John 1:43, 45-51

Enough wine for another wedding

Jesus, His disciples and His mother Mary were at a wedding in Cana. There was a crisis – the wine was finished! Mary asked Jesus to help. Water was changed into the most wonderful wine – Jesus' first miracle. This incident also shows how Jesus feels about life – enjoy it.

¹The next day there was a wedding celebration in the village of Cana in Galilee. Jesus' mother was there, ²and Jesus and his disciples were also invited to the celebration. ³The wine supply ran out during the festivities, so Jesus' mother told him, "They have no more wine."

⁴"Dear woman, that's not our problem," Jesus replied. "My time has not yet come."

⁵But his mother told the servants, "Do whatever he tells you."

⁶Standing nearby were six stone water jars, used for Jewish ceremonial washing. Each could hold twenty to thirty gallons. ⁷Jesus told the servants, "Fill the jars with water." When the jars had been filled, ⁸he said, "Now dip some out, and take it to the master of ceremonies." So the servants followed his instructions.

⁹When the master of ceremonies tasted the water that was now wine, not knowing where it had come from (though, of course, the servants knew), he called the bridegroom over. ¹⁰"A host always serves the best wine first," he said. "Then, when everyone has had a lot to drink, he brings out the less expensive wine. But you have kept the best until now!"

John 2:1-10

Protecting the things that count

Jesus was angry with the people who exploited the believers who came to the temple to worship God. Jesus was upset that His Father was being dishonored and that the temple was being abused. Get angry about the right things, otherwise you will just waste your energy.

[13]It was nearly time for the Jewish Passover celebration, so Jesus went to Jerusalem.

[14]In the Temple area he saw merchants selling cattle, sheep, and doves for sacrifices; he also saw dealers at tables exchanging foreign money. [15]Jesus made a whip from some ropes and chased them all out of the Temple. He drove out the sheep and cattle, scattered the money changers' coins over the floor, and turned over their tables. [16]Then, going over to the people who sold doves, he told them, "Get these things out of here. Stop turning my Father's house into a marketplace!"

[17]Then his disciples remembered this prophecy from the Scriptures: "Passion for God's house will consume me."

[18]But the Jewish leaders demanded, "What are you doing? If God gave you authority to do this, show us a miraculous sign to prove it."

[19]"All right," Jesus replied. "Destroy this temple, and in three days I will raise it up."

[20]"What!" they exclaimed. "It has taken forty-six years to build this Temple, and you can rebuild it in three days?" [21]But when Jesus said "this temple," he meant his own body. [22]After he was raised from the dead, his disciples remembered he had said this, and they believed both the Scriptures and what Jesus had said.

John 2:13-22

For God loved
the world so much ...

Nicodemus didn't really grasp Jesus' explanation of being born again. He wondered how it was possible that he, an old man, could be born again! Then Jesus said the famous words of John 3:16. Thank you, Nicodemus, for your night visit! For God loved the world so much ...

[2]After dark one evening, he came to speak with Jesus. "Rabbi," he said, "we all know that God has sent you to teach us. Your miraculous signs are evidence that God is with you."

[3]Jesus replied, "I tell you the truth, unless you are born again, you cannot see the Kingdom of God."

[4]"What do you mean?" exclaimed Nicodemus. "How can an old man go back into his mother's womb and be born again?"

[5]Jesus replied, "I assure you, no one can enter the Kingdom of God without being born of water and the Spirit.

[9]"How are these things possible?" Nicodemus asked.

[10]Jesus replied, "You are a respected Jewish teacher, and yet you don't understand these things? [11]I assure you, we tell you what we know and have seen, and yet you won't believe our testimony.

[13]"No one has ever gone to heaven and returned. But the Son of Man has come down from heaven.

[16]"For God loved the world so much that he gave his one and only Son, so that everyone who believes in him will not perish but have eternal life."

John 3:2-5, 9-11, 13, 16

Look for life
in the right place

Here is a woman who looked for life in all the wrong places, until she met Jesus. He asked the woman for water, but then He showed her her own need for living water – Jesus! He knew all about her and through their meeting she and many others in her town became believers.

[4]He had to go through Samaria on the way. [5]Eventually he came to the Samaritan village of Sychar, near the field that Jacob gave to his son Joseph. [6]Jacob's well was there; and Jesus, tired from the long walk, sat wearily beside the well about noontime. [7]Soon a Samaritan woman came to draw water, and Jesus said to her, "Please give me a drink."

[9]The woman was surprised, for Jews refuse to have anything to do with Samaritans. She said to Jesus, "You are a Jew, and I am a Samaritan woman. Why are you asking me for a drink?"

[10]Jesus replied, "If you only knew the gift God has for you and who you are speaking to, you would ask me, and I would give you living water."

[11]"But sir, you don't have a rope or a bucket," she said, "and this well is very deep. Where would you get this living water?

[13]Jesus replied, "Anyone who drinks this water will soon become thirsty again. [14]But those who drink the water I give will never be thirsty again. It becomes a fresh, bubbling spring within them, giving them eternal life."

[15]"Please, sir," the woman said, "give me this water! Then I'll never be thirsty again, and I won't have to come here to get water."

John 4:4-7, 9-11, 13-15

A little in our hands is always a lot in His

In today's story there were twelve baskets of food left over, which the disciples then gave to the poor. What a miracle! Where did the baskets come from? The twelve disciples probably each had their own basket. No Jew went on a journey without one!

[5]Jesus soon saw a huge crowd of people coming to look for him. Turning to Philip, he asked, "Where can we buy bread to feed all these people?" [6]He was testing Philip, for he already knew what he was going to do.

[7]Philip replied, "Even if we worked for months, we wouldn't have enough money to feed them!"

[8]Then Andrew, Simon Peter's brother, spoke up. [9]"There's a young boy here with five barley loaves and two fish. But what good is that with this huge crowd?"

[10]"Tell everyone to sit down," Jesus said. So they all sat down on the grassy slopes. (The men alone numbered about 5,000.) [11]Then Jesus took the loaves, gave thanks to God, and distributed them to the people. Afterward he did the same with the fish. And they all ate as much as they wanted. [12]After everyone was full, Jesus told his disciples, "Now gather the leftovers, so that nothing is wasted." [13]So they picked up the pieces and filled twelve baskets with scraps left by the people who had eaten from the five barley loaves.

[14]When the people saw him do this miraculous sign, they exclaimed, "Surely, he is the Prophet we have been expecting!"

John 6:5-14

Stones belong on the ground – not in the hand!

You cannot understand John 8 properly if you are like the Pharisees and carry a stone around with you; always ready to criticize and put other people down. When we discover that we are all sinners, then we understand grace. You are wrong if you think that John 8 means you get a free pass to sin. Nope, live a new life!

²But early the next morning he was back again at the Temple. A crowd soon gathered, and he sat down and taught them. ³As he was speaking, the teachers of religious law and the Pharisees brought a woman who had been caught in the act of adultery. They put her in front of the crowd.

⁴"Teacher," they said to Jesus, "this woman was caught in the act of adultery. ⁵The law of Moses says to stone her. What do you say?"

⁶They were trying to trap him into saying something they could use against him, but Jesus stooped down and wrote in the dust with his finger. ⁷They kept demanding an answer, so he said, "All right, but let the one who has never sinned throw the first stone!" ⁸Then he stooped down again and wrote in the dust.

⁹When the accusers heard this, they slipped away one by one, beginning with the oldest, until only Jesus was left in the middle of the crowd with the woman. ¹⁰Then Jesus stood up again and said to the woman, "Where are your accusers? Didn't even one of them condemn you?"

¹¹"No, Lord," she said. And Jesus said, "Neither do I. Go and sin no more."

John 8:2-11

How well can you see?

Jesus' disciples wondered who was to blame for the man's blindness. Jesus said that it was senseless to look at the world like that because He is the Light of the world who can heal the blind – especially those who are spiritually blind. He healed the blind man. The rest of the story shows us who is really blind – the Pharisees.

¹As Jesus was walking along, he saw a man who had been blind from birth. ²"Rabbi," his disciples asked him, "why was this man born blind? Was it because of his own sins or his parents' sins?"

³"It was not because of his sins or his parents' sins," Jesus answered. "This happened so the power of God could be seen in him."

⁶Then he spit on the ground, made mud with the saliva, and spread the mud over the blind man's eyes. ⁷He told him, "Go wash yourself in the pool of Siloam" (Siloam means "sent"). So the man went and washed and came back seeing!

³⁵When Jesus heard what had happened, he found the man and asked, "Do you believe in the Son of Man?"

³⁹Then Jesus told him, "I entered this world to render judgment—to give sight to the blind and to show those who think they see that they are blind."

⁴⁰Some Pharisees who were standing nearby heard him and asked, "Are you saying we're blind?"

⁴¹"If you were blind, you wouldn't be guilty," Jesus replied. "But you remain guilty because you claim you can see."

John 9:1-3, 6-7, 35, 39-41

An abundant, overflowing life

The Good Shepherd came to give us a quality life that overflows with grace, peace, joy and love! You can trust Him to do exactly what He has promised. To make sure that you live this quality life that God gives you, listen to His voice always.

[1]"I tell you the truth, anyone who sneaks over the wall of a sheepfold, rather than going through the gate, must surely be a thief and a robber! [2]But the one who enters through the gate is the shepherd of the sheep. [3]The gatekeeper opens the gate for him, and the sheep recognize his voice and come to him. He calls his own sheep by name and leads them out. [4]After he has gathered his own flock, he walks ahead of them, and they follow him because they know his voice. [5]They won't follow a stranger; they will run from him because they don't know his voice."

[6]Those who heard Jesus use this illustration didn't understand what he meant, [7]so he explained it to them: "I tell you the truth, I am the gate for the sheep. [8]All who came before me were thieves and robbers. But the true sheep did not listen to them. [9]Yes, I am the gate. Those who come in through me will be saved. They will come and go freely and will find good pastures. [10]The thief's purpose is to steal and kill and destroy. My purpose is to give them a rich and satisfying life.

[11]"I am the good shepherd. The good shepherd sacrifices his life for the sheep.

[14]"I am the good shepherd; I know my own sheep, and they know me, [15]just as my Father knows me and I know the Father. So I sacrifice my life for the sheep."

John 10:1-11, 14-15

Death is not the end

After Jesus heard that Lazarus was very ill, He stayed where He was for two more days. When He eventually returned, Lazarus was already dead. Martha told Jesus that if He had come sooner, her brother would have lived. But Jesus reminded her that He is the Resurrection and the Life.

[20]When Martha got word that Jesus was coming, she went to meet him. But Mary stayed in the house. [21]Martha said to Jesus, "Lord, if only you had been here, my brother would not have died. [22]But even now I know that God will give you whatever you ask."

[23]Jesus told her, "Your brother will rise again."

[24]"Yes," Martha said, "he will rise when everyone else rises, at the last day."

[25]Jesus told her, "I am the resurrection and the life. Anyone who believes in me will live, even after dying. [26]Everyone who lives in me and believes in me will never ever die. Do you believe this, Martha?"

[27]"Yes, Lord," she told him. "I have always believed you are the Messiah, the Son of God, the one who has come into the world from God."

John 11:20-27

Be like Jesus!

The shortest verse in the Bible is very powerful: "Then Jesus wept" (John 11:35). Jesus was not embarrassed to show His emotions; He cried at Lazarus's grave because He cared about Lazarus! Anything that is good enough for Jesus is good enough for us too!

[33]When Jesus saw her weeping and saw the other people wailing with her, a deep anger welled up within him, and he was deeply troubled. [34]"Where have you put him?" he asked them.

They told him, "Lord, come and see." [35]Then Jesus wept. [36]The people who were standing nearby said, "See how much he loved him!"

[38]Jesus was still angry as he arrived at the tomb, a cave with a stone rolled across its entrance. [39]"Roll the stone aside," Jesus told them.

But Martha, the dead man's sister, protested, "Lord, he has been dead for four days. The smell will be terrible."

[40]Jesus responded, "Didn't I tell you that you would see God's glory if you believe?" [41]So they rolled the stone aside. Then Jesus looked up to heaven and said, "Father, thank you for hearing me. [42]You always hear me, but I said it out loud for the sake of all these people standing here, so that they will believe you sent me." [43]Then Jesus shouted, "Lazarus, come out!"

[44]And the dead man came out, his hands and feet bound in graveclothes, his face wrapped in a headcloth. Jesus told them, "Unwrap him and let him go!"

John 11:33-36, 38-44

What a friend we have in Jesus!

Jesus washed His disciples' feet! This is just one way in which Jesus showed His love for people. This humble action proves that Jesus is a Friend who we can turn to any time – because we matter to Him!

⁴So he got up from the table, took off his robe, wrapped a towel around his waist, ⁵and poured water into a basin. Then he began to wash the disciples' feet, drying them with the towel he had around him.

⁶When Jesus came to Simon Peter, Peter said to him, "Lord, are you going to wash my feet?"

⁷Jesus replied, "You don't understand now what I am doing, but someday you will."

⁸"No," Peter protested, "you will never ever wash my feet!"

Jesus replied, "Unless I wash you, you won't belong to me."

⁹Simon Peter exclaimed, "Then wash my hands and head as well, Lord, not just my feet!"

¹⁰Jesus replied, "A person who has bathed all over does not need to wash, except for the feet, to be entirely clean. And you disciples are clean, but not all of you."

¹²After washing their feet, he put on his robe again and sat down and asked, "Do you understand what I was doing? ¹³You call me 'Teacher' and 'Lord,' and you are right, because that's what I am. ¹⁴And since I, your Lord and Teacher, have washed your feet, you ought to wash each other's feet. ¹⁵I have given you an example to follow. Do as I have done to you."

John 13:4-10, 12-15

The new commandment

After Judas took the bread, he went off into the night. It was also night in his soul and it would just get darker for him. And yet, Jesus loved Judas, and so too must we love others (John 13:34).

²¹Now Jesus was deeply troubled, and he exclaimed, "I tell you the truth, one of you will betray me!"

²²The disciples looked at each other, wondering whom he could mean. ²³The disciple Jesus loved was sitting next to Jesus at the table. ²⁴Simon Peter motioned to him to ask, "Who's he talking about?" ²⁵So that disciple leaned over to Jesus and asked, "Lord, who is it?"

²⁶Jesus responded, "It is the one to whom I give the bread I dip in the bowl." And when he had dipped it, he gave it to Judas, son of Simon Iscariot. ²⁷When Judas had eaten the bread, Satan entered into him. Then Jesus told him, "Hurry and do what you're going to do." ³⁰So Judas left at once, going out into the night.

³¹As soon as Judas left the room, Jesus said, "The time has come for the Son of Man to enter into his glory, and God will be glorified because of him. ³²And since God receives glory because of the Son, he will soon give glory to the Son. ³³Dear children, I will be with you only a little longer. And as I told the Jewish leaders, you will search for me, but you can't come where I am going. ³⁴So now I am giving you a new commandment: Love each other. Just as I have loved you, you should love each other. ³⁵Your love for one another will prove to the world that you are my disciples."

John 13:21-27, 30-35

His own eulogy

In John 14:1-14 Jesus gives His own eulogy or funeral speech. He says to everyone:

1. Don't be upset; death happens but it doesn't have the final say.
2. Trust Jesus and the Father on this.
3. There is a home for you with God.

What an amazing speech! What a true comfort!

[1]"Don't let your hearts be troubled. Trust in God, and trust also in me. [2]There is more than enough room in my Father's home. If this were not so, would I have told you that I am going to prepare a place for you? [3]When everything is ready, I will come and get you, so that you will always be with me where I am. [4]And you know the way to where I am going."

[5]"No, we don't know, Lord," Thomas said. "We have no idea where you are going, so how can we know the way?"

[6]Jesus told him, "I am the way, the truth, and the life. No one can come to the Father except through me. [7]If you had really known me, you would know who my Father is. From now on, you do know him and have seen him!"

John 14:1-7

October

Jesus calls us His friends

Jesus uses the image of a vine and a branch to explain his relationship with us. He is the vine and we are the branch. In order for us to grow, it is necessary for us to be pruned by the Gardener, God the Father. But we can trust Jesus through the whole process because He calls us His friends and loves us.

[1]"I am the true grapevine, and my Father is the gardener. [2]He cuts off every branch of mine that doesn't produce fruit, and he prunes the branches that do bear fruit so they will produce even more. [3]You have already been pruned and purified by the message I have given you. [4]Remain in me, and I will remain in you. For a branch cannot produce fruit if it is severed from the vine, and you cannot be fruitful unless you remain in me.

[10]"When you obey my commandments, you remain in my love, just as I obey my Father's commandments and remain in his love.

[12]"This is my commandment: Love each other in the same way I have loved you. [13]There is no greater love than to lay down one's life for one's friends. [14]You are my friends if you do what I command. [15]I no longer call you slaves, because a master doesn't confide in his slaves. Now you are my friends, since I have told you everything the Father told me. [16]You didn't choose me. I chose you. I appointed you to go and produce lasting fruit, so that the Father will give you whatever you ask for, using my name."

John 15:1-4, 10, 12-16

Be brave –
we have the Spirit!

We are not alone in the world. We have the Spirit who lives in us, teaches us and helps us to live like Jesus. Following Jesus is not always easy, but Jesus didn't have it easy either. Don't get discouraged if you are going through a hard time, think of Jesus' victory and take heart!

[5]"But now I am going away to the one who sent me, and not one of you is asking where I am going. [6]Instead, you grieve because of what I've told you. [7]But in fact, it is best for you that I go away, because if I don't, the Advocate won't come. If I do go away, then I will send him to you. [8]And when he comes, he will convict the world of its sin, and of God's righteousness, and of the coming judgment. [9]The world's sin is that it refuses to believe in me. [10]Righteousness is available because I go to the Father, and you will see me no more. [11]Judgment will come because the ruler of this world has already been judged."

[31]Jesus asked, "Do you finally believe? [32]But the time is coming—indeed it's here now—when you will be scattered, each one going his own way, leaving me alone. Yet I am not alone because the Father is with me. [33]I have told you all this so that you may have peace in me. Here on earth you will have many trials and sorrows. But take heart, because I have overcome the world."

John 16:5-11, 31-33

Last words

Jesus only spoke seven sentences on the cross, but each of them is life changing. Eventually He died with a single word on His lips: *tetelestai* (meaning "It is finished" in Greek). It was the very same word that was written on ancient accounts to say that a debt had been paid in full. Jesus paid a high price to settle the debt for everyone and to set everyone free.

23When the soldiers had crucified Jesus, they divided his clothes among the four of them. They also took his robe, but it was seamless, woven in one piece from top to bottom. 24So they said, "Rather than tearing it apart, let's throw dice for it." This fulfilled the Scripture that says, "They divided my garments among themselves and threw dice for my clothing." So that is what they did.

25Standing near the cross were Jesus' mother, and his mother's sister, Mary (the wife of Clopas), and Mary Magdalene. 26When Jesus saw his mother standing there beside the disciple he loved, he said to her, "Dear woman, here is your son." 27And he said to this disciple, "Here is your mother." And from then on this disciple took her into his home.

28Jesus knew that his mission was now finished, and to fulfill Scripture he said, "I am thirsty." 29A jar of sour wine was sitting there, so they soaked a sponge in it, put it on a hyssop branch, and held it up to his lips. 30When Jesus had tasted it, he said, "It is finished!" Then he bowed his head and released his spirit.

John 19:23-30

Nicodemus and Joseph were leading men in the Jewish community, but they were also secret followers of Jesus. After Jesus' death they decided to no longer hide it and they openly showed that they were on His side.

[31]It was the day of preparation, and the Jewish leaders didn't want the bodies hanging there the next day, which was the Sabbath (and a very special Sabbath, because it was the Passover). So they asked Pilate to hasten their deaths by ordering that their legs be broken. Then their bodies could be taken down. [32]So the soldiers came and broke the legs of the two men crucified with Jesus. [33]But when they came to Jesus, they saw that he was already dead, so they didn't break his legs.

[38]Afterward Joseph of Arimathea, who had been a secret disciple of Jesus (because he feared the Jewish leaders), asked Pilate for permission to take down Jesus' body. When Pilate gave permission, Joseph came and took the body away. [39]With him came Nicodemus, the man who had come to Jesus at night. He brought about seventy-five pounds of perfumed ointment made from myrrh and aloes. [40]Following Jewish burial custom, they wrapped Jesus' body with the spices in long sheets of linen cloth.

[41]The place of crucifixion was near a garden, where there was a new tomb, never used before. [42]And so, because it was the day of preparation for the Jewish Passover and since the tomb was close at hand, they laid Jesus there.

John 19:31-33, 38-42

Resurrection day

Early on the third day after Jesus' crucifixion, Mary Magdalene went to His tomb – but the stone had been rolled away and Jesus' body was gone! As soon as Peter and John heard the news they ran to the tomb and discovered that it was indeed empty! Jesus had risen from the dead!

¹Early on Sunday morning, while it was still dark, Mary Magdalene came to the tomb and found that the stone had been rolled away from the entrance. ²She ran and found Simon Peter and the other disciple, the one whom Jesus loved. She said, "They have taken the Lord's body out of the tomb, and we don't know where they have put him!"

³Peter and the other disciple started out for the tomb. ⁶Peter arrived and went inside. He also noticed the linen wrappings lying there, ⁷while the cloth that had covered Jesus' head was folded up and lying apart from the other wrappings.

¹¹Mary was standing outside the tomb crying, and as she wept, she stooped and looked in. ¹²She saw two white-robed angels, one sitting at the head and the other at the foot of the place where the body of Jesus had been lying. ¹³"Dear woman, why are you crying?" the angels asked her. "Because they have taken away my Lord," she replied, "and I don't know where they have put him."

¹⁶"Mary!" Jesus said. She turned to him and cried out, "Rabboni!" (which is Hebrew for "Teacher").

¹⁷"Don't cling to me," Jesus said, "for I haven't yet ascended to the Father. But go find my brothers and tell them, 'I am ascending to my Father and your Father, to my God and your God.'"

John 20:1-3, 6-7, 11-13, 16-17

When in doubt,
trust Jesus

Even though Jesus had risen, the disciples were still scared of the Jews. For this reason Jesus appeared before them – even though all the doors were locked! His resurrection emphasizes that nothing is impossible for Him. Thomas doubted, but once he saw Jesus with his own eyes, all his doubts disappeared!

¹⁹That Sunday evening the disciples were meeting behind locked doors because they were afraid of the Jewish leaders. Suddenly, Jesus was standing there among them! "Peace be with you," he said. ²⁰As he spoke, he showed them the wounds in his hands and his side. They were filled with joy when they saw the Lord!

²⁴One of the twelve disciples, Thomas (nicknamed the Twin), was not with the others when Jesus came. ²⁵They told him, "We have seen the Lord!" But he replied, "I won't believe it unless I see the nail wounds in his hands, put my fingers into them, and place my hand into the wound in his side."

²⁶Eight days later the disciples were together again, and this time Thomas was with them. The doors were locked; but suddenly, as before, Jesus was standing among them. "Peace be with you," he said. ²⁷Then he said to Thomas, "Put your finger here, and look at my hands. Put your hand into the wound in my side. Don't be faithless any longer. Believe!"

²⁸"My Lord and my God!" Thomas exclaimed.

²⁹Then Jesus told him, "You believe because you have seen me. Blessed are those who believe without seeing me."

John 20:19-20, 24-29

Breakfast
on the beach

There are many explanations for the 153 fish in John 21:11. One version is that it refers to the different kinds of fish they caught. This could symbolize that the church must include all people. But one thing stands out: After the miracle fishing, the disciples knew that it was the resurrected Jesus who had made their breakfast.

⁴At dawn Jesus was standing on the beach, but the disciples couldn't see who he was. ⁵He called out, "Fellows, have you caught any fish?" "No," they replied.

⁶Then he said, "Throw out your net on the right-hand side of the boat, and you'll get some!" So they did, and they couldn't haul in the net because there were so many fish in it.

⁷Then the disciple Jesus loved said to Peter, "It's the Lord!" When Simon Peter heard that it was the Lord, he put on his tunic (for he had stripped for work), jumped into the water, and headed to shore. ⁸The others stayed with the boat and pulled the loaded net to the shore, for they were only about a hundred yards from shore. ⁹When they got there, they found breakfast waiting for them—fish cooking over a charcoal fire, and some bread.

¹⁰"Bring some of the fish you've just caught," Jesus said. ¹¹So Simon Peter went aboard and dragged the net to the shore. There were 153 large fish, and yet the net hadn't torn.

¹²"Now come and have some breakfast!" Jesus said. None of the disciples dared to ask him, "Who are you?" They knew it was the Lord. ¹³Then Jesus served them the bread and the fish.

John 21:4-13

Grace helps you
pick up the pieces

The three times that Jesus asked Peter if he loved Him (John 21:15-17) links to the number of times Peter denied Jesus. Jesus gave Peter a chance to declare his love for Him and to wipe away his denials. That's grace! That's how Jesus works!

15After breakfast Jesus asked Simon Peter, "Simon son of John, do you love me more than these?"

"Yes, Lord," Peter replied, "you know I love you."

"Then feed my lambs," Jesus told him.

16Jesus repeated the question: "Simon son of John, do you love me?"

"Yes, Lord," Peter said, "you know I love you."

"Then take care of my sheep," Jesus said.

17A third time he asked him, "Simon son of John, do you love me?" Peter was hurt that Jesus asked the question a third time. He said, "Lord, you know everything. You know that I love you."

Jesus said, "Then feed my sheep.

18"I tell you the truth, when you were young, you were able to do as you liked; you dressed yourself and went wherever you wanted to go. But when you are old, you will stretch out your hands, and others will dress you and take you where you don't want to go." 19Jesus said this to let him know by what kind of death he would glorify God. Then Jesus told him, "Follow me."

John 21:15-19

Power and the cloud

Jesus' followers received the Holy Spirit, which was so powerful it was like an earthquake that shook the whole world. Incidentally, the cloud that carried Jesus away is not just any cloud, but the same cloud that symbolized God's presence in the Old Testament. The Father came to take His Son to be with Him in heaven.

[4]Once when he was eating with them, he commanded them, "Do not leave Jerusalem until the Father sends you the gift he promised, as I told you before. [5]John baptized with water, but in just a few days you will be baptized with the Holy Spirit."

[6]So when the apostles were with Jesus, they kept asking him, "Lord, has the time come for you to free Israel and restore our kingdom?"

[7]He replied, "The Father alone has the authority to set those dates and times, and they are not for you to know. [8]But you will receive power when the Holy Spirit comes upon you. And you will be my witnesses, telling people about me everywhere—in Jerusalem, throughout Judea, in Samaria, and to the ends of the earth."

[9]After saying this, he was taken up into a cloud while they were watching, and they could no longer see him. [10]As they strained to see him rising into heaven, two white-robed men suddenly stood among them. [11]"Men of Galilee," they said, "why are you standing here staring into heaven? Jesus has been taken from you into heaven, but someday he will return from heaven in the same way you saw him go!"

Acts 1:4-11

Forward, march!

Jesus' followers received the Holy Spirit just like Jesus promised. They began to spread the Word all over the world. In the same way it was impossible for death to keep Jesus captive, there is also no stopping the church. Nothing and no one can stop the church of Jesus.

¹On the day of Pentecost all the believers were meeting together in one place. ²Suddenly, there was a sound from heaven like the roaring of a mighty windstorm, and it filled the house where they were sitting. ³Then, what looked like flames or tongues of fire appeared and settled on each of them. ⁴And everyone present was filled with the Holy Spirit and began speaking in other languages, as the Holy Spirit gave them this ability.

⁵At that time there were devout Jews from every nation living in Jerusalem. ⁶When they heard the loud noise, everyone came running, and they were bewildered to hear their own languages being spoken by the believers.

⁷They were completely amazed. "How can this be?" they exclaimed. "These people are all from Galilee, ⁸and yet we hear them speaking in our own native languages! ⁹Here we are— Parthians, Medes, Elamites, people from Mesopotamia, Judea, Cappadocia, Pontus, the province of Asia, ¹⁰Phrygia, Pamphylia, Egypt, and the areas of Libya around Cyrene, visitors from Rome ¹¹(both Jews and converts to Judaism), Cretans, and Arabs. And we all hear these people speaking in our own languages about the wonderful things God has done!" ¹²They stood there amazed and perplexed. "What can this mean?" they asked each other.

Acts 2:1-12

Give to others,
for Jesus' sake

The family of Jesus work together so they can help each other and others whenever they can. As new creations we live out the love of God so that others can joyfully praise God for the change that He has brought into their lives.

[43]A deep sense of awe came over them all, and the apostles performed many miraculous signs and wonders. [44]And all the believers met together in one place and shared everything they had.

[45]They sold their property and possessions and shared the money with those in need. [46]They worshiped together at the Temple each day, met in homes for the Lord's Supper, and shared their meals with great joy and generosity—[47]all the while praising God and enjoying the goodwill of all the people. And each day the Lord added to their fellowship those who were being saved.

Acts 2:43-47

Be an encourager

We should still follow Barnabas's example today. He played a big part in the development of the early church. Why? Because everyone, at some point in their lives, needs to be encouraged. Therefore, be a Barnabas. His name literally means son (*Bar*) of encouragement (*nabas*).

4 [32] All the believers were united in heart and mind. And they felt that what they owned was not their own, so they shared everything they had. [33] The apostles testified powerfully to the resurrection of the Lord Jesus, and God's great blessing was upon them all. [34] There were no needy people among them, because those who owned land or houses would sell them [35] and bring the money to the apostles to give to those in need.

[36] For instance, there was Joseph, the one the apostles nicknamed Barnabas (which means "Son of Encouragement"). He was from the tribe of Levi and came from the island of Cyprus. [37] He sold a field he owned and brought the money to the apostles.

11 [22] When the church at Jerusalem heard what had happened, they sent Barnabas to Antioch. [23] When he arrived and saw this evidence of God's blessing, he was filled with joy, and he encouraged the believers to stay true to the Lord. [24] Barnabas was a good man, full of the Holy Spirit and strong in faith. And many people were brought to the Lord.

Acts 4:32-37; 11:22-24

If it is from God, no one can stop it

The disciples could not stop preaching and were arrested (Acts 5:26). It was quite serious because when the whole Jewish council got together, they meant business. Thankfully, Gamaliel, who was described as respected expert in the Law, put a stop to their plans with his wise words.

[26]The captain went with his Temple guards and arrested the apostles. [27]Then they brought the apostles before the high council, where the high priest confronted them. [28]"Didn't we tell you never again to teach in this man's name?" he demanded. "Instead, you have filled all Jerusalem with your teaching about him, and you want to make us responsible for his death!"

[29]But Peter and the apostles replied, "We must obey God rather than any human authority."

[33]When they heard this, the high council was furious and decided to kill them. [34]But one member, a Pharisee named Gamaliel, who was an expert in religious law and respected by all the people, stood up and ordered that the men be sent outside the council chamber for a while. [35]Then he said to his colleagues, "Men of Israel, take care what you are planning to do to these men!

[38]"So my advice is, leave these men alone. Let them go. If they are planning and doing these things merely on their own, it will soon be overthrown. [39]But if it is from God, you will not be able to overthrow them. You may even find yourselves fighting against God!"

[40]The others accepted his advice. They called in the apostles and had them flogged. Then they ordered them never again to speak in the name of Jesus, and they let them go.

Acts 5:26-29, 33-35, 38-40

It is dangerous to believe in Jesus

Stephen was the first martyr to die for his faith. Later, the other apostles were also killed for their faith. Even in the face of punishment and death, Stephen never lost his faith.

6 ⁹But one day some men from the Synagogue of Freed Slaves, as it was called, started to debate with him. They were Jews from Cyrene, Alexandria, Cilicia, and the province of Asia. ¹⁰None of them could stand against the wisdom and the Spirit with which Stephen spoke.

¹¹So they persuaded some men to lie about Stephen, saying, "We heard him blaspheme Moses, and even God." ¹²This roused the people, the elders, and the teachers of religious law. So they arrested Stephen and brought him before the high council.

¹⁵At this point everyone in the high council stared at Stephen, because his face became as bright as an angel's.

7 ⁵⁵But Stephen, full of the Holy Spirit, gazed steadily into heaven and saw the glory of God, and he saw Jesus standing in the place of honor at God's right hand. ⁵⁶And he told them, "Look, I see the heavens opened and the Son of Man standing in the place of honor at God's right hand!"

⁵⁷Then they put their hands over their ears and began shouting. They rushed at him ⁵⁸and dragged him out of the city and began to stone him. His accusers took off their coats and laid them at the feet of a young man named Saul.

⁵⁹As they stoned him, Stephen prayed, "Lord Jesus, receive my spirit." ⁶⁰He fell to his knees, shouting, "Lord, don't charge them with this sin!" And with that, he died.

Acts 6:9-12, 15; 7:55-60

A persecutor becomes a follower

Paul was a student of Gamaliel and a persecutor of the church. But one day Paul had an encounter with God and God used Paul's passion to grow His church. If God could turn Paul around, imagine what other surprises are in store for His followers!

²He requested letters addressed to the synagogues in Damascus, asking for their cooperation in the arrest of any followers of the Way he found there. He wanted to bring them—both men and women—back to Jerusalem in chains.

³As he was approaching Damascus on this mission, a light from heaven suddenly shone down around him. ⁴He fell to the ground and heard a voice saying to him, "Saul! Saul! Why are you persecuting me?"

⁵"Who are you, lord?" Saul asked. And the voice replied, "I am Jesus, the one you are persecuting! ⁶Now get up and go into the city, and you will be told what you must do."

¹⁰Now there was a believer in Damascus named Ananias. The Lord spoke to him in a vision, calling, "Ananias!" "Yes, Lord!" he replied. ¹¹The Lord said, "Go over to Straight Street, to the house of Judas. When you get there, ask for a man from Tarsus named Saul. ¹²I have shown him a vision of a man named Ananias coming in and laying hands on him so he can see again."

¹⁷So Ananias went and found Saul. He laid his hands on him and said, "Brother Saul, the Lord Jesus, who appeared to you on the road, has sent me so that you might regain your sight and be filled with the Holy Spirit." ¹⁸Instantly something like scales fell from Saul's eyes, and he regained his sight. Then he got up and was baptized.

Acts 9:2-6, 10-12, 17-18

Keep your heart open

Paul lived his life according to this slogan: "Go M.A.D. Go **M**ake **A D**ifference." Paul made a difference in a prison guard's life and the guard became a believer. He treated Silas and Paul's wounds and invited them to eat with him and his family. If your faith does not make you love others then it is only skin deep.

[25]Around midnight Paul and Silas were praying and singing hymns to God, and the other prisoners were listening. [26]Suddenly, there was a massive earthquake, and the prison was shaken to its foundations. All the doors immediately flew open, and the chains of every prisoner fell off! [27]The jailer woke up to see the prison doors wide open. He assumed the prisoners had escaped, so he drew his sword to kill himself. [28]But Paul shouted to him, "Stop! Don't kill yourself! We are all here!"

[29]The jailer called for lights and ran to the dungeon and fell down trembling before Paul and Silas. [30]Then he brought them out and asked, "Sirs, what must I do to be saved?"

[31]They replied, "Believe in the Lord Jesus and you will be saved, along with everyone in your household." [32]And they shared the word of the Lord with him and with all who lived in his household. [33]Even at that hour of the night, the jailer cared for them and washed their wounds. Then he and everyone in his household were immediately baptized. [34]He brought them into his house and set a meal before them, and he and his entire household rejoiced because they all believed in God.

Acts 16:25-34

Don't throw your weight around

You can be deceived by authorities who throw their weight around. However, Paul reminds us that Jesus is the true Authority. His power and influence are everywhere, whether we recognize it or not. The Lord is not dependant on us for power. He is Almighty.

¹This letter is from Paul, a slave of Christ Jesus, chosen by God to be an apostle and sent out to preach his Good News. ²God promised this Good News long ago through his prophets in the holy Scriptures.

³The Good News is about his Son. In his earthly life he was born into King David's family line, ⁴and he was shown to be the Son of God when he was raised from the dead by the power of the Holy Spirit. He is Jesus Christ our Lord. ⁵Through Christ, God has given us the privilege and authority as apostles to tell Gentiles everywhere what God has done for them, so that they will believe and obey him, bringing glory to his name.

⁶And you are included among those Gentiles who have been called to belong to Jesus Christ. ⁷I am writing to all of you in Rome who are loved by God and are called to be his own holy people. May God our Father and the Lord Jesus Christ give you grace and peace.

Romans 1:1-7

We can't save ourselves

If you are drowning in the sea, you can't save yourself. You need a lifesaver. The same principle applies to your spiritual life. Jesus is our only Lifesaver! Therefore it is good to talk about Him and all that He has done for you, and talk less about yourself.

²¹But now God has shown us a way to be made right with him without keeping the requirements of the law, as was promised in the writings of Moses and the prophets long ago. ²²We are made right with God by placing our faith in Jesus Christ. And this is true for everyone who believes, no matter who we are.

²³For everyone has sinned; we all fall short of God's glorious standard. ²⁴Yet God, with undeserved kindness, declares that we are righteous. He did this through Christ Jesus when he freed us from the penalty for our sins.

²⁵For God presented Jesus as the sacrifice for sin. People are made right with God when they believe that Jesus sacrificed his life, shedding his blood. This sacrifice shows that God was being fair when he held back and did not punish those who sinned in times past, ²⁶for he was looking ahead and including them in what he would do in this present time. God did this to demonstrate his righteousness, for he himself is fair and just, and he declares sinners to be right in his sight when they believe in Jesus.

²⁷Can we boast, then, that we have done anything to be accepted by God? No, because our acquittal is not based on obeying the law. It is based on faith.

Romans 3:21-27

The Good News

We are forgiven (Rom. 5:1) and we are loved (v. 5, 8)! We are blessed with a bag full of gifts: peace with God (v. 1), grace for our mistakes (v. 2), a share in God's glory (v. 2), endurance (v. 3), a trustworthy character (v. 4), hope (v. 5), and the Spirit who works in us (v. 5).

¹Therefore, since we have been made right in God's sight by faith, we have peace with God because of what Jesus Christ our Lord has done for us. ²Because of our faith, Christ has brought us into this place of undeserved privilege where we now stand, and we confidently and joyfully look forward to sharing God's glory.

³We can rejoice, too, when we run into problems and trials, for we know that they help us develop endurance. ⁴And endurance develops strength of character, and character strengthens our confident hope of salvation. ⁵And this hope will not lead to disappointment. For we know how dearly God loves us, because he has given us the Holy Spirit to fill our hearts with his love.

⁶When we were utterly helpless, Christ came at just the right time and died for us sinners. ⁷Now, most people would not be willing to die for an upright person, though someone might perhaps be willing to die for a person who is especially good. ⁸But God showed his great love for us by sending Christ to die for us while we were still sinners. ⁹And since we have been made right in God's sight by the blood of Christ, he will certainly save us from God's condemnation.

Romans 5:1-9

A solution in two words

Sometimes we struggle to be the Christians we would like to be. A Paul says, "I want to do what is right, but I inevitably do what is wrong." Fortunately there is a two-word solution to this dilemma: Jesus Christ!

[18]And I know that nothing good lives in me, that is, in my sinful nature. I want to do what is right, but I can't. [19]I want to do what is good, but I don't. I don't want to do what is wrong, but I do it anyway. [20]But if I do what I don't want to do, I am not really the one doing wrong; it is sin living in me that does it.

[21]I have discovered this principle of life—that when I want to do what is right, I inevitably do what is wrong. [22]I love God's law with all my heart. [23]But there is another power within me that is at war with my mind. This power makes me a slave to the sin that is still within me. [24]Oh, what a miserable person I am! Who will free me from this life that is dominated by sin and death?

[25]Thank God! The answer is in Jesus Christ our Lord. So you see how it is: In my mind I really want to obey God's law, but because of my sinful nature I am a slave to sin.

Romans 7:18-25

Spiritual makeover

"Every time we say, 'I believe in the Holy Spirit,' we mean that we believe that there is a living God able and willing to enter human personality and change it" (J. B. Philips). If you've said yes to God then you have said yes to a spiritual makeover.

¹So now there is no condemnation for those who belong to Christ Jesus. ²And because you belong to him, the power of the life-giving Spirit has freed you from the power of sin that leads to death. ³The law of Moses was unable to save us because of the weakness of our sinful nature. So God did what the law could not do. He sent his own Son in a body like the bodies we sinners have. And in that body God declared an end to sin's control over us by giving his Son as a sacrifice for our sins. ⁴He did this so that the just requirement of the law would be fully satisfied for us, who no longer follow our sinful nature but instead follow the Spirit.

⁵Those who are dominated by the sinful nature think about sinful things, but those who are controlled by the Holy Spirit think about things that please the Spirit.

⁹But you are not controlled by your sinful nature. You are controlled by the Spirit if you have the Spirit of God living in you. (And remember that those who do not have the Spirit of Christ living in them do not belong to him at all.)

Romans 8:1-5, 9

Things don't always go according to plan

Things don't always go according to plan and sometimes a person doesn't know what to pray for anymore. At times like these remember that you have a Prayer Helper. The Holy Spirit is your interpreter and He will translate your prayer into heavenly language for God the Father. In this way He makes everything work out well for His children.

[15]So you have not received a spirit that makes you fearful slaves. Instead, you received God's Spirit when he adopted you as his own children. Now we call him, "Abba, Father." [16]For his Spirit joins with our spirit to affirm that we are God's children. [17]And since we are his children, we are his heirs. In fact, together with Christ we are heirs of God's glory. But if we are to share his glory, we must also share his suffering.

[26]And the Holy Spirit helps us in our weakness. For example, we don't know what God wants us to pray for. But the Holy Spirit prays for us with groanings that cannot be expressed in words. [27]And the Father who knows all hearts knows what the Spirit is saying, for the Spirit pleads for us believers in harmony with God's own will.

[28]And we know that God causes everything to work together for the good of those who love God and are called according to his purpose for them. [29]For God knew his people in advance, and he chose them to become like his Son, so that his Son would be the firstborn among many brothers and sisters. [30]And having chosen them, he called them to come to him. And having called them, he gave them right standing with himself. And having given them right standing, he gave them his glory.

Romans 8:15-17, 26-30

Victorious

Verse 37 says that "overwhelming victory" is ours. This is not because we are so wonderful, but because God is so great and wonderful. Absolutely nothing can separate us from God's love. Absolutely nothing.

³¹What shall we say about such wonderful things as these? If God is for us, who can ever be against us? ³²Since he did not spare even his own Son but gave him up for us all, won't he also give us everything else? ³³Who dares accuse us whom God has chosen for his own? No one—for God himself has given us right standing with himself. ³⁴Who then will condemn us? No one—for Christ Jesus died for us and was raised to life for us, and he is sitting in the place of honor at God's right hand, pleading for us.

³⁵Can anything ever separate us from Christ's love? Does it mean he no longer loves us if we have trouble or calamity, or are persecuted, or hungry, or destitute, or in danger, or threatened with death? ³⁶(As the Scriptures say, "For your sake we are killed every day; we are being slaughtered like sheep.") ³⁷No, despite all these things, overwhelming victory is ours through Christ, who loved us.

³⁸And I am convinced that nothing can ever separate us from God's love. Neither death nor life, neither angels nor demons, neither our fears for today nor our worries about tomorrow—not even the powers of hell can separate us from God's love. ³⁹No power in the sky above or in the earth below—indeed, nothing in all creation will ever be able to separate us from the love of God that is revealed in Christ Jesus our Lord.

Romans 8:31-39

An important message

Romans 10:9-10 is of great importance. Every person must confess:

1. Jesus is Lord, in other words, He is the crucified One who took all our sins upon Himself.
2. Jesus was resurrected and this implies that He still lives today.
3. You must not only believe this, you must tell others about it too.

[8]"The message is very close at hand; it is on your lips and in your heart." And that message is the very message about faith that we preach: [9]If you confess with your mouth that Jesus is Lord and believe in your heart that God raised him from the dead, you will be saved. [10]For it is by believing in your heart that you are made right with God, and it is by confessing with your mouth that you are saved.

[11]As the Scriptures tell us, "Anyone who trusts in him will never be disgraced." [12]Jew and Gentile are the same in this respect. They have the same Lord, who gives generously to all who call on him. [13]For "Everyone who calls on the name of the LORD will be saved."

[14]But how can they call on him to save them unless they believe in him? And how can they believe in him if they have never heard about him? And how can they hear about him unless someone tells them? [15]And how will anyone go and tell them without being sent? That is why the Scriptures say, "How beautiful are the feet of messengers who bring good news!"

Romans 10:8-15

A symphony of praise

God is incomprehensible but you can still trust
Him. He deserves all of our praise. In Romans 11
Paul changes from a theologian to a poet, and
these words are what every believer can say to
God.

²²Notice how God is both kind and severe. He is severe toward
those who disobeyed, but kind to you if you continue to trust in
his kindness. But if you stop trusting, you also will be cut off.

³³Oh, how great are God's riches and wisdom and knowledge!
How impossible it is for us to understand his decisions and his
ways! ³⁴For who can know the LORD's thoughts? Who knows
enough to give him advice? ³⁵And who has given him so much
that he needs to pay it back?

³⁶For everything comes from him and exists by his power and
is intended for his glory. All glory to him forever! Amen.

Romans 11:22, 33-36

Focus on Jesus

Paul says that a person's inner self must go through a metamorphosis (like the stages of a butterfly's life). Remember, it's not a once-off change, but a lifelong growing process. Allow the Holy Spirit to change your focus to Jesus. He does this by giving you the mind of Christ.

[1]And so, dear brothers and sisters, I plead with you to give your bodies to God because of all he has done for you. Let them be a living and holy sacrifice—the kind he will find acceptable. This is truly the way to worship him.

[2]Don't copy the behavior and customs of this world, but let God transform you into a new person by changing the way you think. Then you will learn to know God's will for you, which is good and pleasing and perfect.

Romans 12:1-2

Stand out for Jesus!

In the Scripture passage below Paul gives us a guideline of what the Christian life should look like in our everyday lives. He gives rules for us to follow. We must not just blend into society, we must stand out for Jesus.

9Don't just pretend to love others. Really love them. Hate what is wrong. Hold tightly to what is good. 10Love each other with genuine affection, and take delight in honoring each other. 11Never be lazy, but work hard and serve the Lord enthusiastically. 12Rejoice in our confident hope. Be patient in trouble, and keep on praying. 13When God's people are in need, be ready to help them. Always be eager to practice hospitality.

14Bless those who persecute you. Don't curse them; pray that God will bless them. 15Be happy with those who are happy, and weep with those who weep. 16Live in harmony with each other. Don't be too proud to enjoy the company of ordinary people. And don't think you know it all!

17Never pay back evil with more evil. Do things in such a way that everyone can see you are honorable. 18Do all that you can to live in peace with everyone.

Romans 12:9-18

Get up!

When your alarm clock goes off it means one thing: it's time to get up! You have a choice: you can either ignore it and go back to sleep, or you can get up. God says that wisdom will convince people to get up out of their sins and live fully for Jesus.

⁸Owe nothing to anyone—except for your obligation to love one another. If you love your neighbor, you will fulfill the requirements of God's law. ⁹For the commandments say, "You must not commit adultery. You must not murder. You must not steal. You must not covet." These—and other such commandments—are summed up in this one commandment: "Love your neighbor as yourself." ¹⁰Love does no wrong to others, so love fulfills the requirements of God's law.

¹¹This is all the more urgent, for you know how late it is; time is running out. Wake up, for our salvation is nearer now than when we first believed. ¹²The night is almost gone; the day of salvation will soon be here. So remove your dark deeds like dirty clothes, and put on the shining armor of right living.

¹³Because we belong to the day, we must live decent lives for all to see. Don't participate in the darkness of wild parties and drunkenness, or in sexual promiscuity and immoral living, or in quarreling and jealousy. ¹⁴Instead, clothe yourself with the presence of the Lord Jesus Christ. And don't let yourself think about ways to indulge your evil desires.

Romans 13:8-14

A good example

A good example to follow is the one that Paul mentions below: Jesus. Then we will be able to accept others for who they are – just as Jesus does it with us. Verses 19-20 are a good goal for our lives. The secret of God's love (v. 25) is out, we see it in the example of Jesus Christ's love.

15⁵May God, who gives this patience and encouragement, help you live in complete harmony with each other, as is fitting for followers of Christ Jesus. ⁶Then all of you can join together with one voice, giving praise and glory to God, the Father of our Lord Jesus Christ.

⁷Therefore, accept each other just as Christ has accepted you so that God will be given glory.

¹³I pray that God, the source of hope, will fill you completely with joy and peace because you trust in him. Then you will over-flow with confident hope through the power of the Holy Spirit.

16¹⁹But everyone knows that you are obedient to the Lord. This makes me very happy. I want you to be wise in doing right and to stay innocent of any wrong. ²⁰The God of peace will soon crush Satan under your feet. May the grace of our Lord Jesus be with you.

²⁵Now all glory to God, who is able to make you strong, just as my Good News says. This message about Jesus Christ has revealed his plan for you Gentiles, a plan kept secret from the beginning of time. ²⁶But now as the prophets foretold and as the eternal God has commanded, this message is made known to all Gentiles everywhere, so that they too might believe and obey him.

Romans 15:5-7, 13; 16:19-20, 25-26

The signature of Christ

The cross is the signature of Christ, because it is the power of God. A person who doesn't understand that has no wisdom, no matter how intelligent they are. There is a right way of thinking and a right way of living, so do what's right.

[18]The message of the cross is foolish to those who are headed for destruction! But we who are being saved know it is the very power of God. [19]As the Scriptures say, "I will destroy the wisdom of the wise and discard the intelligence of the intelligent."

[20]So where does this leave the philosophers, the scholars, and the world's brilliant debaters? God has made the wisdom of this world look foolish. [21]Since God in his wisdom saw to it that the world would never know him through human wisdom, he has used our foolish preaching to save those who believe. [22]It is foolish to the Jews, who ask for signs from heaven. And it is foolish to the Greeks, who seek human wisdom. [23]So when we preach that Christ was crucified, the Jews are offended and the Gentiles say it's all nonsense.

[24]But to those called by God to salvation, both Jews and Gentiles, Christ is the power of God and the wisdom of God. [25]This foolish plan of God is wiser than the wisest of human plans, and God's weakness is stronger than the greatest of human strength.

1 Corinthians 1:18-25

You are a walking temple of God

Technically it is incorrect to say, "Come, let's go to church." Why? Because all Christians are churches (temples). Therefore we must carefully examine how we live, because for people who are looking for the church, we are the address. True worship is when you give your life to God every day, because you are His walking temple.

3⁵After all, who is Apollos? Who is Paul? We are only God's servants through whom you believed the Good News. Each of us did the work the Lord gave us. ⁶I planted the seed in your hearts, and Apollos watered it, but it was God who made it grow. ⁷It's not important who does the planting, or who does the watering. What's important is that God makes the seed grow. ⁸The one who plants and the one who waters work together with the same purpose. And both will be rewarded for their own hard work. ⁹For we are both God's workers. And you are God's field. You are God's building.

¹⁶Don't you realize that all of you together are the temple of God and that the Spirit of God lives in you? ¹⁷God will destroy anyone who destroys this temple. For God's temple is holy, and you are that temple.

6¹⁹ Don't you realize that your body is the temple of the Holy Spirit, who lives in you and was given to you by God? You do not belong to yourself, ²⁰for God bought you with a high price. So you must honor God with your body.

1 Corinthians 3:5-9, 16-17; 6:19-20

November

A hit love song

In 1 Corinthians 13, Paul wrote one of the greatest love songs ever. The Greek word that he uses is *agape*, which means God's love or Jesus' love. He explains love:

1. Life without it is meaningless (vv. 1-3)
2. The ins and outs of love (vv. 4-7)
3. Love lasts forever (vv. 8-13)

¹If I could speak all the languages of earth and of angels, but didn't love others, I would only be a noisy gong or a clanging cymbal. ²If I had the gift of prophecy, and if I understood all of God's secret plans and possessed all knowledge, and if I had such faith that I could move mountains, but didn't love others, I would be nothing. ³If I gave everything I have to the poor and even sacrificed my body, I could boast about it; but if I didn't love others, I would have gained nothing.

⁴Love is patient and kind. Love is not jealous or boastful or proud ⁵or rude. It does not demand its own way. It is not irritable, and it keeps no record of being wronged. ⁶It does not rejoice about injustice but rejoices whenever the truth wins out. ⁷Love never gives up, never loses faith, is always hopeful, and endures through every circumstance. ⁸Prophecy and speaking in unknown languages and special knowledge will become useless. But love will last forever!

¹³Three things will last forever—faith, hope, and love—and the greatest of these is love.

1 Corinthians 13:1-8, 13

By this we stand and fall

Christianity is the only religion that is built on something that is empty – Jesus' empty tomb. Other religions visit their founders' graves. Our God lives! The Bible does not explain the resurrection, the resurrection explains the Bible. The resurrection is not a note in the margin of the Christian faith, it *is* the Christian faith.

[12]But tell me this—since we preach that Christ rose from the dead, why are some of you saying there will be no resurrection of the dead? [13]For if there is no resurrection of the dead, then Christ has not been raised either. [14]And if Christ has not been raised, then all our preaching is useless, and your faith is useless. [17]And if Christ has not been raised, then your faith is useless and you are still guilty of your sins.

[50]What I am saying, dear brothers and sisters, is that our physical bodies cannot inherit the Kingdom of God. These dying bodies cannot inherit what will last forever.

[51]But let me reveal to you a wonderful secret. We will not all die, but we will all be transformed! [52]It will happen in a moment, in the blink of an eye, when the last trumpet is blown. For when the trumpet sounds, those who have died will be raised to live forever. And we who are living will also be transformed. [53]For our dying bodies must be transformed into bodies that will never die; our mortal bodies must be transformed into immortal bodies.

1 Corinthians 15:12-14, 17, 50-53

Tough times

Tough times can't make God abandon you. Paul clearly teaches us that God's arms are around us in our struggles. He will always deliver us. Therefore you can also help others who are going through tough times. Your care reminds those who are struggling that God really does care for them!

[3]All praise to God, the Father of our Lord Jesus Christ. God is our merciful Father and the source of all comfort. [4]He comforts us in all our troubles so that we can comfort others. When they are troubled, we will be able to give them the same comfort God has given us.

[5]For the more we suffer for Christ, the more God will shower us with his comfort through Christ. [6]Even when we are weighed down with troubles, it is for your comfort and salvation! For when we ourselves are comforted, we will certainly comfort you. Then you can patiently endure the same things we suffer. [7]We are confident that as you share in our sufferings, you will also share in the comfort God gives us.

2 Corinthians 1:3-7

Fragile!
Handle with care!

Clay pots were the only containers available in Paul's time and they broke easily. Wine, grain and many other things were stored in these clay pots. The contents stored were much more important than the actual container. It's the same with us. Therefore, God's light shines through our cracks (2 Cor. 4:6).

4 ⁵We don't go around preaching about ourselves. We preach that Jesus Christ is Lord, and we ourselves are your servants for Jesus' sake. ⁶For God, who said, "Let there be light in the darkness," has made this light shine in our hearts so we could know the glory of God that is seen in the face of Jesus Christ.

⁷We now have this light shining in our hearts, but we ourselves are like fragile clay jars containing this great treasure. This makes it clear that our great power is from God, not from ourselves.

5 ¹⁶So we have stopped evaluating others from a human point of view. At one time we thought of Christ merely from a human point of view. How differently we know him now! ¹⁷This means that anyone who belongs to Christ has become a new person. The old life is gone; a new life has begun!

¹⁸And all of this is a gift from God, who brought us back to himself through Christ. And God has given us this task of reconciling people to him. ¹⁹For God was in Christ, reconciling the world to himself, no longer counting people's sins against them. ²⁰So we are Christ's ambassadors. We speak for Christ when we plead, "Come back to God!" ²¹For God made Christ, who never sinned, to be the offering for our sin, so that we could be made right with God through Christ.

Strength for your weakness

In 2 Corinthians 12 Paul tells of a God experience, and he speaks about the thorn in his flesh. No one knows what the thorn was. Some people believe that Paul suffered from epilepsy or bad eyesight, but in his weakness he discovered that God is strong, and that is all that matters.

[2] I was caught up to the third heaven fourteen years ago. Whether I was in my body or out of my body, I don't know—only God knows. [3] Yes, only God knows whether I was in my body or outside my body. But I do know [4] that I was caught up to paradise and heard things so astounding that they cannot be expressed in words, things no human is allowed to tell.

[5] That experience is worth boasting about, but I'm not going to do it. I will boast only about my weaknesses. [6] If I wanted to boast, I would be no fool in doing so, because I would be telling the truth. But I won't do it, because I don't want anyone to give me credit beyond what they can see in my life or hear in my message, [7] even though I have received such wonderful revelations from God. So to keep me from becoming proud, I was given a thorn in my flesh, a messenger from Satan to torment me and keep me from becoming proud.

[8] Three different times I begged the Lord to take it away. [9] Each time he said, "My grace is all you need. My power works best in weakness." So now I am glad to boast about my weaknesses, so that the power of Christ can work through me. [10] That's why I take pleasure in my weaknesses, and in the insults, hardships, persecutions, and troubles that I suffer for Christ. For when I am weak, then I am strong.

2 Corinthians 12:2-10

The old me is gone, long live the new me!

In Galatians Paul doesn't beat around the bush; he expresses his surprise at how quickly the people's faith cooled down. In chapter two he tries to explain his changed life by saying that his old life died. It was crucified with Jesus, but a new Paul was resurrected with Jesus!

1 ¹This letter is from Paul, an apostle. I was not appointed by any group of people or any human authority, but by Jesus Christ himself and by God the Father, who raised Jesus from the dead.

²All the brothers and sisters here join me in sending this letter to the churches of Galatia.

³May God our Father and the Lord Jesus Christ give you grace and peace. ⁴Jesus gave his life for our sins, just as God our Father planned, in order to rescue us from this evil world in which we live.

2 ¹⁷But suppose we seek to be made right with God through faith in Christ and then we are found guilty because we have abandoned the law. Would that mean Christ has led us into sin? Absolutely not! ¹⁸Rather, I am a sinner if I rebuild the old system of law I already tore down. ¹⁹For when I tried to keep the law, it condemned me. So I died to the law—I stopped trying to meet all its requirements—so that I might live for God. ²⁰My old self has been crucified with Christ. It is no longer I who live, but Christ lives in me. So I live in this earthly body by trusting in the Son of God, who loved me and gave himself for me.

²¹I do not treat the grace of God as meaningless. For if keeping the law could make us right with God, then there was no need for Christ to die.

Galatians 1:1-4; 2:17-21

What sort of fruit grows on your tree?

The Holy Spirit makes our lives brand new. Just like fruit growing on a tree is a sign that the tree is healthy, the Spirit produces fruit as a sign of the new life in us. From the nine qualities in Galatians 5:22-23 people will be able to see how much you love Jesus and also how serious you are about living like He did.

13For you have been called to live in freedom, my brothers and sisters. But don't use your freedom to satisfy your sinful nature. Instead, use your freedom to serve one another in love. 14For the whole law can be summed up in this one command: "Love your neighbor as yourself."

16So I say, let the Holy Spirit guide your lives. Then you won't be doing what your sinful nature craves. 17The sinful nature wants to do evil, which is just the opposite of what the Spirit wants. And the Spirit gives us desires that are the opposite of what the sinful nature desires. These two forces are constantly fighting each other, so you are not free to carry out your good intentions. 18But when you are directed by the Spirit, you are not under obligation to the law of Moses.

22But the Holy Spirit produces this kind of fruit in our lives: love, joy, peace, patience, kindness, goodness, faithfulness, 23gentleness, and self-control. There is no law against these things!

24Those who belong to Christ Jesus have nailed the passions and desires of their sinful nature to his cross and crucified them there. 25Since we are living by the Spirit, let us follow the Spirit's leading in every part of our lives. 26Let us not become conceited, or provoke one another, or be jealous of one another.

Galatians 5:13-14, 16-18, 22-26

You reap what you sow

If you sow goodness, you will definitely reap good somewhere down the line. But if you continuously sow the weed of unkindness in-between the goodness, the weed will soon take over. This is the way that weeds work. Therefore Paul reminds believers to not grow tired of doing good!

¹Dear brothers and sisters, if another believer is overcome by some sin, you who are godly should gently and humbly help that person back onto the right path. And be careful not to fall into the same temptation yourself. ²Share each other's burdens, and in this way obey the law of Christ. ³If you think you are too important to help someone, you are only fooling yourself. You are not that important.

⁴Pay careful attention to your own work, for then you will get the satisfaction of a job well done, and you won't need to compare yourself to anyone else. ⁵For we are each responsible for our own conduct.

⁶Those who are taught the word of God should provide for their teachers, sharing all good things with them.

⁷Don't be misled—you cannot mock the justice of God. You will always harvest what you plant. ⁸Those who live only to satisfy their own sinful nature will harvest decay and death from that sinful nature. But those who live to please the Spirit will harvest everlasting life from the Spirit. ⁹So let's not get tired of doing what is good. At just the right time we will reap a harvest of blessing if we don't give up. ¹⁰Therefore, whenever we have the opportunity, we should do good to everyone—especially to those in the family of faith.

Galatians 6:1-10

Greatest deposit of all time

God doesn't buy anything without paying for it in full. Therefore, He did not just ransom us from our debt of sin with Jesus' blood, but He also made the greatest deposit imaginable. The Holy Spirit was the deposit, the guarantee (*arrabon* was a term used in ancient economy) meaning the "sales transaction" was settled.

³All praise to God, the Father of our Lord Jesus Christ, who has blessed us with every spiritual blessing in the heavenly realms because we are united with Christ. ⁴Even before he made the world, God loved us and chose us in Christ to be holy and without fault in his eyes. ⁵God decided in advance to adopt us into his own family by bringing us to himself through Jesus Christ. This is what he wanted to do, and it gave him great pleasure.

⁶So we praise God for the glorious grace he has poured out on us who belong to his dear Son. ⁷He is so rich in kindness and grace that he purchased our freedom with the blood of his Son and forgave our sins. ⁸He has showered his kindness on us, along with all wisdom and understanding. ⁹God has now revealed to us his mysterious plan regarding Christ, a plan to fulfill his own good pleasure.

¹³And now you Gentiles have also heard the truth, the Good News that God saves you. And when you believed in Christ, he identified you as his own by giving you the Holy Spirit, whom he promised long ago. ¹⁴The Spirit is God's guarantee that he will give us the inheritance he promised and that he has purchased us to be his own people. He did this so we would praise and glorify him.

Ephesians 1:3-9, 13-14

The staircase to God

The prayer in Ephesians 3 works like a staircase. On the first step lies the blessing of *power* that you can hold on to. On the second step lies the *faith* to see all that God has done and still will do. Then lies *love* to understand how much God loves us. On the next step lies the *fullness of God* that allows us to live with joy. Right at the top of the staircase is *God*, so that you will never think that God is small!

¹⁴When I think of all this, I fall to my knees and pray to the Father, ¹⁵the Creator of everything in heaven and on earth. ¹⁶I pray that from his glorious, unlimited resources he will empower you with inner strength through his Spirit. ¹⁷Then Christ will make his home in your hearts as you trust in him. Your roots will grow down into God's love and keep you strong.

¹⁸And may you have the power to understand, as all God's people should, how wide, how long, how high, and how deep his love is. ¹⁹May you experience the love of Christ, though it is too great to understand fully. Then you will be made complete with all the fullness of life and power that comes from God.

²⁰Now all glory to God, who is able, through his mighty power at work within us, to accomplish infinitely more than we might ask or think. ²¹Glory to him in the church and in Christ Jesus through all generations forever and ever! Amen.

Ephesians 3:14-21

We don't all
have to be the same

Unity doesn't mean that everyone has to be the same and think the same. No, it implies that we respect and appreciate each other's uniqueness. It also means that there are no bad feelings, irreconcilable differences, or division between believers.

¹Therefore I, a prisoner for serving the Lord, beg you to lead a life worthy of your calling, for you have been called by God. ²Always be humble and gentle. Be patient with each other, making allowance for each other's faults because of your love. ³Make every effort to keep yourselves united in the Spirit, binding yourselves together with peace. ⁴For there is one body and one Spirit, just as you have been called to one glorious hope for the future. ⁵There is one Lord, one faith, one baptism, ⁶and one God and Father, who is over all and in all and living through all.

⁷However, he has given each one of us a special gift through the generosity of Christ.

¹⁵Instead, we will speak the truth in love, growing in every way more and more like Christ, who is the head of his body, the church. ¹⁶He makes the whole body fit together perfectly. As each part does its own special work, it helps the other parts grow, so that the whole body is healthy and growing and full of love.

¹⁷With the Lord's authority I say this: Live no longer as the Gentiles do, for they are hopelessly confused.

Ephesians 4:1-7, 15-17

There is a visible difference

There is a very visible difference between how Christians and non-Christians live. At least, there should be a difference! Christians should stand out as images of God (Eph. 4:24).

4 ²¹Since you have heard about Jesus and have learned the truth that comes from him, ²²throw off your old sinful nature and your former way of life, which is corrupted by lust and deception. ²³Instead, let the Spirit renew your thoughts and attitudes. ²⁴Put on your new nature, created to be like God—truly righteous and holy.

²⁵So stop telling lies. Let us tell our neighbors the truth, for we are all parts of the same body. ²⁶And "don't sin by letting anger control you." Don't let the sun go down while you are still angry, ²⁷for anger gives a foothold to the devil.

²⁸If you are a thief, quit stealing. Instead, use your hands for good hard work, and then give generously to others in need. ²⁹Don't use foul or abusive language. Let everything you say be good and helpful, so that your words will be an encouragement to those who hear them.

³¹Get rid of all bitterness, rage, anger, harsh words, and slander, as well as all types of evil behavior. ³²Instead, be kind to each other, tenderhearted, forgiving one another, just as God through Christ has forgiven you.

5 ¹Imitate God, therefore, in everything you do, because you are his dear children.

Ephesians 4:21-29, 31–5:1

True light

In Ephesians 5, Paul reminds us that we work for God's Light company, a light company that has power 24/7. Don't live in darkness! Plug in to the true Source of power. Paul describes a condition without Christ as darkness. But if the light of Jesus shines on you, you live without fear and walk in the light.

[8]For once you were full of darkness, but now you have light from the Lord. So live as people of light! [9]For this light within you produces only what is good and right and true.

[10]Carefully determine what pleases the Lord. [11]Take no part in the worthless deeds of evil and darkness; instead, expose them. [12]It is shameful even to talk about the things that ungodly people do in secret. [13]But their evil intentions will be exposed when the light shines on them, [14]for the light makes everything visible. This is why it is said, "Awake, O sleeper, rise up from the dead, and Christ will give you light."

[15]So be careful how you live. Don't live like fools, but like those who are wise. [16]Make the most of every opportunity in these evil days. [17]Don't act thoughtlessly, but understand what the Lord wants you to do. [18]Don't be drunk with wine, because that will ruin your life. Instead, be filled with the Holy Spirit, [19]singing psalms and hymns and spiritual songs among yourselves, and making music to the Lord in your hearts. [20]And give thanks for everything to God the Father in the name of our Lord Jesus Christ.

Ephesians 5:8-20

Be prepared

In the Scripture verses below Paul uses an image that the people of his time were very familiar with – a Roman soldier. And it was even more familiar to Paul because when he was imprisoned, he was handcuffed to a Roman soldier's wrist! Paul matches this with spiritual meaning. Remember to put your armor on 24/7.

[11]Put on all of God's armor so that you will be able to stand firm against all strategies of the devil. [12]For we are not fighting against flesh-and-blood enemies, but against evil rulers and authorities of the unseen world, against mighty powers in this dark world, and against evil spirits in the heavenly places.

[13]Therefore, put on every piece of God's armor so you will be able to resist the enemy in the time of evil. Then after the battle you will still be standing firm. [14]Stand your ground, putting on the belt of truth and the body armor of God's righteousness. [15]For shoes, put on the peace that comes from the Good News so that you will be fully prepared. [16]In addition to all of these, hold up the shield of faith to stop the fiery arrows of the devil. [17]Put on salvation as your helmet, and take the sword of the Spirit, which is the word of God.

[18]Pray in the Spirit at all times and on every occasion. Stay alert and be persistent in your prayers for all believers everywhere.

[19]And pray for me, too. Ask God to give me the right words so I can boldly explain God's mysterious plan that the Good News is for Jews and Gentiles alike. [20]I am in chains now, still preaching this message as God's ambassador. So pray that I will keep on speaking boldly for him, as I should.

Ephesians 6:11-20

God finishes what He starts

Of one thing every believer can be sure – God will finish the work He has begun in every one of us. God doesn't just leave us on the side of the road when we fall down. The Bible is full of stories of people who "fell down", like Jacob and David, and God was with them until the end. God loves us in spite of our mistakes.

[3]Every time I think of you, I give thanks to my God. [4]Whenever I pray, I make my requests for all of you with joy, [5]for you have been my partners in spreading the Good News about Christ from the time you first heard it until now. [6]And I am certain that God, who began the good work within you, will continue his work until it is finally finished on the day when Christ Jesus returns.

[7]So it is right that I should feel as I do about all of you, for you have a special place in my heart. You share with me the special favor of God, both in my imprisonment and in defending and confirming the truth of the Good News. [8]God knows how much I love you and long for you with the tender compassion of Christ Jesus.

[9]I pray that your love will overflow more and more, and that you will keep on growing in knowledge and understanding. [10]For I want you to understand what really matters, so that you may live pure and blameless lives until the day of Christ's return. [11]May you always be filled with the fruit of your salvation—the righteous character produced in your life by Jesus Christ—for this will bring much glory and praise to God.

Philippians 1:3-11

This song tells a story

In Philippians 2 Paul tries to do the impossible. He tries to describe what Christ had in mind when He became human. That's a tall order! Paul isn't quite sure how to say it, so he turns to an early Christian praise song (vv. 6-11). Follow Jesus – that's what it means to bow your knee.

¹Is there any encouragement from belonging to Christ? Any comfort from his love? Any fellowship together in the Spirit? Are your hearts tender and compassionate? ²Then make me truly happy by agreeing wholeheartedly with each other, loving one another, and working together with one mind and purpose.

³Don't be selfish; don't try to impress others. Be humble, thinking of others as better than yourselves. ⁴Don't look out only for your own interests, but take an interest in others, too.

⁵You must have the same attitude that Christ Jesus had. ⁶Though he was God, he did not think of equality with God as something to cling to. ⁷Instead, he gave up his divine privileges; he took the humble position of a slave and was born as a human being. When he appeared in human form, ⁸he humbled himself in obedience to God and died a criminal's death on a cross.

⁹Therefore, God elevated him to the place of highest honor and gave him the name above all other names, ¹⁰that at the name of Jesus every knee should bow, in heaven and on earth and under the earth, ¹¹and every tongue confess that Jesus Christ is Lord, to the glory of God the Father.

Philippians 2:1-11

The finish line lies ahead

No one wins a race by looking back or by running backwards. The finish line is always in front and a person only gets to it by running forward. To help you stay focused, make Christ your all and don't think about how great you are. Greatness will get you nowhere, so focus on Jesus.

[7]I once thought these things were valuable, but now I consider them worthless because of what Christ has done. [8]Yes, everything else is worthless when compared with the infinite value of knowing Christ Jesus my Lord. For his sake I have discarded everything else, counting it all as garbage, so that I could gain Christ [9]and become one with him. I no longer count on my own righteousness through obeying the law; rather, I become righteous through faith in Christ. For God's way of making us right with himself depends on faith.

[10]I want to know Christ and experience the mighty power that raised him from the dead. I want to suffer with him, sharing in his death, [11]so that one way or another I will experience the resurrection from the dead!

[12]I don't mean to say that I have already achieved these things or that I have already reached perfection. But I press on to possess that perfection for which Christ Jesus first possessed me. [13]No, dear brothers and sisters, I have not achieved it, but I focus on this one thing: Forgetting the past and looking forward to what lies ahead, [14]I press on to reach the end of the race and receive the heavenly prize for which God, through Christ Jesus, is calling us.

Philippians 3:7-14

There are always going to be problems and things to complain about. And there will be good things too – things to be thankful for. It is our choice whether to be positive or negative! Guide your thoughts according to Philippians 4:8. What you think will determine how you act.

[1]Therefore, my dear brothers and sisters, stay true to the Lord. I love you and long to see you, dear friends, for you are my joy and the crown I receive for my work.

[2]Now I appeal to Euodia and Syntyche. Please, because you belong to the Lord, settle your disagreement. [3]And I ask you, my true partner, to help these two women, for they worked hard with me in telling others the Good News. They worked along with Clement and the rest of my co-workers, whose names are written in the Book of Life.

[4]Always be full of joy in the Lord. I say it again—rejoice! [5]Let everyone see that you are considerate in all you do. Remember, the Lord is coming soon.

[6]Don't worry about anything; instead, pray about everything. Tell God what you need, and thank him for all he has done. [7]Then you will experience God's peace, which exceeds anything we can understand. His peace will guard your hearts and minds as you live in Christ Jesus.

[8]And now, dear brothers and sisters, one final thing. Fix your thoughts on what is true, and honorable, and right, and pure, and lovely, and admirable. Think about things that are excellent and worthy of praise. [9]Keep putting into practice all you learned and received from me—everything you heard from me and saw me doing. Then the God of peace will be with you.

Philippians 4:1-9

From, in, by and through

In Colossians 1 Paul again uses a well-known Christian song that was popular during his time. Today we no longer know how the tune went, but through Paul's help we at least have the song's deep words. Its meaning can be summed up like this: To be a Christian means to be from Christ, in Christ, by Christ and through Christ.

[11]We also pray that you will be strengthened with all his glorious power so you will have all the endurance and patience you need. May you be filled with joy, [12]always thanking the Father. He has enabled you to share in the inheritance that belongs to his people, who live in the light. [13]For he has rescued us from the kingdom of darkness and transferred us into the Kingdom of his dear Son, [14]who purchased our freedom and forgave our sins.

[15]Christ is the visible image of the invisible God. He existed before anything was created and is supreme over all creation, [16]for through him God created everything in the heavenly realms and on earth. He made the things we can see and the things we can't see—such as thrones, kingdoms, rulers, and authorities in the unseen world. Everything was created through him and for him. [17]He existed before anything else, and he holds all creation together. [18]Christ is also the head of the church, which is his body. He is the beginning, supreme over all who rise from the dead. So he is first in everything.

[19]For God in all his fullness was pleased to live in Christ, [20]and through him God reconciled everything to himself. He made peace with everything in heaven and on earth by means of Christ's blood on the cross.

Colossians 1:11-20

Dressed
in the best

In Colossians 3 Paul compares our old lives with dirty clothes that we must take off and throw out. It is not fitting for a believer to walk around in dirty clothes. Rather put on the new clothes that have the brand name *Jesus* on. God has given you a cupboard full of new clothes – wear them 24/7.

⁵So put to death the sinful, earthly things lurking within you. Have nothing to do with sexual immorality, impurity, lust, and evil desires. Don't be greedy, for a greedy person is an idolater, worshiping the things of this world. ⁶Because of these sins, the anger of God is coming.

⁷You used to do these things when your life was still part of this world. ⁸But now is the time to get rid of anger, rage, malicious behavior, slander, and dirty language. ⁹Don't lie to each other, for you have stripped off your old sinful nature and all its wicked deeds. ¹⁰Put on your new nature, and be renewed as you learn to know your Creator and become like him. ¹¹In this new life, it doesn't matter if you are a Jew or a Gentile, circumcised or uncircumcised, barbaric, uncivilized, slave, or free. Christ is all that matters, and he lives in all of us.

¹²Since God chose you to be the holy people he loves, you must clothe yourselves with tenderhearted mercy, kindness, humility, gentleness, and patience. ¹³Make allowance for each other's faults, and forgive anyone who offends you. Remember, the Lord forgave you, so you must forgive others. ¹⁴Above all, clothe yourselves with love, which binds us all together in perfect harmony.

Colossians 3:5-14

Your relationships

In the Scripture passage below Paul emphasizes that all your relationships must bear the stamp of your new life in Jesus. That's why the word "Lord" is used so often in the passage before; it emphasizes the fact that in all our relationships our behavior must reflect the will of God.

3 [16]Let the message about Christ, in all its richness, fill your lives. Teach and counsel each other with all the wisdom he gives. Sing psalms and hymns and spiritual songs to God with thankful hearts. [17]And whatever you do or say, do it as a representative of the Lord Jesus, giving thanks through him to God the Father.

[18]Wives, submit to your husbands, as is fitting for those who belong to the Lord.

[19]Husbands, love your wives and never treat them harshly.

[20]Children, always obey your parents, for this pleases the Lord. [21]Fathers, do not aggravate your children, or they will become discouraged.

[22]Slaves, obey your earthly masters in everything you do. Try to please them all the time, not just when they are watching you. Serve them sincerely because of your reverent fear of the Lord. [23]Work willingly at whatever you do, as though you were working for the Lord rather than for people. [24]Remember that the Lord will give you an inheritance as your reward, and that the Master you are serving is Christ.

4 [1]Masters, be just and fair to your slaves. Remember that you also have a Master—in heaven.

Colossians 3:16-24; 4:1

The three signs

Paul knew the believers in Thessalonica belonged to God because of these three signs:

1. Their deeds showed they believed.
2. Their love showed they cared for their community and they tried to make a difference.
3. Their hope was strong. The result of this is that they became an example to others.

³As we pray to our God and Father about you, we think of your faithful work, your loving deeds, and the enduring hope you have because of our Lord Jesus Christ.

⁴We know, dear brothers and sisters, that God loves you and has chosen you to be his own people. ⁵For when we brought you the Good News, it was not only with words but also with power, for the Holy Spirit gave you full assurance that what we said was true. And you know of our concern for you from the way we lived when we were with you. ⁶So you received the message with joy from the Holy Spirit in spite of the severe suffering it brought you. In this way, you imitated both us and the Lord. ⁷As a result, you have become an example to all the believers in Greece—throughout both Macedonia and Achaia.

⁸And now the word of the Lord is ringing out from you to people everywhere, for wherever we go we find people telling us about your faith in God. We don't need to tell them about it, ⁹for they keep talking about the wonderful welcome you gave us and how you turned away from idols to serve the living and true God. ¹⁰And they speak of how you are looking forward to the coming of God's Son from heaven—Jesus, whom God raised from the dead. He is the one who has rescued us from the terrors of the coming judgment.

1 Thessalonians 1:3-10

We cry differently

Christians cry differently at a funeral. We cry tears of hope, because we know that we will see the person again. We know that death is a highway to heaven, and not a dead-end street. As Christians, we do not say a final goodbye, but only "bye for now" because we will meet again in heaven.

¹Finally, dear brothers and sisters, we urge you in the name of the Lord Jesus to live in a way that pleases God, as we have taught you. You live this way already, and we encourage you to do so even more.

¹⁴For since we believe that Jesus died and was raised to life again, we also believe that when Jesus returns, God will bring back with him the believers who have died.

¹⁵We tell you this directly from the Lord: We who are still living when the Lord returns will not meet him ahead of those who have died. ¹⁶For the Lord himself will come down from heaven with a commanding shout, with the voice of the archangel, and with the trumpet call of God. First, the Christians who have died will rise from their graves. ¹⁷Then, together with them, we who are still alive and remain on the earth will be caught up in the clouds to meet the Lord in the air. Then we will be with the Lord forever. ¹⁸So encourage each other with these words.

1 Thessalonians 4:1, 14-18

The Second Coming is a fact – just like the fact that the sun rises and sets every day. That's why we should live our lives as if Jesus could return at any moment. Such an attitude makes a heavenly difference to your life and other people's lives.

[1]Now concerning how and when all this will happen, dear brothers and sisters, we don't really need to write you. [2]For you know quite well that the day of the Lord's return will come unexpectedly, like a thief in the night. [3]When people are saying, "Everything is peaceful and secure," then disaster will fall on them as suddenly as a pregnant woman's labor pains begin. And there will be no escape.

[4]But you aren't in the dark about these things, dear brothers and sisters, and you won't be surprised when the day of the Lord comes like a thief. [5]For you are all children of the light and of the day; we don't belong to darkness and night. [6]So be on your guard, not asleep like the others. Stay alert and be clearheaded. [7]Night is the time when people sleep and drinkers get drunk. [8]But let us who live in the light be clearheaded, protected by the armor of faith and love, and wearing as our helmet the confidence of our salvation.

[9]For God chose to save us through our Lord Jesus Christ, not to pour out his anger on us. [10]Christ died for us so that, whether we are dead or alive when he returns, we can live with him forever. [11]So encourage each other and build each other up, just as you are already doing.

1 Thessalonians 5:1-11

These three things are necessary

Always be glad because nothing and no one can take away your joy. Never stop praying. Be connected to God 24/7. Be thankful in all circumstances. Hear the refrain in the three verses (1 Thess. 5:16-18): always, never stop, all circumstances. This is God's will for you. God's will is joy, prayer and thankfulness.

[12]Dear brothers and sisters, honor those who are your leaders in the Lord's work. They work hard among you and give you spiritual guidance. [13]Show them great respect and wholehearted love because of their work. And live peacefully with each other.

[14]Brothers and sisters, we urge you to warn those who are lazy. Encourage those who are timid. Take tender care of those who are weak. Be patient with everyone.

[15]See that no one pays back evil for evil, but always try to do good to each other and to all people.

[16]Always be joyful. [17]Never stop praying. [18]Be thankful in all circumstances, for this is God's will for you who belong to Christ Jesus.

[19]Do not stifle the Holy Spirit. [20]Do not scoff at prophecies, [21]but test everything that is said. Hold on to what is good. [22]Stay away from every kind of evil.

[23]Now may the God of peace make you holy in every way, and may your whole spirit and soul and body be kept blameless until our Lord Jesus Christ comes again. [24]God will make this happen, for he who calls you is faithful.

1 Thessalonians 5:12-24

Characteristics of a Christian

Paul encouraged the believers in Thessalonica by showing them what they were doing well (the characteristics of a Christian), so that they would continue to give their best.

1. Their faith increased.
2. Their love for each other increased.
3. They didn't give up – they persevered.
4. They loved things that were good.

³Dear brothers and sisters, we can't help but thank God for you, because your faith is flourishing and your love for one another is growing. ⁴We proudly tell God's other churches about your endurance and faithfulness in all the persecutions and hardships you are suffering. ⁵And God will use this persecution to show his justice and to make you worthy of his Kingdom, for which you are suffering. ⁶In his justice he will pay back those who persecute you.

⁷And God will provide rest for you who are being persecuted and also for us when the Lord Jesus appears from heaven. He will come with his mighty angels.

¹⁰When he comes on that day, he will receive glory from his holy people—praise from all who believe. And this includes you, for you believed what we told you about him.

¹¹So we keep on praying for you, asking our God to enable you to live a life worthy of his call. May he give you the power to accomplish all the good things your faith prompts you to do.

2 Thessalonians 1:3-7, 10-11

Don't stop working
on this relationship

Timothy was the son that Paul never had. Therefore he spoke to Timothy like a loving father
would to his son. He constantly showed Timothy
how to work on His relationship with the Lord,
because the deeper our relationship with the Lord
is, the clearer our consciences (v. 19).

¹This letter is from Paul, an apostle of Christ Jesus, appointed
by the command of God our Savior and Christ Jesus, who gives
us hope.

²I am writing to Timothy, my true son in the faith. May God
the Father and Christ Jesus our Lord give you grace, mercy,
and peace.

³When I left for Macedonia, I urged you to stay there in
Ephesus and stop those whose teaching is contrary to the truth.

¹⁷All honor and glory to God forever and ever! He is the eternal King, the unseen one who never dies; he alone is God.
Amen.

¹⁸Timothy, my son, here are my instructions for you, based on
the prophetic words spoken about you earlier. May they help
you fight well in the Lord's battles. ¹⁹Cling to your faith in Christ,
and keep your conscience clear. For some people have deli-
berately violated their consciences; as a result, their faith has
been shipwrecked.

1 Timothy 1:1-3, 17-19

There is no one like Jesus

As you read the passage below you will realize one thing: there is no one like Jesus. He deserves nothing less than your complete, undivided love! The last part of 1 Timothy 3:16 was probably a Christian song that the early church sang to help them focus on the uniqueness of Jesus and His story.

2 ¹I urge you, first of all, to pray for all people. Ask God to help them; intercede on their behalf, and give thanks for them. ²Pray this way for kings and all who are in authority so that we can live peaceful and quiet lives marked by godliness and dignity. ³This is good and pleases God our Savior, ⁴who wants everyone to be saved and to understand the truth. ⁵For there is only one God and one Mediator who can reconcile God and humanity—the man Christ Jesus. ⁶He gave his life to purchase freedom for everyone. This is the message God gave to the world at just the right time.

3 ¹⁴I am writing these things to you now, even though I hope to be with you soon, ¹⁵so that if I am delayed, you will know how people must conduct themselves in the household of God. This is the church of the living God, which is the pillar and foundation of the truth.

¹⁶Without question, this is the great mystery of our faith: Christ was revealed in a human body and vindicated by the Spirit. He was seen by angels and announced to the nations. He was believed in throughout the world and taken to heaven in glory.

1 Timothy 2:1-6; 3:14-16

A significant difference

Many people think life is all about being success-ful and wealthy. But material things can only make you happy to a certain point. Instead, be someone who makes a significant impact on the world while you are here.

⁶Yet true godliness with contentment is itself great wealth. ⁷After all, we brought nothing with us when we came into the world, and we can't take anything with us when we leave it. ⁸So if we have enough food and clothing, let us be content.

⁹But people who long to be rich fall into temptation and are trapped by many foolish and harmful desires that plunge them into ruin and destruction. ¹⁰For the love of money is the root of all kinds of evil. And some people, craving money, have wandered from the true faith and pierced themselves with many sorrows.

¹¹But you, Timothy, are a man of God; so run from all these evil things. Pursue righteousness and a godly life, along with faith, love, perseverance, and gentleness. ¹²Fight the good fight for the true faith. Hold tightly to the eternal life to which God has called you, which you have confessed so well before many witnesses.

¹³And I charge you before God, who gives life to all, and before Christ Jesus, who gave a good testimony before Pontius Pilate, ¹⁴that you obey this command without wavering. Then no one can find fault with you from now until our Lord Jesus Christ comes again.

1 Timothy 6:6-14

Potential for growth

Don't give up, because the Spirit gives you the following: the same power that resurrected Jesus from the dead; the same love that God has for you; and self-control to do what God expects from you. Therefore you should never be too shy to share the gospel with others. Words are not always necessary, because your life should be a message too!

³Timothy, I thank God for you—the God I serve with a clear conscience, just as my ancestors did. Night and day I constantly remember you in my prayers.

⁵I remember your genuine faith, for you share the faith that first filled your grandmother Lois and your mother, Eunice. And I know that same faith continues strong in you. ⁶This is why I remind you to fan into flames the spiritual gift God gave you when I laid my hands on you. ⁷For God has not given us a spirit of fear and timidity, but of power, love, and self-discipline.

⁸So never be ashamed to tell others about our Lord. And don't be ashamed of me, either, even though I'm in prison for him. With the strength God gives you, be ready to suffer with me for the sake of the Good News. ⁹For God saved us and called us to live a holy life. He did this, not because we deserved it, but because that was his plan from before the beginning of time— to show us his grace through Christ Jesus.

¹⁰And now he has made all of this plain to us by the appearing of Christ Jesus, our Savior. He broke the power of death and illuminated the way to life and immortality through the Good News.

2 Timothy 1:3, 5-10

December

Believers are ...

Stay focused on Jesus, just like a good soldier performs his task no matter what the circumstances. Always follow the rules, just like an athlete. You will, like a farmer, enjoy a good harvest. And you can know that God will stand by you through thick and thin.

[1]Timothy, my dear son, be strong through the grace that God gives you in Christ Jesus.

[3]Endure suffering along with me, as a good soldier of Christ Jesus. [4]Soldiers don't get tied up in the affairs of civilian life, for then they cannot please the officer who enlisted them. [5]And athletes cannot win the prize unless they follow the rules. [6]And hardworking farmers should be the first to enjoy the fruit of their labor.

[8]Always remember that Jesus Christ, a descendant of King David, was raised from the dead. This is the Good News I preach. [9]And because I preach this Good News, I am suffering and have been chained like a criminal. But the word of God cannot be chained. [10]So I am willing to endure anything if it will bring salvation and eternal glory in Christ Jesus to those God has chosen.

[11]This is a trustworthy saying: If we die with him, we will also live with him. [12]If we endure hardship, we will reign with him. If we deny him, he will deny us. [13]If we are unfaithful, he remains faithful, for he cannot deny who he is.

2 Timothy 2:1, 3-6, 8-13

The Bible is our Guidebook to an abundant life in Jesus. In the Bible we discover who Jesus is, what He does, how we can know Him personally, who we are, and what we should do in our relationships. But there's a warning: If you use it once, it can become addictive. But it also works like an energy drink – it keeps you going to the end!

3 ¹⁴But you must remain faithful to the things you have been taught. You know they are true, for you know you can trust those who taught you. ¹⁵You have been taught the holy Scriptures from childhood, and they have given you the wisdom to receive the salvation that comes by trusting in Christ Jesus. ¹⁶All Scripture is inspired by God and is useful to teach us what is true and to make us realize what is wrong in our lives. It corrects us when we are wrong and teaches us to do what is right. ¹⁷God uses it to prepare and equip his people to do every good work.

4 ¹I solemnly urge you in the presence of God and Christ Jesus, who will someday judge the living and the dead when he appears to set up his Kingdom: ²Preach the word of God. Be prepared, whether the time is favorable or not. Patiently correct, rebuke, and encourage your people with good teaching.

³For a time is coming when people will no longer listen to sound and wholesome teaching. They will follow their own desires and will look for teachers who will tell them whatever their itching ears want to hear. ⁴They will reject the truth and chase after myths.

⁵But you should keep a clear mind in every situation. Don't be afraid of suffering for the Lord. Work at telling others the Good News, and fully carry out the ministry God has given you.

2 Timothy 3:14-4:5

Keep your balance

Sometimes you might feel like a tightrope walker struggling to keep your balance. But God's grace, love and undeserved goodness allow you to stay focused. God makes you righteous and devoted so that you will be able to stay balanced on the tightrope of life. So always be God-confident and self-confident.

[11]For the grace of God has been revealed, bringing salvation to all people. [12]And we are instructed to turn from godless living and sinful pleasures. We should live in this evil world with wisdom, righteousness, and devotion to God, [13]while we look forward with hope to that wonderful day when the glory of our great God and Savior, Jesus Christ, will be revealed.

[14]He gave his life to free us from every kind of sin, to cleanse us, and to make us his very own people, totally committed to doing good deeds.

[15]You must teach these things and encourage the believers to do them. You have the authority to correct them when necessary, so don't let anyone disregard what you say.

Titus 2:11-15

If it wasn't for God's grace ...

In his letter, Paul refers no less than thirteen times to Titus, a convert from Greek heathenism. Titus is proof that God can turn a dead-end life around so that a person can live in the wide-open spaces of His grace!

¹Remind the believers to submit to the government and its officers. They should be obedient, always ready to do what is good. ²They must not slander anyone and must avoid quarreling. Instead, they should be gentle and show true humility to everyone.

³Once we, too, were foolish and disobedient. We were misled and became slaves to many lusts and pleasures. Our lives were full of evil and envy, and we hated each other.

⁴But—"When God our Savior revealed his kindness and love, ⁵he saved us, not because of the righteous things we had done, but because of his mercy. He washed away our sins, giving us a new birth and new life through the Holy Spirit. ⁶He generously poured out the Spirit upon us through Jesus Christ our Savior.

⁷Because of his grace he declared us righteous and gave us confidence that we will inherit eternal life." ⁸This is a trustworthy saying, and I want you to insist on these teachings so that all who trust in God will devote themselves to doing good. These teachings are good and beneficial for everyone.

Titus 3:1-8

From useless to useful

Paul let Philemon know that his runaway slave, Onesimus (meaning "Useful") had become a new person in Jesus Christ. For the first time he was living up to his name – Useful! Incidentally there is a story that "Useful" later became the bishop of a church in Smyrna. We don't know if that's true. But for God anything is possible!

¹⁰I appeal to you to show kindness to my child, Onesimus. I became his father in the faith while here in prison. ¹¹Onesimus hasn't been of much use to you in the past, but now he is very useful to both of us. ¹²I am sending him back to you, and with him comes my own heart.

¹³I wanted to keep him here with me while I am in these chains for preaching the Good News, and he would have helped me on your behalf. ¹⁴But I didn't want to do anything without your consent. I wanted you to help because you were willing, not because you were forced. ¹⁵It seems you lost Onesimus for a little while so that you could have him back forever. ¹⁶He is no longer like a slave to you. He is more than a slave, for he is a beloved brother, especially to me. Now he will mean much more to you, both as a man and as a brother in the Lord.

¹⁷So if you consider me your partner, welcome him as you would welcome me. ¹⁸If he has wronged you in any way or owes you anything, charge it to me. ¹⁹I, Paul, write this with my own hand: I will repay it. And I won't mention that you owe me your very soul!

²⁰Yes, my brother, please do me this favor for the Lord's sake. Give me this encouragement in Christ. ²¹I am confident as I write this letter that you will do what I ask and even more!

Philemon 10-21

The best older brother you can have

Jesus showed us how God meant for His people to live. In Jesus we can once again become the people God planned for us to become so long ago. No matter what life deals us, we have an older brother in Jesus; He will stand by us.

[6]For in one place the Scriptures say, "What are mere mortals that you should think about them, or a son of man that you should care for him? [7]Yet you made them only a little lower than the angels and crowned them with glory and honor. [8]You gave them authority over all things." Now when it says "all things," it means nothing is left out. But we have not yet seen all things put under their authority.

[9]What we do see is Jesus, who was given a position "a little lower than the angels"; and because he suffered death for us, he is now "crowned with glory and honor." Yes, by God's grace, Jesus tasted death for everyone. [10]God, for whom and through whom everything was made, chose to bring many children into glory. And it was only right that he should make Jesus, through his suffering, a perfect leader, fit to bring them into their salvation.

[11]So now Jesus and the ones he makes holy have the same Father. That is why Jesus is not ashamed to call them his brothers and sisters.

[16]We also know that the Son did not come to help angels; he came to help the descendants of Abraham. [17]Therefore, it was necessary for him to be made in every respect like us, his brothers and sisters, so that he could be our merciful and faithful High Priest before God. Then he could offer a sacrifice that would take away the sins of the people.

Hebrews 2:6-11, 16-17

Today is still the Lord's day

It's important to understand the word *today* (Heb. 4:7). It's as if the Hebrews writer wants to say: Don't ever think you arrived too late in the history of the world. Never think, *If only I had lived in those days* ... The time you live in is still God's "today"! God is still the same today as He was yesterday and way before. His Word looks right into our souls and teaches us this.

⁷So God set another time for entering his rest, and that time is today. God announced this through David much later in the words already quoted: "Today when you hear his voice, don't harden your hearts."

⁸Now if Joshua had succeeded in giving them this rest, God would not have spoken about another day of rest still to come. ⁹So there is a special rest still waiting for the people of God. ¹⁰For all who have entered into God's rest have rested from their labors, just as God did after creating the world. ¹¹So let us do our best to enter that rest. But if we disobey God, as the people of Israel did, we will fall.

¹²For the word of God is alive and powerful. It is sharper than the sharpest two-edged sword, cutting between soul and spirit, between joint and marrow. It exposes our innermost thoughts and desires. ¹³Nothing in all creation is hidden from God. Everything is naked and exposed before his eyes, and he is the one to whom we are accountable.

Hebrews 4:7-13

See more through faith

Faith is not a one-man show. No, your faith makes you part of a family. There are three good habits that believers should do together:

1. Spur each other on to love and do good deeds.
2. Worship together.
3. Encourage each other.

These three things strengthen your eyes of faith so that you can see things that others don't.

10 ¹⁹And so, dear brothers and sisters, we can boldly enter heaven's Most Holy Place because of the blood of Jesus. ²⁰By his death, Jesus opened a new and life-giving way through the curtain into the Most Holy Place.

²¹And since we have a great High Priest who rules over God's house, ²²let us go right into the presence of God with sincere hearts fully trusting him. For our guilty consciences have been sprinkled with Christ's blood to make us clean, and our bodies have been washed with pure water.

²³Let us hold tightly without wavering to the hope we affirm, for God can be trusted to keep his promise. ²⁴Let us think of ways to motivate one another to acts of love and good works.

11 ¹Faith is the confidence that what we hope for will actually happen; it gives us assurance about things we cannot see.

Hebrews 10:19-24; 11:1

Believers
run a marathon

Faith is not a 100m sprint you can finish quickly. No, it's a marathon. Keep your eyes focused on Jesus during the race. He is the example that inspires you not to give up. However, remember that you cannot run the race if you are carrying baggage with you. Give your baggage to Jesus. Run light. Always listen to the "running tips" from your Trainer – God the Father. It's for your own good!

[1] Therefore, since we are surrounded by such a huge crowd of witnesses to the life of faith, let us strip off every weight that slows us down, especially the sin that so easily trips us up. And let us run with endurance the race God has set before us. [2] We do this by keeping our eyes on Jesus, the champion who initiates and perfects our faith. Because of the joy awaiting him, he endured the cross, disregarding its shame. Now he is seated in the place of honor beside God's throne. [3] Think of all the hostility he endured from sinful people; then you won't become weary and give up.

[11] No discipline is enjoyable while it is happening—it's painful! But afterward there will be a peaceful harvest of right living for those who are trained in this way.

[12] So take a new grip with your tired hands and strengthen your weak knees. [13] Mark out a straight path for your feet so that those who are weak and lame will not fall but become strong.

Hebrews 12:1-3, 11-13

Make God happy

In the first few verses of Hebrews 13 the writer gives practical guidelines on how to live out your faith. Then he reminds us that God is always the same and makes the point that praising God is more than just making music and singing together. With what you say and do, let all glory fall on God. A life like this fills God's heart with joy!

¹Keep on loving each other as brothers and sisters. ²Don't forget to show hospitality to strangers, for some who have done this have entertained angels without realizing it! ³Remember those in prison, as if you were there yourself. Remember also those being mistreated, as if you felt their pain in your own bodies.

⁴Give honor to marriage, and remain faithful to one another in marriage. God will surely judge people who are immoral and those who commit adultery.

⁵Don't love money; be satisfied with what you have. For God has said, "I will never fail you. I will never abandon you."

⁷Remember your leaders who taught you the word of God. Think of all the good that has come from their lives, and follow the example of their faith.

⁸Jesus Christ is the same yesterday, today, and forever.

¹⁵Therefore, let us offer through Jesus a continual sacrifice of praise to God, proclaiming our allegiance to his name. ¹⁶And don't forget to do good and to share with those in need. These are the sacrifices that please God.

Hebrews 13:1-5, 7-8, 15-16

Wisdom is a gift from God

If you want more knowledge you have to learn more. Therefore you enroll in school or university. But wisdom is something different. You can only get it from God. He gives it to you for free when you serve Him. It allows you to make sense of the ups and downs of life so that you can live meaningfully here and now.

[1]This letter is from James, a slave of God and of the Lord Jesus Christ. I am writing to the "twelve tribes"—Jewish believers scattered abroad. Greetings!

[2]Dear brothers and sisters, when troubles come your way, consider it an opportunity for great joy. [3]For you know that when your faith is tested, your endurance has a chance to grow. [4]So let it grow, for when your endurance is fully developed, you will be perfect and complete, needing nothing.

[5]If you need wisdom, ask our generous God, and he will give it to you. He will not rebuke you for asking. [6]But when you ask him, be sure that your faith is in God alone. Do not waver, for a person with divided loyalty is as unsettled as a wave of the sea that is blown and tossed by the wind. [7]Such people should not expect to receive anything from the Lord. [8]Their loyalty is divided between God and the world, and they are unstable in everything they do.

James 1:1-8

A recipe for lemonade

Sometimes we get mad when life gives us lemons. In James 1:19 we are given a recipe for turning lemons into lemonade:

1. Step one: Be quick to listen. To who and what? We must listen to God!
2. Step two: Don't be too quick to speak. Hurtful words can't be taken back.
3. Step three: Don't get angry easily. Be patient. God will change your − into a +.

[19]Understand this, my dear brothers and sisters: You must all be quick to listen, slow to speak, and slow to get angry. [20]Human anger does not produce the righteousness God desires. [21]So get rid of all the filth and evil in your lives, and humbly accept the word God has planted in your hearts, for it has the power to save your souls.

[22]But don't just listen to God's word. You must do what it says. Otherwise, you are only fooling yourselves. [23]For if you listen to the word and don't obey, it is like glancing at your face in a mirror. [24]You see yourself, walk away, and forget what you look like. [25]But if you look carefully into the perfect law that sets you free, and if you do what it says and don't forget what you heard, then God will bless you for doing it.

[26]If you claim to be religious but don't control your tongue, you are fooling yourself, and your religion is worthless. [27]Pure and genuine religion in the sight of God the Father means caring for orphans and widows in their distress and refusing to let the world corrupt you.

James 1:19-27

Do you build up or break down?

Who do you work for: a demolition company or a construction company? Because your tongue can break someone down or build them up. Most of us would rather be known as a builder; someone who builds others up. So be careful, once you say something, you can't take it back.

¹Dear brothers and sisters, not many of you should become teachers in the church, for we who teach will be judged more strictly. ²Indeed, we all make many mistakes. For if we could control our tongues, we would be perfect and could also control ourselves in every other way.

³We can make a large horse go wherever we want by means of a small bit in its mouth. ⁴And a small rudder makes a huge ship turn wherever the pilot chooses to go, even though the winds are strong. ⁵In the same way, the tongue is a small thing that makes grand speeches.

But a tiny spark can set a great forest on fire. ⁶And the tongue is a flame of fire. It is a whole world of wickedness, corrupting your entire body. It can set your whole life on fire, for it is set on fire by hell itself.

⁷People can tame all kinds of animals, ⁸but no one can tame the tongue. It is restless and evil, full of deadly poison. ⁹Sometimes it praises our Lord and Father, and sometimes it curses those who have been made in the image of God. ¹⁰And so blessing and cursing come pouring out of the same mouth. Surely, this is not right! ¹¹Does a spring of water bubble out with both fresh water and bitter water? ¹²Does a fig tree produce olives, or a grapevine produce figs? No, and you can't draw fresh water from a salty spring.

James 3:1-12

Think twice

For Peter, Jesus is present but invisible (see 1 Pet. 1:8), but will become visible at His second coming. So we must live with the knowledge that Jesus is still with us, even though we can't see Him right now. Think a bit about the difference between "Jesus is gone" and "Jesus is invisible" when you have to make a decision.

³All praise to God, the Father of our Lord Jesus Christ. It is by his great mercy that we have been born again, because God raised Jesus Christ from the dead. Now we live with great expectation, ⁴and we have a priceless inheritance—an inheritance that is kept in heaven for you, pure and undefiled, beyond the reach of change and decay. ⁵And through your faith, God is protecting you by his power until you receive this salvation, which is ready to be revealed on the last day for all to see.

⁶So be truly glad. There is wonderful joy ahead, even though you have to endure many trials for a little while.

⁸You love him even though you have never seen him. Though you do not see him now, you trust him; and you rejoice with a glorious, inexpressible joy. ⁹The reward for trusting him will be the salvation of your souls.

¹³So think clearly and exercise self-control. Look forward to the gracious salvation that will come to you when Jesus Christ is revealed to the world. ¹⁴So you must live as God's obedient children. Don't slip back into your old ways of living to satisfy your own desires. You didn't know any better then. ¹⁵But now you must be holy in everything you do, just as God who chose you is holy.

1 Peter 1:3-6, 8-9, 13-15

Jesus' earthly address

God is not static or bound to a building, He is dynamic. He is on the move. Therefore the people who follow Him become His new address. This is what Peter emphasizes in 1 Peter 2:1-12. We are living bricks of the church. So we had better behave like followers of Jesus!

¹So get rid of all evil behavior. Be done with all deceit, hypocrisy, jealousy, and all unkind speech. ²Like newborn babies, you must crave pure spiritual milk so that you will grow into a full experience of salvation. Cry out for this nourishment, ³now that you have had a taste of the Lord's kindness.

⁴You are coming to Christ, who is the living cornerstone of God's temple. He was rejected by people, but he was chosen by God for great honor.

⁵And you are living stones that God is building into his spiritual temple. What's more, you are his holy priests. Through the mediation of Jesus Christ, you offer spiritual sacrifices that please God. ⁶As the Scriptures say, "I am placing a cornerstone in Jerusalem, chosen for great honor, and anyone who trusts in him will never be disgraced."

⁷Yes, you who trust him recognize the honor God has given him. But for those who reject him, "The stone that the builders rejected has now become the cornerstone."

1 Peter 2:1-7

Tracing the alphabet

Jesus is our example, or in Greek our *hupogram-mon*. A *hupogrammon* was a pattern or a stencil of the Greek alphabet that children used to trace to learn how to write. Christians should be like first graders doing their homework and tracing Jesus' life in their own lives.

¹⁸You who are slaves must accept the authority of your masters with all respect. Do what they tell you—not only if they are kind and reasonable, but even if they are cruel. ¹⁹For God is pleased with you when you do what you know is right and patiently endure unfair treatment. ²⁰Of course, you get no credit for being patient if you are beaten for doing wrong. But if you suffer for doing good and endure it patiently, God is pleased with you.

²¹For God called you to do good, even if it means suffering, just as Christ suffered for you. He is your example, and you must follow in his steps.

²²He never sinned, nor ever deceived anyone.

²³He did not retaliate when he was insulted, nor threaten revenge when he suffered. He left his case in the hands of God, who always judges fairly.

²⁴He personally carried our sins in his body on the cross so that we can be dead to sin and live for what is right. By his wounds you are healed.

²⁵Once you were like sheep who wandered away. But now you have turned to your Shepherd, the Guardian of your souls.

1 Peter 2:18-25

The five habits of believers

In an upside-down and confused world Peter gives five habits that will help us stand out for Jesus. We must:

1. be humble (1 Pet. 5:5)
2. not worry (v. 7)
3. stay alert (v. 8)
4. stand firm (v. 9)
5. persevere (v. 10)

⁵In the same way, you younger men must accept the authority of the elders. And all of you, serve each other in humility, for "God opposes the proud but favors the humble."

⁶So humble yourselves under the mighty power of God, and at the right time he will lift you up in honor. ⁷Give all your worries and cares to God, for he cares about you.

⁸Stay alert! Watch out for your great enemy, the devil. He prowls around like a roaring lion, looking for someone to devour. ⁹Stand firm against him, and be strong in your faith. Remember that your Christian brothers and sisters all over the world are going through the same kind of suffering you are.

¹⁰In his kindness God called you to share in his eternal glory by means of Christ Jesus. So after you have suffered a little while, he will restore, support, and strengthen you, and he will place you on a firm foundation. ¹¹All power to him forever! Amen.

1 Peter 5:5-11

God's ground crew

Believers are God's ground crew. 2 Peter 1:3-11 says in principle that God will not do anything without His ground crew, but that we (His ground crew) cannot do anything without God. St. Augustine illustrated this point well when he said, "Without God, we cannot. Without us, God will not."

³By his divine power, God has given us everything we need for living a godly life. We have received all of this by coming to know him, the one who called us to himself by means of his marvelous glory and excellence. ⁴And because of his glory and excellence, he has given us great and precious promises. These are the promises that enable you to share his divine nature and escape the world's corruption caused by human desires.

⁵In view of all this, make every effort to respond to God's promises. Supplement your faith with a generous provision of moral excellence, and moral excellence with knowledge, ⁶and knowledge with self-control, and self-control with patient endurance, and patient endurance with godliness, ⁷and godliness with brotherly affection, and brotherly affection with love for everyone.

⁸The more you grow like this, the more productive and useful you will be in your knowledge of our Lord Jesus Christ.

¹⁰So, dear brothers and sisters, work hard to prove that you really are among those God has called and chosen. Do these things, and you will never fall away.

2 Peter 1:3-8, 10

it's not news to God

God knows people inside-out; that's why we can confess to Him when we are struggling with sin. He will not just push us to the side; He will forgive us and give us a fresh start. Don't be so silly as to deny it!

¹We proclaim to you the one who existed from the beginning, whom we have heard and seen. We saw him with our own eyes and touched him with our own hands. He is the Word of life. ²This one who is life itself was revealed to us, and we have seen him. And now we testify and proclaim to you that he is the one who is eternal life. He was with the Father, and then he was revealed to us. ³We proclaim to you what we ourselves have actually seen and heard so that you may have fellowship with us. And our fellowship is with the Father and with his Son, Jesus Christ. ⁴We are writing these things so that you may fully share our joy.

⁵This is the message we heard from Jesus and now declare to you: God is light, and there is no darkness in him at all. ⁶So we are lying if we say we have fellowship with God but go on living in spiritual darkness; we are not practicing the truth. ⁷But if we are living in the light, as God is in the light, then we have fellowship with each other, and the blood of Jesus, his Son, cleanses us from all sin.

⁸If we claim we have no sin, we are only fooling ourselves and not living in the truth. ⁹But if we confess our sins to him, he is faithful and just to forgive us our sins and to cleanse us from all wickedness. ¹⁰If we claim we have not sinned, we are calling God a liar and showing that his word has no place in our hearts.

1 John 1:1-10

Live like Jesus

"If a man does not keep pace with his companions, perhaps it is because he hears a different drummer" (Henry Thoreau). Of Woodrow Wilson, the American president, it is said, "He speaks like Jesus Christ" because he listened to another Drummer. This meant that he acted differently to others, like Jesus did! May this be true of you too!

¹We have an advocate who pleads our case before the Father. He is Jesus Christ, the one who is truly righteous. ²He himself is the sacrifice that atones for our sins—and not only our sins but the sins of all the world.

³And we can be sure that we know him if we obey his commandments. ⁴If someone claims, "I know God," but doesn't obey God's commandments, that person is a liar and is not living in the truth. ⁵But those who obey God's word truly show how completely they love him. That is how we know we are living in him. ⁶Those who say they live in God should live their lives as Jesus did.

¹²I am writing to you who are God's children because your sins have been forgiven through Jesus. ¹³I am writing to you who are mature in the faith because you know Christ, who existed from the beginning. I am writing to you who are young in the faith because you have won your battle with the evil one.

¹⁴I have written to you who are God's children because you know the Father. I have written to you who are mature in the faith because you know Christ, who existed from the beginning. I have written to you who are young in the faith because you are strong. God's word lives in your hearts.

1 John 2:1-6, 12-14

Climb higher

The test of the authenticity of your love for God can be seen in how deep, wide, high and long your love for others stretches. We love God only as much as the person we love the least. Whatever we do for the least person, we do for God too! It makes you think, doesn't it? Remember, if you help someone up a hill, you climb higher too.

¹³So don't be surprised, dear brothers and sisters, if the world hates you.

¹⁴If we love our Christian brothers and sisters, it proves that we have passed from death to life. But a person who has no love is still dead.

¹⁶We know what real love is because Jesus gave up his life for us. So we also ought to give up our lives for our brothers and sisters. If someone has enough money to live well and sees a brother or sister in need but shows no compassion—how can God's love be in that person?

¹⁸Dear children, let's not merely say that we love each other; let us show the truth by our actions.

²²And we will receive from him whatever we ask because we obey him and do the things that please him.

²³And this is his commandment: We must believe in the name of his Son, Jesus Christ, and love one another, just as he commanded us. ²⁴Those who obey God's commandments remain in fellowship with him, and he with them. And we know he lives in us because the Spirit he gave us lives in us.

1 John 3:13-14, 16-18, 22-24

Love is not just a feeling, it is a choice

Love starts in one place: God. He teaches us how love works. He has made a choice to love us no matter what happens. Such love is called unconditional love. This is how we should love too! Unconditional means we choose to love someone even when we don't really want to.

[7]Dear friends, let us continue to love one another, for love comes from God. Anyone who loves is a child of God and knows God.

[10]This is real love—not that we loved God, but that he loved us and sent his Son as a sacrifice to take away our sins.

[11]Dear friends, since God loved us that much, we surely ought to love each other. [12]No one has ever seen God. But if we love each other, God lives in us, and his love is brought to full expression in us.

[13]And God has given us his Spirit as proof that we live in him and he in us.

[16]We know how much God loves us, and we have put our trust in his love. God is love, and all who live in love live in God, and God lives in them.

[17]And as we live in God, our love grows more perfect. So we will not be afraid on the day of judgment, but we can face him with confidence because we live like Jesus here in this world.

[19]We love each other because he loved us first.

1 John 4:7, 10-13, 16-17, 19

Love is to
live what you believe

"Elder" was the nickname Christians used for the white-haired apostle John. The "lady and her children" doesn't refer to a family, but a congregation. The truth without love is hard and ungracious and love without the truth is empty and meaningless. Love and Truth is a pair that can change the world, so that's how believers must live.

¹This letter is from John, the elder. I am writing to the chosen lady and to her children, whom I love in the truth—as does everyone else who knows the truth—²because the truth lives in us and will be with us forever.

³Grace, mercy, and peace, which come from God the Father and from Jesus Christ—the Son of the Father—will continue to be with us who live in truth and love.

⁴How happy I was to meet some of your children and find them living according to the truth, just as the Father commanded.

⁵I am writing to remind you, dear friends, that we should love one another. This is not a new commandment, but one we have had from the beginning. ⁶Love means doing what God has commanded us, and he has commanded us to love one another, just as you heard from the beginning.

2 John 1-6

A prayer request against the Diotrephes illness

In 3 John 2 there is a wish: "I hope all is well with you and that you are as healthy in body as you are strong in spirit." Who can achieve such a wish? Some people are so weak spiritually that these words seem more like a curse! Sometimes things are spiritually bad because of the Diotrephes illness – me at the center, and everything revolving around me. Rather put Jesus first, then you will be hospitable, practical and full of love for others.

²Dear friend, I hope all is well with you and that you are as healthy in body as you are strong in spirit.

⁵Dear friend, you are being faithful to God when you care for the traveling teachers who pass through, even though they are strangers to you. ⁶They have told the church here of your loving friendship. Please continue providing for such teachers in a manner that pleases God.

⁸So we ourselves should support them so that we can be their partners as they teach the truth.

⁹I wrote to the church about this, but Diotrephes, who loves to be the leader, refuses to have anything to do with us. ¹⁰When I come, I will report some of the things he is doing and the evil accusations he is making against us. Not only does he refuse to welcome the traveling teachers, he also tells others not to help them. And when they do help, he puts them out of the church.

¹¹Dear friend, don't let this bad example influence you. Follow only what is good. Remember that those who do good prove that they are God's children, and those who do evil prove that they do not know God.

3 John 2, 5-6, 8-11

That's grace!

The letters from Jude and James were probably written by Jesus' two brothers. James was the leader of the Jerusalem community and, after he was murdered, Jude took over. Jesus' brothers, who initially didn't believe (see Matt. 13:57), became important church leaders after His resurrection. This is grace! This is the same grace that makes all Christians family of Jesus!

[17]But you, my dear friends, must remember what the apostles of our Lord Jesus Christ said. [18]They told you that in the last times there would be scoffers whose purpose in life is to satisfy their ungodly desires. [19]These people are the ones who are creating divisions among you. They follow their natural instincts because they do not have God's Spirit in them.

[20]But you, dear friends, must build each other up in your most holy faith, pray in the power of the Holy Spirit, [21]and await the mercy of our Lord Jesus Christ, who will bring you eternal life. In this way, you will keep yourselves safe in God's love.

[22]And you must show mercy to those whose faith is wavering. [23]Rescue others by snatching them from the flames of judgment. Show mercy to still others, but do so with great caution, hating the sins that contaminate their lives.

[24]Now all glory to God, who is able to keep you from falling away and will bring you with great joy into his glorious presence without a single fault.

Jude 17-24

First and Last

Often no one wants to be the first to do something. You might ruin your reputation or maybe you are just too scared. But no one wants to be last either. Jesus says to His followers: "Don't be afraid! I am the First and the Last." We are safe with Jesus, because He's got the front and back line covered.

[12]When I turned to see who was speaking to me, I saw seven gold lampstands. [13]And standing in the middle of the lampstands was someone like the Son of Man. He was wearing a long robe with a gold sash across his chest. [14]His head and his hair were white like wool, as white as snow. And his eyes were like flames of fire. [15]His feet were like polished bronze refined in a furnace, and his voice thundered like mighty ocean waves. [16]He held seven stars in his right hand, and a sharp two-edged sword came from his mouth. And his face was like the sun in all its brilliance.

[17]When I saw him, I fell at his feet as if I were dead. But he laid his right hand on me and said, "Don't be afraid! I am the First and the Last. [18]I am the living one. I died, but look—I am alive forever and ever! And I hold the keys of death and the grave.

[19]"Write down what you have seen—both the things that are now happening and the things that will happen. [20]This is the meaning of the mystery of the seven stars you saw in my right hand and the seven gold lampstands: The seven stars are the angels of the seven churches, and the seven lampstands are the seven churches."

Revelation 1:12-20

A faithful and reliable witness

The "Amen" (see Rev. 3:14) means that Jesus' promises are true and that you can trust them. In biblical times three things were necessary to be a faithful and reliable witness:

1. You had to see for yourself what you were witnessing about.
2. You had to honestly and accurately share what you saw.
3. You had to have the ability to witness so that people actually listened.

Jesus could share about God – He is God's Son. We can count on His words. No one has ever spoken like He did!

[14]"Write this letter to the angel of the church in Laodicea. This is the message from the one who is the Amen—the faithful and true witness, the beginning of God's new creation:

[15]"I know all the things you do, that you are neither hot nor cold. I wish that you were one or the other! [16]But since you are like lukewarm water, neither hot nor cold, I will spit you out of my mouth! [19]I correct and discipline everyone I love. So be diligent and turn from your indifference.

[20]"Look! I stand at the door and knock. If you hear my voice and open the door, I will come in, and we will share a meal together as friends. [21]Those who are victorious will sit with me on my throne, just as I was victorious and sat with my Father on his throne.

[22]"Anyone with ears to hear must listen to the Spirit and understand what he is saying to the churches."

Revelation 3:14-16, 19-22

No one like God!

Even though John was reluctant to describe God Himself, he describes God's appearance. He does this by comparing God to different precious stones, each of which in those days had a fixed characteristic: Jasper (transparent – *purity*), carnelian (red – *judgment*), and emerald (green – *grace*).

¹Then as I looked, I saw a door standing open in heaven, and the same voice I had heard before spoke to me like a trumpet blast. The voice said, "Come up here, and I will show you what must happen after this."

²And instantly I was in the Spirit, and I saw a throne in heaven and someone sitting on it. ³The one sitting on the throne was as brilliant as gemstones—like jasper and carnelian. And the glow of an emerald circled his throne like a rainbow. ⁴Twenty-four thrones surrounded him, and twenty-four elders sat on them. They were all clothed in white and had gold crowns on their heads.

⁵From the throne came flashes of lightning and the rumble of thunder. And in front of the throne were seven torches with burning flames. This is the sevenfold Spirit of God. ⁶In front of the throne was a shiny sea of glass, sparkling like crystal.

Revelation 4:1-6

True life

True life is to praise God, and to praise God is to live! No wonder the rabbis in the ancient days always answered the question, "Where is the Lord?" with: "The Lord is seated on the throne through the praise of His children." Our praises confirm that Jesus is Lord; that He sits on the throne. Our praises remind us who the King is and helps us to truly live!

[8]And when he took the scroll, the four living beings and the twenty-four elders fell down before the Lamb. Each one had a harp, and they held gold bowls filled with incense, which are the prayers of God's people. [9]And they sang a new song with these words: "You are worthy to take the scroll and break its seals and open it. For you were slaughtered, and your blood has ransomed people for God from every tribe and language and people and nation. [10]And you have caused them to become a Kingdom of priests for our God. And they will reign on the earth."

[11]Then I looked again, and I heard the voices of thousands and millions of angels around the throne and of the living beings and the elders. [12]And they sang in a mighty chorus: "Worthy is the Lamb who was slaughtered—to receive power and riches and wisdom and strength and honor and glory and blessing."

[13]And then I heard every creature in heaven and on earth and under the earth and in the sea. They sang: "Blessing and honor and glory and power belong to the one sitting on the throne and to the Lamb forever and ever."

[14]And the four living beings said, "Amen!" And the twenty-four elders fell down and worshiped the Lamb.

Revelation 5:8-14

Heaven on earth

These two words – "heaven" and "earth" – can never be considered separately, because it is God's workplace. Like Eugene Peterson said, "Heaven is not simply a dream to retreat to when things get messy on earth. We have access to heaven now: it is the invisibility in which we are immersed, that is developing into visibility, and that one day will be thoroughly visible."

¹Then I saw a new heaven and a new earth, for the old heaven and the old earth had disappeared. And the sea was also gone. ²And I saw the holy city, the new Jerusalem, coming down from God out of heaven like a bride beautifully dressed for her husband.

³I heard a loud shout from the throne, saying, "Look, God's home is now among his people! He will live with them, and they will be his people. God himself will be with them. ⁴He will wipe every tear from their eyes, and there will be no more death or sorrow or crying or pain. All these things are gone forever."

⁵And the one sitting on the throne said, "Look, I am making everything new!" And then he said to me, "Write this down, for what I tell you is trustworthy and true."

Revelation 21:1-5

it's not about you!

Revelation points out the following: It's about God – and worshiping Him alone. Obedience starts with the first day of the week's worship; it forms and determines the rest of your week and life. Therefore this book wants to emphasize just one thing: Focus on God! This makes you happy and brings you success.

[12]"Look, I am coming soon, bringing my reward with me to repay all people according to their deeds. [13]I am the Alpha and the Omega, the First and the Last, the Beginning and the End."

[16]"I, Jesus, have sent my angel to give you this message for the churches. I am both the source of David and the heir to his throne. I am the bright morning star."

[17]The Spirit and the bride say, "Come." Let anyone who hears this say, "Come." Let anyone who is thirsty come. Let anyone who desires drink freely from the water of life. [18]And I solemnly declare to everyone who hears the words of prophecy written in this book: If anyone adds anything to what is written here, God will add to that person the plagues described in this book. [19]And if anyone removes any of the words from this book of prophecy, God will remove that person's share in the tree of life and in the holy city that are described in this book.

[20]He who is the faithful witness to all these things says, "Yes, I am coming soon!" Amen! Come, Lord Jesus!

[21]May the grace of the Lord Jesus be with God's holy people.

Revelation 22:12-13, 16-21

Scripture Index